New Mexico's
Wilderness Areas

THE COMPLETE GUIDE

TEXT BY
BOB JULYAN

PHOTOGRAPHY BY
TOM TILL

WESTCLIFFE PUBLISHERS

Dedication

This one's for you, Mom, with love and gratitude.

Hoodoos
Ah-shi-sle-pah Wilderness Study Area

Table of Contents

ISBN: 1-56579-291-2

PHOTOGRAPHY COPYRIGHT: Tom Till, 1998. All rights reserved.

TEXT COPYRIGHT: Robert Julyan, 1998. All rights reserved.

PRODUCTION MANAGER: Harlene Finn

EDITOR: Kristen Iversen

DESIGN AND PRODUCTION: Rebecca Finkel, F + P Graphic Design; Boulder, CO

PUBLISHED BY: Westcliffe Publishers, Inc.
P.O. Box 1261
Englewood, Colorado 80150

PRINTED IN: Hong Kong
PRINTED THROUGH: World Print Ltd.

LIBRARY OF CONGRESS CATALOGING-IN-PUBLICATION DATA

Julyan, Bob.
New Mexico's wilderness areas : the complete guide / text
by Bob Julyan : photography by Tom Till.
p. cm.
Includes bibliographical references (p.   ) and index.
ISBN: 1-56579-291-2
1. Hiking—New Mexico—Guidebooks. 2. Wilderness
areas—New Mexico—Guidebooks. 3. New Mexico—
Guidebooks. I. Till, Tom. II. Title.
GV199.42.N6J85 1998   98-19238
796.51'09789—dc21   CIP

*For more information
about other fine books and
calendars from Westcliffe
Publishers, please call your
local bookstore, contact us
at 1-800-523-3692, or write
for our free color catalog.*

COVER:
*Pinnacle and badlands,
Bisti—De-na-zin
Wilderness*

PLEASE NOTE:
Risk is always a factor in backcountry, high-mountain, and desert travel.
Many of the activities described in this book can be dangerous, especially
when weather is adverse or unpredictable, and when unforeseen events
or conditions create a hazardous situation. The author has done his best
to provide the reader with accurate information about backcountry travel,
as well as to point out some of its potential hazards. It is the responsibility
of the users of this guide to learn the necessary skills for safe backcountry
travel, and to exercise caution in potentially hazardous areas. The author
and publisher disclaim any liability for injury or other damage caused by
backcountry traveling, mountain biking, or performing any other activity
described in this book.

Acknowledgments

I WOULD LIKE TO GRATEFULLY ACKNOWLEDGE
the following people for their kind assistance: Janet Baca
and Lee Thornhill of the Lincoln National Forest; Nancy
Brouillard and the New Mexico Mountain Club; Rob
Deyerberg of the Carson National Forest (Questa Ranger
District); Ed Frederickson of Las Cruces; Monica Gallion
at the Cibola National Forest (Mountainair Ranger
District); Joseph Gendron of Mimbres; Joan Hellen of
the Gila National Forest (Glenwood Ranger District);
Alita Knight of Carlsbad Caverns National Park; Martin
Frentzel of the New Mexico Department of Game and
Fish; The New Mexico Natural Heritage Program; Jerry
Payne and Tim Pohlman of the Gila National Forest
(Black Range Ranger District); Carl Smith of Albuquerque;
Eric Smith and the New Mexico Wilderness Alliance;
William Stone of Albuquerque; Sam Tobias of the
District Lincoln National Forest (Smokey Bear Ranger
District); Kathy Walter, Wilderness and Outdoor
Recreation Planner, Bureau of Land Management office
in Albuquerque; Jerold G. Widdison of Albuquerque;
Mary Wyant and the staff of the Map and Geographic
Information Center at the University of New Mexico;
and the staff of the Cibola National Forest (Sandia and
Magdalena Ranger Districts).

And finally, the members of my family: my wife,
Mary, and my daughters, Megan and Robyn, for their
encouragement and support.

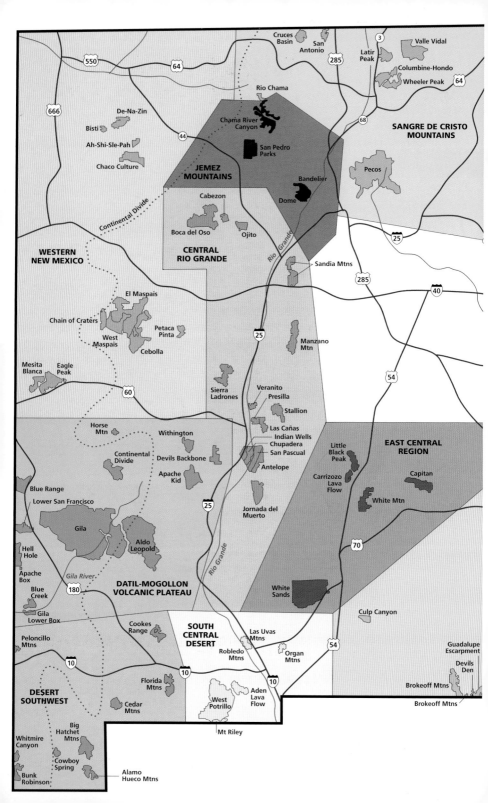

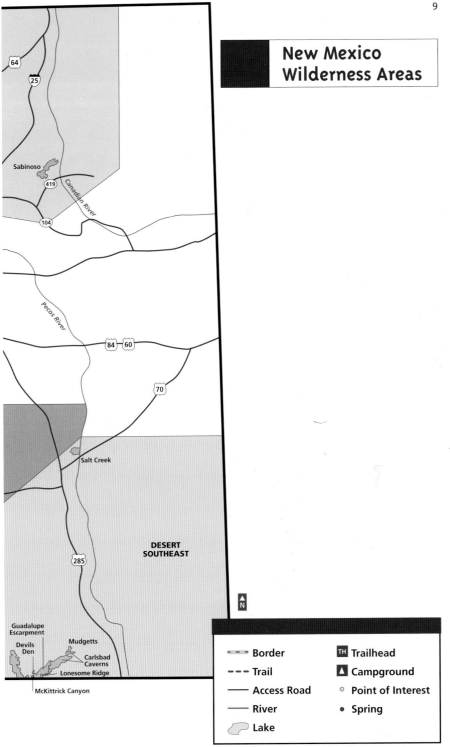

New Mexico Wilderness Areas

64
25

Sabinoso
419

Canadian River

104

Pecos River

84 60

70

Salt Creek

DESERT SOUTHEAST

285

N

Guadalupe Escarpment
Mudgetts
Devils Den
Carlsbad Caverns
Lonesome Ridge
McKittrick Canyon

Legend

▪▪▪ Border
--- Trail
— Access Road
— River
⬮ Lake

TH Trailhead
▲ Campground
○ Point of Interest
● Spring

Please refer to this legend for all maps.

Preface

LET ME TELL YOU A LITTLE about how I came to be in New Mexico. My wife, Mary, our infant daughter, Megan, and I had been living for several years in northern New England, among the Green Mountains of Vermont and the White Mountains of New Hampshire. Truly beautiful areas, but as time passed I began to realize I was missing something: a sense of excitement, of adventure, of discovery. Born and raised in Colorado's Front Range, I had the intuitive feeling that what I was missing could be found out West.

So one Thanksgiving we accepted an invitation to spend the holiday at the ranch of Mary's stepmother, Connie Dempsey, outside La Jara, New Mexico. There the warm sun burnished the aspen leaves golden against a sky more blue than any I'd seen before (and we had left New England in a blizzard). Everywhere were vistas begging to be explored, mountain ranges, plains, and deserts. I'd found what I'd been missing. Nine months later we were living in New Mexico.

That was 20 years ago. Since then, I've traveled extensively throughout New Mexico. When I undertook to write *The Place Names of New Mexico* for the University of New Mexico Press, I had to visit each of New Mexico's 33 counties, many of them several times, driving down thousands of miles of back roads and ferreting out obscure places. When I undertook to write *Best Hikes with Children in New Mexico*, I was obliged to find appropriate hikes throughout the state. This was in addition to the many hikes and trips I'd taken by myself or with my family, just for the fun of it.

And despite that, the excitement, the sense of adventure and discovery I felt 20 years ago has not faded. I'm still enjoying new wonders, new mysteries, new delights, new challenges. Even places I've visited many times always seem to have something new to reveal to me.

This is especially true in New Mexico's wildernesses. To claim I know everything about the state's wilderness areas would be the height of presumption. Indeed, I'm still discovering new trails and new areas in the small Sandia Mountain Wilderness, and I've been exploring there at least once a week for 18 years!

Reflections along the trail
Bandelier National Monument

Wilderness in New Mexico

IMAGINE, if you will, the land here as seen by the first humans to enter what is now New Mexico. At Blackwater Draw near Clovis and Folsom Site near Folsom, stone tools and the bones of extinct animals were found indicating that humans lived in this part of the world at least ten thousand years ago. The climate would have been subtly different then—cooler, moister—and the wildlife vastly more diverse. Yet landscapes still exist in New Mexico where you can, without too much difficulty, see the land as it was then: open, wild, and innocent of boundaries.

The concept of wilderness likely did not exist then, for wilderness as a concept requires its opposite: civilization. Thus, the languages of the Native American peoples who have continued to inhabit New Mexico down the years since those first Paleo-Indians have few, if any, words that translate as "wilderness." Vincent Lujan Sr., former governor of Taos Pueblo, put it well when he said, "The so-called wilderness was never wilderness to us, because we are part of that wilderness."

For somewhat similar reasons, the early Spanish explorers of New Mexico never labeled any area as wilderness. Even if they had, they likely would have used the Spanish words for wilderness, *desierto* and *yermo,* both meaning "deserted," "uninhabited," or "desert." Curiously, that's what the English word for wilderness meant in its Middle English form. How could the concept of wilderness as we know it today exist when there was little else?

In 1630, Father Alonso de Benavides visited New Mexico to report on the state of the new province. He wrote about the land's fertility, mineral potential, and the abundance of fish and game. He described piñon nuts, prickly pear fruit, and the indigenous people. Nowhere did he mention the beautiful wilderness he passed through.

Rather, New Mexico's early Spanish-speaking settlers looked east and west from their villages along the Rio Grande and viewed the wilderness on either side with fear and suspicion. It was from the wilderness that hostile Indians launched their relentless raids. Grizzly bears, mountain lions, and wolves lived in the wilderness, threatening livestock and the shepherds who tended them. We can scarcely imagine the pervasive sense of danger these early peoples felt. I feel much safer in the wilderness today than I do, say, in Albuquerque. When a twig snaps near my campsite at night, I never fear for my life. But to these early settlers, fear was a reality, and for good reason.

Yet at the same time wilderness was a place of many gifts: timber for building, firewood, fish and game, and medicinal and edible plants. Later it was where the settlers grazed their livestock. The lives of people living in isolated, rural communities were bound up with wilderness in ways urban people today find difficult to understand. Judith Espinosa, former Secretary of the New Mexico Environment Department, stated it well: "Wilderness is involved in the sustainability of culture. It isn't just setting aside land but also involves the people and their use of the land."

This fact reveals itself in northern New Mexico today, where resistance to wilderness is often high, primarily because the rural Hispanics fear wilderness designation will threaten their traditional uses of the land and consequently their traditional culture.

When English-speaking settlers began arriving in New Mexico in the latter 1800s, they viewed wilderness similarly to the Indians and Hispanics. In a report filed in 1848 by Lt. J.W. Abert of the U.S. Army Topographical Engineers, he, like Benavides 200 years earlier, spoke matter-of-factly about the plants, animals, and potential of minerals. He discussed the location of villages and the possibility of further settlement. But nowhere did he effuse about the beautiful wilderness he passed through. The only time he waxed poetic in the account of his expedition was when he gratefully returned to Kansas. "We now felt at home," he wrote, "and as the sun rose there seemed to be a cheering brightness in his rays which is not to be seen in New Mexico, nor on the prairies."

The settlers had conflicting feelings about wilderness. A harsh, dangerous place, yes, but also the provider of sustenance and livelihood. They exploited the wildlands more intensely, but that had much to do with greater access to markets and technology. Without a doubt, at some level the settlers felt an appreciation for New Mexico's wild lands, but if someone had proposed setting aside land to protect its wild character, their response certainly would have been, "Huh? Come again?"

No, it was not until wilderness began to disappear that the seemingly infinite was revealed as finite. We began to notice wilderness and define it. Here in New Mexico, that began in the mid-to-late nineteenth century. Once the wilderness-eradicating forces were set in motion, they proceeded with the destructive inevitability of an avalanche.

Wildlife in New Mexico suffered a virtual holocaust. By the late 1800s, bison had been hunted to extinction on the eastern plains. By 1888, elk had disappeared from the vast Pecos Wilderness. Twelve years later, by 1900, no elk lived anywhere in New Mexico—none! Rocky Mountain bighorn sheep, once common throughout northern New Mexico, utterly vanished, and desert bighorn sheep were on the verge of extinction. By 1917, only 1,700 pronghorn were left in the entire state in just 35 bands (slightly more than one band per present county). Wild turkey populations were decimated. The last grizzly was killed in the Pecos in 1923; the last one in the state at Rain Creek in the Gila Country in 1931. During the 1915 hunting season, deer were so sparse in the million-acre Carson National Forest that hunters killed only eight.

Wildlife was not the only casualty. As railroads penetrated the state's more remote regions, forests were stripped of timber for ties and construction camps. The Zuni Mountains were logged almost bare. The so-called Cloud-Climbing Railroad that ran from Alamogordo to Cloudcroft opened the forests of the Sacramento Mountains to loggers. In northern New Mexico, lumber camps such as La Madera and Lumberton processed board feet at an untold rate.

At the same time, overgrazing turned grasslands into deserts. Sheep were especially destructive. Today, sheep seem relatively absent from the landscape, but a hundred years ago they dwarfed cattle in numbers. Indeed, many of the livestock empires of early Territorial New Mexico were based on sheep rather than cows. In 1919, during the heyday of the cattle drives, 21,677 cattle and 150,000 sheep passed over the "Hoof Highway"—the Magdalena Livestock Driveway leading to the stock-yards in Magdalena. Now most of the sheep are gone, but livestock grazing continues throughout the state with varying degrees of impact. Grazing is allowed in the national forests and wilderness areas. (It's been estimated that a third of New Mexico's wilder-nesses are grazed; hikers wonder, "Where are the other two-thirds hidden?") Grazing in wilderness has become an increasingly sensitive and controversial issue as environ-mentalists seek to reduce or altogether eliminate grazing allotments, while ranchers try to preserve a way of life already threatened from other directions. Ironically, ranchers in the Gila Country, where antiwilderness feelings are most intense, were among the main supporters of the creation of the Gila Wilderness; they saw it as a means of protecting their grazing lands.

This was the New Mexico that Aldo Leopold, a 22-year-old forest ranger, found when he arrived in southwestern New Mexico in 1909. Through writings based on his wilderness experiences, Leopold forever changed American wilderness thinking. But his philosophy, as articulated in the books *A Sand County Almanac* (1949) and *Round River* (1953), evolved gradually. When Leopold first arrived in New Mexico, he was an avid hunter. In 1916, writing about the prospects of restoring Arizona's wildlife, he said, "Nature is with us; only man and predatory animals are against us." He enthusiastically sought the extermination of wolves. But years later, in *A Sand County Almanac,* he wrote: "I was young then, and full of trigger-itch; I thought that because fewer wolves meant more deer, that no wolves would mean hunter's paradise."

Leopold—whose books are still in print today—rose rapidly in the Forest Service. He became supervisor of the Carson National Forest, where his employees included a young man of similar age, Elliott Barker. Barker shared Leopold's concern about vanishing wildlife and wildlands, and they formed a lifelong partnership. Leopold was eventually transferred to the regional office in Albuquerque, where he formed alliances with other people whose thinking paralleled his own: Gifford Pinchot, head of the Forest Service, and Arthur Carhart, the Forest Service planner at Trapper Lake in Colorado. When asked to make a recommendation as to what to do with Trapper Lake, Carhart replied: "Nothing." He felt it should be left in its wild state. A novel idea at the time.

In 1924, the Gila Wilderness was created—the first area in the country to be set aside solely to preserve its character as wilderness. This executive proclamation by the U.S. Secretary of Agriculture was in direct response to an initiative led by Aldo Leopold.

In New Mexico, other initiatives quickly followed. In 1931, the San Pedro Parks were designated a Forest Service Primitive Area; in 1933, the Pecos received the same designation. This coincided with a rapid evolution in public and governmental thinking about wilderness. Bob Marshall of the Forest Service emerged as an articulate and passionate spokesperson for protecting the nation's wild lands. Taking the next significant step, Marshall, Leopold, and other prominent conservationists formed the Wilderness Society in 1935.

Still, the nation lacked a comprehensive system of protecting wilderness areas, and it wasn't until well after World War II that the idea gained momentum. In 1956, Howard Zahniser, executive director of the Wilderness Society, drafted the first version of the Wilderness Act. The times were not right, however, and the act faced fierce opposition. Eight years and 66 revisions later, the Wilderness Act was finally signed into law in 1964. The Act was significant in its definition, for the first time, of the concept of wilderness: "A wilderness, in contrast with those areas where man and his own works dominate the landscape, is hereby recognized as an area where the earth and its community of life are untrammeled by man, where man himself is a visitor who does not remain."

Snow-covered chollas and mesas,
Ojito Wilderness Study Area

As the Wilderness Act struggled through Congress, it had powerful allies from New Mexico. United States Senator Clinton P. Anderson was chairman of the committee that wrote the legislation; he had hiked the Gila Country with Leopold. And Elliott Barker, descendant of a pioneer New Mexico ranching family and a rugged outdoorsman himself, provided strong testimony. When he spoke about the value of experiencing wilderness, people listened.

Yet curiously, the 1964 Wilderness Act had relatively little immediate impact upon New Mexico. The White Mountains and San Pedro Parks became formal wilderness areas, but given its exact definition of wilderness, the Wilderness Act seemed to exclude many potential areas. In 1972, the Forest Service took another step when it conducted a Roadless Area Review Evaluation (RARE) to identify other wildernesses. Regrettably, the process had rather strict criteria, and few areas met them. Wilderness advocates cried foul. The Forest Service responded by initiating another inventory, RARE II, with looser criteria.

Nevertheless, this prompted a group of private citizens to organize, conduct their own inventory, and make their own recommendations. They called themselves the New Mexico Wilderness Study Committee, and their effect upon wilderness in New Mexico has been enormous. Dedicated and diligent, they went to the wilderness study areas and walked the boundaries themselves. They evaluated human impacts (such as windmills, stock tanks, and old roads), documented their observations, and proposed alternatives. In 1980 their efforts culminated with the introduction and passage of the nation's first post-RARE II wilderness bill. This resulted in several new wilderness areas in the state, including Apache Kid, Withington, Capitan Mountains, Dome, Latir Peak, and Cruces Basin.

At the same time, the U.S. Bureau of Land Management (BLM)—responding to the mandate of the 1976 Federal Land Policy Management Act—was making an inventory of its own extensive holdings in New Mexico. And again, a group of private citizens, many of them affiliated with the New Mexico Wilderness Study Committee, began their own wilderness evaluation of the BLM's land. In 1991 the BLM released its findings and recommendations, and advised wilderness status for 487,186 acres within 23 wilderness study areas. They also recommended that 420,000 acres within 39 other study areas be released for uses other than wilderness. However, because no legislation was attached to the recommendations, they have remained only that.

Lobbying efforts continue. In 1997, the New Mexico Wilderness Alliance was formally organized to continue efforts for wilderness protection. In the absence of legislation, the BLM Wilderness Study Areas, whether recommended for wilderness or not, continue to be managed to protect their wilderness character, as mandated by law.

Public and government attitudes continue to evolve. Emphasis is increasingly shifting from wilderness as scenery and recreation toward preservation of habitat for plant and animal species. The implications are significant for New Mexico, where many wildlands are only marginally scenic in the traditional postcard sense. The Alamo Hueco Mountains will likely never be attractive to tourists, for example, yet as habitat for rare and endangered species they are as vital as the Pecos Wilderness.

Another idea gaining currency is the concept of connecting wild lands through wilderness "corridors" where populations of endangered species can be self-sustaining. The Wildlands Project would link several areas around the Gila Wilderness into such a complex. This relates to the concept of wilderness fostering so-called "umbrella species": animals at the top of the food chain, whose survival is indicative of the viability of the species beneath them. In the Gila Country, these umbrella species would include bears (perhaps even grizzly bears), mountain lions, jaguars, and wolves. Wolves have already been released into the wild in Arizona's Blue Range Primitive Area.

As human attitudes change, the land itself changes as well. I recall a friendly conversation with a rancher as I was about to pass through the gate into the Cebolla Wilderness. "Look at this land," he declared. "It ain't wilderness. The land on this side of the fence is the same as the land on that side, and this side ain't wilderness. Hell, there's roads and cut timber and water dams all through this country. Just puttin' up a fence and a sign don't make it wilderness."

He was right. After I'd passed through the gate and started hiking down an old dirt road, I found signs of human presence everywhere: sawed stumps, tin cans, earthen dams, abandoned homesteader cabins, and ranchers' line camps. In the words of the Wilderness Act, it had been thoroughly trammeled! But fifty years from now, those well-worn pickup-truck roads will be footpaths, the tin cans will rust into oblivion, the earthen dams will erode beyond recognition, and the sawed stumps will decay into humus. The land will have untrammeled itself.

At present, New Mexico's formal wilderness areas total 1.6 million acres, just two percent of the state's total land area. Of the 13 western states, only three—Utah, Nevada, and Hawaii—have less total land in wilderness; only two—Utah and Nevada—have a smaller percentage. Yet New Mexico is the nation's fifth largest state.

Geography and history are at least partly responsible. In New Mexico, mountain areas are generally small and isolated, not large and contiguous as they are in other western states. This has resulted in a Balkanization of the state's wilderness areas. Also, New Mexico has a much longer human history than most western states. Twenty-two years before Plymouth Colony was founded in Massachusetts, New Mexico was established as a colony. Humans have had a longer time here to leave their mark upon wilderness.

Nevertheless, New Mexico has a low population (only 1.6 million), and most of them live in the Albuquerque–Santa Fe corridor. Some counties are virtually unpopulated; many wildlands have fewer human visitors now than they did 100 years ago. New Mexico remains a state of vast spaces, long vistas uninterrupted by towns or any human endeavor whatsoever, and nameless mountains and mesas cresting interminably like waves reaching far into the distance.

At the beginning of this history, I asked you to imagine the land as it existed when the first humans arrived here so many millennia ago. When I hike in the beautiful wilderness areas of New Mexico, time and time again I appreciate the fact that to imagine such a scene isn't much of a stretch at all.

Native Americans in New Mexico

OF THE NATIVE AMERICAN PEOPLES the Spaniards encountered 400 years ago when they arrived in New Mexico many are still here, most still living on the same tribal lands. Granted, the Plains Indians, like the buffalo, are gone from the Llano Estacado; Utes no longer roam the Sangre de Cristo Mountains; Chiricahua and Mimbres Apaches are absent from southwestern New Mexico; and the Piro and Tompiro pueblos, south of Albuquerque, are just anonymous mounds of rubble. But the state still has 19 inhabited pueblos. The Navajo Nation, encompassing traditional Navajo lands, is the nation's largest reservation, and the Mescalero and Jicarilla Apaches also have reservations within their tribal homelands.

For wilderness users, this long-continuing Indian presence has several implications. The wilderness experience is made richer by the knowledge that the landscape has a human history going back at least 10,000 years. Ancient people likely camped or hiked exactly where you're camping and hiking. The New Mexico wilderness is filled with echoes and ghosts.

It is also filled with artifacts. You can't hike in New Mexico without coming across pottery shards, worked pieces of flint, projectile points, manos and metates, remains of dwellings and structures, and more. As I reiterate later in this introduction, please don't disturb the fragile ruins, and resist the temptation to take artifacts as souvenirs.

Remember that the descendants of the Indians who made those artifacts are still here and still an integral part of the wilderness. The Ramah Navajo Reservation is next to the Chain of Craters Wilderness Study Area. The Bisti—De-na-zin Wilderness and Chaco Culture National Historical Park are surrounded by Navajo land. The Mescalero Apache Reservation abuts the White Mountain Wilderness. The Indians of Santo Domingo, Cochiti, Santa Clara, and probably other pueblos still visit shrines in the Bandelier Backcountry. Blue Lake, Taos Pueblo's most sacred site, is adjacent to the Wheeler Peak Wilderness. Pueblos along the Rio Grande maintain shrines in the Pecos Wilderness and regard the high peaks as sacred. All this imposes upon us a special obligation to treat the land with respect—perhaps sharing with Native Americans the belief that we too are linked spiritually with wild nature, like a child to its parent.

Rainwater pool
El Malpais National Monument

New Mexico's Life Zones

ECOLOGISTS HAVE SAID that New Mexico includes all the life zones in North America except tropical. (During the state's "monsoon season," some residents might even include that!) Certainly the state's biological and topographic diversity are part of the state's appeal among hikers. Not only can they find somewhere to hike in the state at any time of year, they also have an extraordinarily broad array of ecosystems to explore. In the same week they can hear pikas barking among rocks above timberline in the Rocky Mountains and also look for Gila monsters in the Chihuahuan Desert.

The major determining factors behind this diversity are latitude and elevation. New Mexico shares its southern border with Mexico and Texas, in the Chihuahuan Desert, but its northern border is with Colorado and the southern Rocky Mountains. Furthermore, elevations in the state go from 2,817 feet near the Texas border south of Carlsbad to 13,161 feet atop Wheeler Peak in the Sangre de Cristo Mountains northeast of Taos, a vertical relief of more than 10,000 feet. The occurrence of specific plants and animals within this enormous range depends on other factors as well, such as available moisture, temperature, habitat, and so forth, with thousands of micro-ecosystems existing throughout the state. Still, New Mexico can be divided into several major life zones and hikers should be familiar with these, not only because this awareness enhances the experience of hiking but also because each has its own unique characteristics and challenges. Classification systems and labels vary widely among naturalists, and the actual situation is infinitely more complex than what is presented here. Nevertheless, the following classification has been widely used and is easy to understand.

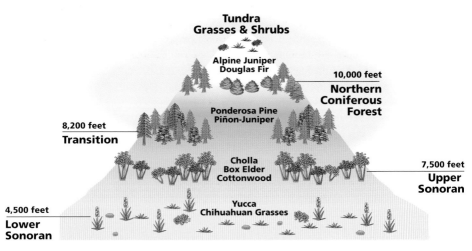

New Mexico's Life Zones

LOWER SONORAN

This occurs below 4,500 feet in New Mexico, and despite the name features the plants of the Chihuahuan Desert rather than the Sonoran Desert, which does not exist in New Mexico. Temperatures are hot for much of the year and evaporation high. Characteristic plants are mesquite, creosote bush, yucca, agave, four-wing saltbush, and Chihuahuan grasses such as burro grass, grama, black grama, dropseed, ricegrass, sacaton, and tobosa.

UPPER SONORAN

Within this zone, generally occurring from 4,500 to 7,500 feet, summers are hot and winters somewhat mild. Precipitation is modest and evaporation is still high. This is the zone of the piñon-juniper forest, New Mexico's most widespread vegetation type. Other characteristic plants are alligator juniper, Chihuahua pine, chamisa, cholla, Apache plume, Gambel oak, and, near water, box elder, tamarisk, and, of course, cottonwood.

TRANSITION

Within this zone, from 7,500 to 8,200 feet, ponderosa pines replace piñon-junipers. Summers are mild and winters cold, often with substantial snowfall. Other native pines grow here, such as the limber and Apache pine. Other typical plants include Rocky Mountain maple, New Mexico locust, and riparian willow.

NORTHERN CONIFEROUS FOREST

This zone, from 8,200 feet to timberline (10,000 to 11,500 feet), is dominated by Douglas fir, white fir, subalpine fir, Engelmann spruce, blue spruce, alpine juniper, limber pine, and, occasionally in the north, bristlecone pine. Aspens are common in disturbed or transition areas. Summers here are cool, winters cold, and mountains with these elevations catch lots of moisture.

TUNDRA

Here above timberline the dominant vegetation is a tough, windswept mat of low, hardy grasses, sedges, and shrubs. Temperatures are cool to cold, even in summer, and evaporation is high because of wind, elevation, and exposure. A considerable amount of snow falls, although most is swept away by high winds. Hikers in this zone should be prepared for severe weather at all times of the year.

The above classification is greatly oversimplified. The elevation cut-offs vary enormously by latitude and whether a slope is facing north or south. Don't worry too much about labels or definitions; just get to know the plants and landscape.

Hiking in New Mexico

Generally people enter New Mexico by one of three Interstate highways. Regrettably, the views from these highways reinforce the stereotype that New Mexico is arid, barren country with some interesting desert ranges—the key word being *desert*.

I'll concede that the state does indeed have an arid climate: 90 percent of New Mexico receives less than 20 inches of moisture annually, while 20–30 percent receives less than 10 inches. The climate can indeed be hot; no one who's been in southern New Mexico in the summer will deny that. You'll note that the phrase "… so you'll need to carry water" occurs frequently in this book. But I also talk about snowpack, areas not open for hiking until June, animals like elk and black bears, and the intense color and variety of alpine wildflowers.

Consequently, it's impossible to generalize about hiking in New Mexico. Preparing for dryness and heat is a good strategy, but other factors, especially elevation and latitude, are important to keep in mind. For example, in the White Mountain Wilderness, you could pick cactus prickers out of your socks in the morning and have to worry about losing your way in a spruce forest in the afternoon—all on the same hike.

Keeping these factors in mind, below are some general guidelines to consider when hiking in New Mexico.

Permits

At present, the only areas requiring permits for backcountry camping are Carlsbad Caverns National Park, Bandelier National Monument, and White Sands National Monument. Chaco Culture National Historical Park does not require permits for its short backcountry trails, but camping is not allowed. In other areas, camping may be allowed generally but prohibited around specific vulnerable areas, such as lakes in the Pecos Wilderness. Certain trails in the Sandia Mountains Wilderness are closed when peregrine falcons are nesting. Some areas impose restrictions when fire danger is extremely high. It's always a good idea to contact the appropriate ranger district or visitor center before entering a particular wilderness, not only to see what regulations might apply but also to check on current conditions.

Leave No Trace

As more and more people use America's wild lands, they have been forced to minimize their impact by adopting an ethic known as "Leave No Trace." This responsibility is even more urgent in New Mexico, where scant rainfall, sparse vegetation, and thin topsoil mean that recovery from damage can take a very long time indeed. Once, while hiking with some range ecologists in the Las Uvas Mountains in southern New Mexico, I asked how long recovery would take from the overgrazing and trampling that had occurred there. Their answer shocked me: if further undisturbed, new soil would form at the rate of a millimeter (the width of a pencil lead) per century.

"Leave No Trace" really isn't difficult. It just means adopting some fairly simple habits and practices.

Natural arch, Bisti—De-na-zin Wilderness

PLAN AND PREPARE

Everything you bring into the wilderness should be taken back out with you. Repackage and store food in reusable containers, and carry plastic bags for packing out trash. If you run across other people's trash, try to pack it out with you.

TRAILS

Stay on designated trails, walking single-file in the middle. Don't take shortcuts on switchbacks. Try to stay on durable surfaces. Use your map, compass, or Global Positioning System unit to eliminate the need to rely on cairns or blazes.

CAMPSITES

Wherever possible, choose camping sites that are already established, preferably those where the soil has previously been worn bare. However, when traveling where few obvious sites exist, try to select a new site rather than one where impacts are just

becoming noticeable. When selecting a campsite in a pristine area, choose a resistant area rather than a more delicate site. Camp at least 200 feet (about 70 adult steps) from lakes and streams.

FIRES

The best advice? Don't build a fire — use a portable stove. Wilderness etiquette and common sense dictate that you should avoid leaving an ugly and ecologically destructive black blemish. If you do build a fire, use an established fire ring. Don't scar the landscape by snapping branches off trees or shrubs—live or dead. Before you leave a site, completely extinguish your fire, making sure it's cold. Remove all unburned trash and scatter the cold ashes over a large area. If you want to build a fire in an area where no fire ring exists, build a mound fire. Find a source of mineral soil, such as a low stream bed or hollow beneath an overturned tree. Scoop up this soil and pile it on a tarp, making a flat-topped mound 6 to 8 inches high. Build a small fire on top. When done, scatter the cold ashes over a wide area, then return the soil to its source.

Many people like a campfire for the warmth, the light, and the camaraderie. I carry a small Ultralite oil lantern, and have found to my surprise that even its tiny flame, while short on warmth, provides much of the psychological comfort of a campfire.

SANITATION

The recommended method of disposing of human wastes is the "cat hole" method, whereby you dig a hole 6 to 8 inches deep with a lightweight aluminum or plastic trowel, and cover and disguise the hole when you're done. Stay at least 200 feet away from water sources. Toilet paper should be used sparingly and packed out (sealed double plastic bags), or you can use a natural alternative.

All trash, including food scraps, should be packed out. Most trash, including paper, doesn't burn well and generally ends up being scattered by wind or animals.

WILD ANIMALS

Don't attract them. Don't feed them. Don't approach or touch them. This not only disrupts wildlife ecology and encourages animals to become dependent on humans, but also exposes people to the possibility of bites and infection by animal-borne diseases such as plague (that's right—Black Death). Hang your food supplies from tree limbs, out of reach, and do all your food preparation and clean up away and downwind from your camp. Most New Mexico wilderness areas don't have a problem with "bum" animals like other areas do, and we should try to keep it that way.

TREAD SOFTLY

In arid regions, the soil often acquires a protective "crust" that, once disturbed, leaves the soil vulnerable to erosion. In areas of sandy soil, a living community of bacteria, fungi, and lichens forms, called cryptobiotic crust or cryptogamic soil. This living soil has a distinctive dark, lumpy appearance, and while it may look like mere soil, it actually is a complex living community. It takes 100 to 200 years for even a thin layer of this crust to develop. Avoid stepping or making camps on this inconspicuous but important part of desert ecology.

Organ Mountains in fog

Dogs

I like pets, and I like dogs. While I concede a dog can be a welcome companion in the wilderness, I feel strongly that you'll have a more successful, more responsible trip if you don't take the dog. On the trail, the dog must be under control at all times so as not to threaten or hinder other hikers. (Even friendly dogs that just run up and sniff can terrify some people, who may have been attacked in the past.) At camp, the dog must also be under control so as not to bother other campers by visiting their camp-sites or chronically barking. And because dogs are predators, they can harass and kill wild birds and animals. Further, domestic animals often behave unpredictably when suddenly placed in wild nature and may run away. I've known more than one hiker whose trip was ruined because the family pet took off and didn't come back. My advice is to make everything much simpler by just leaving the dog at home. (Many areas don't allow dogs anyway.) A final caveat: dogs are fond of catching rodents or snuffing around dead ones. In New Mexico, rodents can carry fleas, and fleas some-times harbor plague bacteria. Need I say more?

Water

Cattle are ubiquitous in New Mexico's wilderness areas and you need to treat all back-country water by filtering, boiling, or adding chemicals such as iodine. I arrived at this conclusion with great regret and reluctance, because I grew up drinking wild water with no ill consequences. But while I've never had the intestinal parasite *Giardia lamblia*, I've known people who have, and they assure me that it's far more serious, debilitating, and difficult to treat than a simple case of the trots. Besides, even diarrhea can ruin a backcountry trip. Not wanting to play those odds, I now treat water and recommend that others do as well.

Maps and Directions

The maps in this book are intended to provide general orientation only and not substitute for more detailed maps, which I've listed for each wilderness area. Similarly, the hike descriptions are intended to guide you to some of the more interesting or representative hikes for the area, but with a few exceptions they are not comprehensive listings of trails within a wilderness. The Gila Wilderness, for example, has 700 miles of trails. For more complete hiking information, please refer to one of the guides listed in the bibliography. I've expressed trail mileages as decimals, but that may imply far greater precision than actually is possible. Still, I've tried to be as accurate as I can.

Pests and Hazards

Please don't be intimidated by the following list. It is meant to be comprehensive; the chance of encountering even one of these hazards on any given trip is small. New Mexico, with its generally mild climate, is a gentle, welcoming environment for hikers. I've ranked the following hazards according to the likelihood of whether or not you might have to deal with them, beginning with the most common.

THE SUN

Skin cancer kills more New Mexicans each year than all the rattlesnakes, scorpions, spiders, flash floods, and plague and hantavirus combined. Yet many hikers who dutifully pack a snakebite kit routinely go out without sun protection.

I've always been a poster boy for skin cancer: fair skinned, redheaded, and freckle faced. But in New Mexico even a tan can't prevent eventual skin damage. Indeed, the darkest tan provides less protection than sunblock rated 15. Three factors make the sun especially searing here. One is latitude; New Mexico is closer to the equator compared to more northern states, and the sun is more directly overhead. Another is aridity; the dry air doesn't have much moisture to block harmful rays. But most important is elevation. Most of the state is around 5,000 feet, give or take a thousand, and mountain areas are usually much higher. Thus, harmful ultraviolet rays have much less atmosphere to penetrate here than at lower elevations.

Protect yourself against the sun by avoiding the outdoors when the sun is directly overhead, wearing a long-sleeved shirt and hat (there was a reason cowboys in the Old West wore broad-brimmed hats), and putting on sunscreen with a sun protection factor of at least 15. A great irony is that many people would shun living near a uranium processing plant for fear of radiation, yet eagerly seek exposure to carcinogenic ultraviolet rays from the sun.

The sun is also responsible for heat-related disorders. Be mindful of the following potential problems.

HEAT CRAMPS

This is caused by the loss of electrolytes, such as salt, through excessive perspiration. Treat heat cramps by drinking fluids that replace electrolytes, such as lightly salted water, lemonade, or a sport drink, and gently stretch the cramped muscle.

HEAT EXHAUSTION

Again, this is caused by failing to replace water and salts lost through sweating. Symptoms include a sense of weakness, instability, or extreme fatigue; wet, clammy skin; and headache, nausea, or even collapse. Treatment involves resting or lying prone in the shade and drinking salt-replacing fluids.

DEHYDRATION EXHAUSTION

This is due to failing to replace water losses over several days, resulting in weight loss and excessive fatigue. Rest and drink plenty of fluids.

HEAT STROKE

This is a very serious condition in which the body's temperature-regulating mechanisms totally collapse. Symptoms include hot, dry skin; high body temperature (as much as 106 degrees Fahrenheit); mental confusion; delirium; loss of consciousness; and convulsions. This is a true medical emergency and treatment must begin immediately. Cool the victim as rapidly as possible, either by immersion in cold water or by soaking his or her clothing and fanning to promote evaporative cooling. Treat for shock, if necessary, once the victim's temperature is lowered. If medical help is available, seek it at once.

Here are some other heat-management tips I've picked up over the years.
- Don't wait until you're thirsty to begin drinking; by then you might already be suffering some dehydration.
- Don't underestimate dehydration; a 2 percent loss of body fluids can result in a 20 percent decrease in performance.
- Be aware that rapid evaporation in dry, desert air can lead you to believe you're not sweating and losing body fluids as much as you actually are.
- Soaking a bandana or similar cloth and wearing it over your head, preferably dangling from a hat, can help cool your head.
- You can gauge how well hydrated you are by the color of your urine. Clear urine is a good sign; increasingly yellow urine means you need to drink more.
- And finally, one of the best heat-management techniques is one adopted by many desert animals: don't go out during midday. Do your hiking early in the morning or late in the afternoon, and hole up and rest during the heat of the day.

HUMANS

Regrettably, I must confess that the hazard I fear most while hiking in New Mexico is other people. No, I don't feel like a jogger in New York's Central Park after dark. I actually feel very safe in the wilderness. But leaving my car at the trailhead is another story. Vandalism and theft can be a problem for New Mexico hikers, especially in the northern part of the state. Here are some suggestions for protecting your vehicle.
- Don't leave anything of value in your vehicle.
- Don't leave valuables in plain view; cover or conceal them.
- Check with the local rangers or public lands managers to see which areas have been safe and which have not.
- Ask someone at the trailhead—a campground host or another camper—to watch your vehicle, or better yet, allow you to park it nearby.

STICKERS AND PRICKLERS

New Mexico has a wonderfully diverse array of cacti as well as other spiny plants such as mesquite. That's one reason my utility knife always includes a pair of tweezers.

POISON IVY

This plant is quite common, especially around moist areas. The only protection is to learn to recognize it, even when its shiny green leaves, in groups of three, are absent. Some studies suggest that washing with soap and water immediately after contact removes at least some of the noxious oil, called urushiol. Otherwise, check with your dermatologist as to the latest treatment.

STINGING NETTLE

This plant, with small toothed leaves covered with tiny hairs, occurs occasionally along streams and upon contact secretes a stinging fluid. The result is mild to moderate skin pain that disappears in an hour or less. Unfortunately, stinging nettle is not too distinctive and often easy to miss, so keep a watchful eye when hiking next to a stream.

Mexican gold poppies and cactus, Cookes Range Wilderness Study Area

RATTLESNAKES

Several species of rattlesnakes—the western diamondback being the most common—are found throughout New Mexico, although they become increasingly rare above 8,000 feet. My home in the southern Sandia Mountains is in rattlesnake habitat, and I go trail running or walking in the Sandia foothills almost every day, not to mention the numerous hikes and outings I take elsewhere in New Mexico. Over the years I've averaged about one rattlesnake sighting a year. I've never been bitten or even struck at, and I am convinced rattlesnakes genuinely want to avoid a confrontation and thus are reluctant to strike. I'm alert to news accounts of rattlesnake bites in New Mexico; they're very uncommon, and almost invariably the person bitten was attempting to handle or provoke the snake.

I hope you find all this reassuring. But if you're still scared spitless of rattlesnakes, that's okay; I understand. They scare the hell out of me when I actually encounter one, and I all but refuse to walk outdoors on warm nights without a flashlight. I was even more fearful when my children were small and constantly clambering over rocks and ledges. Once they went racing down a trail and inadvertently leaped over one stretched across the path—and instantly all those parental warnings were taken more seriously.

The rules for avoiding unpleasant rattlesnake encounters are rather simple:

- Watch where you put your hands and feet; don't reach up to grab ledges without looking first.
- Check around tents, sleeping bags, packs, or anything left on the ground.
- Be aware that rattlesnakes are most active at night and use a flashlight.
- Know that rattlesnakes don't always rattle to alert you to their presence; fewer than half the snakes I've encountered have ever rattled.
- Never attempt to touch, move, annoy, or capture a rattlesnake.
- Never touch or handle a dead rattlesnake; it's amazing how many bites occur from so-called dead snakes.
- Remember that you can avoid rattlesnakes entirely, even in the summer, simply by hiking at higher elevations.

What if you or a member of your party, against all odds, is bitten? The recommended responses for this situation vary widely. Indeed, about the only thing everyone agrees upon is this: seek medical help immediately.

FLASH FLOODS

Until you've seen one, the suddenness and ferocity of a flash flood are difficult to imagine, especially on the sunny days when only sand fills the arroyos. Be mindful of weather conditions as you hike, especially during the summer thundershower season, and not just overhead but also in the distance. When you hike in narrow canyons, ask yourself if you could climb to higher ground if you had to. And don't camp in drainages. Many times I've hiked in dry watercourses and noticed withered waterborne debris tangled in tree branches higher than my head.

MINES AND CAVES

Some areas in this book have natural caves, and if you're hiking the backcountry of the limestone Guadalupe Mountains, for example, your chances are fairly good that you'll encounter what are called "wild caves." Unless you're an experienced caver and have appropriate equipment, leave these caves alone. They can be extremely dangerous.

Even more dangerous are abandoned mine tunnels replete with rotting timbers, unstable rock, and rattlesnakes. Stay out!

SPIDERS

Two dangerous spider species live in New Mexico: black widows and brown recluses. Both are retiring and non-aggressive, and most bites occur when a spider has gotten into clothing or bedding. Symptoms of a bite include pain centered around a red area. However, if you suspect a bite has occurred, don't wait for symptoms: seek medical help immediately. Counter-measures are available. Fortunately, both species are more often found around human dwellings than in wild nature. I've never seen either while hiking in New Mexico.

I have, however, encountered tarantulas and count myself fortunate when I do. These gentle giants are interesting to watch. But while their bite is not dangerous, it still can be painful and get infected, so don't attempt to handle them.

PLAGUE, HANTAVIRUS

Regrettably, New Mexico is among the North American reservoirs for *Yersinia pestis,* the bacillus that causes plague, and each year a few cases, and even a few deaths, are reported. Similarly, hantavirus, a very serious disease, first surfaced in New Mexico, although since then it has been discovered elsewhere.

Your chance of being infected by one of these diseases is minuscule, and the strategy for protecting yourself is very simple: Avoid all contact with rodents, including their droppings, their holes and dens, their dead carcasses, everything. Actually, avoiding contact with all wild animals is a good idea.

SCORPIONS

These exist in the state's warmer regions, but they're rare and retiring; the lethal species is not found in New Mexico. Most stings occur when people are lifting stones or logs, which are where scorpions like to hide. When camping, don't leave clothing, shoes, and bedding out, and inspect and shake these out before using them. In all the hiking I've done in New Mexico, I've only found one scorpion—a dormant one my daughter dug out of a dirt bank in winter.

Equipment

I've seen as many equipment lists as I've seen guidebooks (and that's a lot!). Rather than burden you with yet another basic equipment list which you can pick up in any outdoor store, I'll describe the method I use.

I work from a computer (although that's not necessary), and keep a running checklist of equipment I've found necessary and useful. The list constantly evolves as I discard items and add new ones. I recently added duct tape, for example. When I want to go for a backpack trip I simply print out the list and then cross off items as I put them in my pack or my car. With some items on the list I'll say, "Nah, I don't think I'll need that," but at least the list has forced me to consider them. If you do this conscientiously for several trips, you'll quickly have your own personalized list of essential items.

How to Use This Guide

THIS BOOK IS A GUIDE TO New Mexico's wild lands. It features the state's designated wilderness areas, but also includes more than 50 Wilderness Study Areas as well as lands that don't fit into either category but nonetheless are wild and accessible to the public.

The regions are presented as they exist from roughly the northern to the southern parts of the state. Each wild area is preceded by an information block summarizing special features, general location, size in acres, elevation range, ecosystems, miles of trails (where applicable), which land-management agencies have responsibility for the area, and which topographic maps would be most useful in exploring the area. (See Appendix I for "at-a-glance" information about the areas.)

Wilderness Study Areas (WSAs) are those areas identified by land-management agencies as having wilderness potential, but not formally designated as wilderness. I've included the acreage of the WSAs as they exist now, along with the acreage recommended by the New Mexico Wilderness Alliance, a statewide wilderness advocacy group whose plans include introducing legislation that would change these WSAs into new wilderness areas. I have not included the acreage recommendations of the land-management agencies, particularly the U.S. Bureau of Land Management, because those recommendations were made several years ago. Since then, much has changed in public and agency thinking about wilderness concepts of biodiversity, ecosystem complexes encompassing a variety of designations, and so forth. Thus the previously recommended acreages, while still "official," may not accurately reflect the agency's current thinking regarding wilderness designation.

Following each information block is a more detailed description of the area and its natural history, including geology, plants, animals, ecosystems, endangered species, and anything important to understanding and appreciating that area. I also discuss the area's human history, because in a state like New Mexico, to ignore that is to miss much of the excitement and richness of being here. The administrative history of each area is also included—how it came to be recognized and set aside as a public wildland. I've visited and hiked each of the areas (except for some of the WSAs), and in this general description I pass along some of my experiences and observations I think other hikers might find interesting and useful.

Following the general information are descriptions of specific hikes in the area. Hikes are classified as follows:

DAY HIKES. Trails and destinations that fit an appropriate eight-hour period.

DESTINATION HIKES. Longer hikes to a specific destination that may require an overnight stay.

LOOP HIKES. Routes that circle through the wilderness to return the hiker to the trailhead via a different route. These include both day trips and overnighters.

SHUTTLE HIKES. Hikes that require shuttling vehicles between the start and finish points of a one-way route—typically a multi-day trek through a long canyon or across a mountain pass.

I've endeavored to present a range of hikes, from easy ones suitable for families to more difficult backpack trips. I tend to choose hikes I've done myself, and my selection of hikes is by no means a comprehensive list of good hikes in an area. Each hike has an information block listing distance (usually one-way), low and high elevations, and an estimate of its difficulty. I tend to be conservative when rating difficulty; many hikers will find hikes I label as moderate to be rather easy. When I wrote an earlier book about hiking with children, I learned that it was far better for a group to finish a hike saying, "That was a piece of cake" than "I didn't realize this was going to be a death march!"

Following the trail description, you'll find directions to the trailhead and a brief summary of the hike itself. I recommend that hikers supplement these directions with good maps and perhaps sections from guidebooks specific to the area. I mention hazards only if they're specific to that area. Please note that some wild lands here, especially the WSAs, have no developed trails and can only be explored by going cross-country. For each area I try to pass along some tips and guidelines, but cross-country travel should always be regarded as a special challenge.

Regarding the names in this book, geographic names are subject to change and variation, especially in a multilingual state such as New Mexico. While not denying the validity of name variants, I have used the names approved by the U.S. Board on Geographic Names and listed in the Geographic Names Information System database. By federal law, these are the names approved for federal maps and publications, including the U.S. Geological Survey and its maps, the U.S. Forest Service, the National Park Service, and the U.S. Bureau of Land Management. I felt readers would be best served if the names here are those found in the federal maps of the wilderness areas discussed.

These federal maps must also adhere to the policies and principles of the U.S. Board on Geographic Names, including dropping the possessive apostrophe in names such as Cookes Peak, Saint Peters Dome, and Devils Backbone. My goal in this book is twofold: 1) to give you the basic information you'll need to begin exploring New Mexico's wildernesses yourself; and 2) to share with you what I've found in the hope that it will kindle in you the same fire that was ignited in me so many years ago.

The presentation of the wild lands is followed at the back of this book by an Appendix ranking the wilderness areas by size; it also lists the administrative agency and the date the area was designated a wilderness. Finally, I've included a glossary of Spanish words a hiker might encounter on a map. Then I've included an extensive bibliography of books, both general and specific, about New Mexico and its wild lands. You can't travel and hike in New Mexico without wanting to know more about this most interesting state, and these books are a good place to start.

Abbreviations

USFS   U.S. Forest Service
USGS   U.S. Geological Survey
BLM   U.S. Bureau of Land Management

The Sangre de Cristo Mountains

The Sangre de Cristo Mountains, which are the southern terminus of the great Rocky Mountain chain, dominate north-central New Mexico. Visitors will immediately note this region's resemblance to the Colorado Rockies and with good reason, for the Sangre de Cristos do indeed extend into Colorado. Here are the high alpine summits, glacier-carved valleys, and great pine and spruce-fir forests that one associates with the Rocky Mountains. When people anywhere mention wilderness, images like this come to mind.

In addition to their natural beauty, New Mexico's Sangre de Cristos also have major cultural and historical significance. All of New Mexico's Native Americans converged here at one time or another: Plains Indians, such as the Comanches and Kiowas; nomadic Navajos and Apaches speaking Athabaskan languages; mountain-dwelling Utes; and Puebloan peoples—many of whose pueblos still stand here. They hunted in the vast forests of the Sangre de Cristos and came to trade in towns like Taos. These rendezvous brought together Hispanic traders and settlers as well as American mountain men; Kit Carson knew this region well and made his home here. At a place called San Gabriel (near the confluence of the Rio Grande and the Rio Chama), Spaniards established the first European capital in what is now the United States; traditional Hispanic culture still survives in rural mountain villages here.

The Sangre de Cristo region is loosely bordered on the west by the Rio Grande Rift—one of the earth's most active geological zones. The Rio Grande and its gorge are indeed impressive, but they are only surface artifacts of the great subterranean drama occurring here. With the continued uplift of mountains in the east and of the subsiding basin beneath the Rio Grande, this rift would be six times deeper than the Grand Canyon if emptied of sediments. This geological ferment is evidenced by the numerous volcanic formations in the Taos area, such as hulking San Antonio Mountain near the Colorado border and the basaltic lava columns in the Rio Grande Gorge.

East of the Rio Grande are the Sangre de Cristos, as well as numerous subranges, including the Culebra Range, the Cimarron Range, the Taos Range, the Las Vegas Range, and the Santa Fe Range. These geographic distinctions are lost on most people, however, as the ranges are clearly

Hiker approaching Wheeler Peak

part of the larger whole. To the east, the Sangre de Cristos devolve into the complex landforms of northeastern New Mexico. The Cimarron Range, with peaks exceeding 12,000 feet, runs through this area, helping define the Rocky Mountain character of the Valle Vidal Unit Natural Area. The Sabinoso Wilderness Study Area, an area of mesa and rimrock along the Canadian River, is included in this section of the book for convenience and geographic proximity.

In the south, the 3,000-mile-long Rocky Mountains, which begin in northwestern Alaska, finally taper out in the Santa Fe Range east of Santa Fe; Interstate 25 serves as a convenient demarcation line. It's not an ignoble end, however, for several 12,000-plus-foot peaks are found here, as well as the Pecos Wilderness, which is the second largest in New Mexico and considered one of the crown jewels among New Mexico's wildlands. It is certainly the most heavily used of New Mexico's wildernesses, yet while frequently hiked and highly regulated, the Pecos Country remains a place of wild beauty.

The Pecos Wilderness, encompassing the 13,000-foot Truchas Peaks, extends into the Sangre de Cristo region's core. Three other wildernesses protect the Sangre's wild character as well: the Wheeler Peak Wilderness, which is heavily used due to its close proximity to Taos and the resort town of Red River; the Columbine-Hondo Wilderness Study Area; and the Latir Peak Wilderness. Although Columbine-Hondo and Latir Peaks are more remote and less used than Wheeler Peak, they, too, exemplify the Rocky Mountain high country.

High elevations and northern latitude mean this region captures moisture moving along storm tracks from the west. This results in dense conifer forests, shimmering aspen groves, and lush meadows filled with wildflowers. Blue columbines also occur here. Although lingering spring snowpack and early fall storms shorten the high-elevation hiking season here, summers compensate for the lack of length with breathtaking beauty. Furthermore, this region is among the few in New Mexico where hikers needn't worry about water availability. Rivers tend to be small and little known outside of New Mexico (except for the Pecos), but are numerous. The Rio Mora, the Vermejo River, the Red River, the Rio Hondo, and the Rio Pueblo de Taos, among others, are found here. In the Sangre de Cristo Mountains streams actually get larger as they flow down from the mountains.

The abundant moisture here results in more diverse recreational opportunities than elsewhere in the state. This region is the state's primary focus for downhill and cross-country skiing. Spring runoff on the Rio Grande attracts boaters, and some of New Mexico's best trout streams are found here. An extensive network of forest roads makes for excellent mountain biking.

Wildlife in this region, once decimated by market hunting, has made a dramatic recovery. Mule deer, elk, Rocky Mountain bighorn sheep, black bears, mountain lions, beavers, and many other species are common in the Sangre de Cristos, a region where they once neared extinction. Of all the species the mountain men would have known, only grizzlies, wolves, and Merriams elk are still absent.

While it's unlikely that north-central New Mexico will ever upstage the great mountain recreation areas of the more northerly Rockies—in part because tourist facilities here are still limited—people can no longer claim that New Mexico's Sangre de Cristos are a well-kept secret. Northern New Mexico, and Santa Fe in particular, continue to be an appealing destination for tourists, retirees, and people who want something different than typical coastal destinations for vacations. Santa Fe is the largest population center in the region, followed by Taos and Española, all of which are growing rapidly. Albuquerque, while not directly within this region, is only a short drive away. From my home just outside Albuquerque, I can be in the Pecos Wilderness in about the same amount of time it takes a person in Denver to get to the wildlands of the Front Range.

Due to increasing population and easier accessibility, the pressure of development and recreational land use on these wildlands will intensify, mitigated somewhat by the fact that many of these lands have been preempted by Spanish and Mexican land grants, Native American tribal lands, and public agency holdings. Political situations are complex, as many local Native American and Hispanic peoples increasingly see the influx of outsiders as a threat to traditional culture and to the land itself. But as always, the Sangre de Cristo Mountains continue to fascinate and inspire because they embody New Mexico high country at its best: a glorious finale to North America's greatest mountain chain.

Columbine–Hondo Wilderness Study Area

The Columbine-Hondo is a large and significant wilderness study area in the northern Sangre de Cristo Mountains, featuring 11,000-plus-foot peaks, clear mountain streams, high meadows, and conifer forests.

Columbine blooms

LOCATION	Northeast of Taos, north of the Rio Hondo and south of the Red River
SIZE	30,500 acres
ELEVATION RANGE	7,900 to 12,711 feet at Gold Hill
MILES OF TRAILS	Approximately 75
ECOSYSTEMS	Spruce-fir, high grassy meadows, alpine tundra
ADMINISTRATION	Carson National Forest
TOPOGRAPHIC MAPS	Carson National Forest — Latir Peak and Wheeler Peak Wildernesses
BEST SEASONS	Summer, early fall
GETTING THERE	Access is via Highway 38 on the north or Highway 150 on the south; both have several Forest Service campgrounds.
HIKING	The Columbine–Hondo WSA offers outstanding opportunities for extended hiking and backpacking via an extensive network of developed scenic trails.

Located between the Latir Peak and Wheeler Peak Wildernesses, the Columbine–Hondo WSA is larger than these sister areas but comparable in terms of scenery and wilderness character. Columbine–Hondo has an extensive and well-developed trail system, yet the area is relatively unknown to the public and is visited far less often. It's a perfect place to go for solitude.

This was not the case about a hundred years ago. Prospectors scoured the mountains for ore bodies similar to the ones that created boomtowns such as nearby Red River. Indeed, many trails here were first trod by prospectors, and the Columbine Twining National Recreation Trail follows a route used during the mining boom by miners and prospectors traveling between the gold camps of the Red River Valley and the mining camp of Twining (now Taos Ski Valley).

As happened so often in New Mexico, the boom eventually went bust, the mining camps were abandoned or nearly so, and the remote mountain area was dormant and ignored. Then in the 1950s another boom began, this time based upon a resource that proved far more valuable than underground minerals—snow. Skis and ski lifts replaced shovels and tunnels.

Hikers with backpacks replaced prospectors with burros. While the Columbine–Hondo WSA includes numerous pleasant day hikes, its size and terrain make it more suitable for backpacking. The trails are often long, and because many ascend from valleys to ridges, they can be steep. The two most popular trailheads are the Twining Campground on the south and the Columbine Campground on the north.

From the Twining Campground Trailhead, a strenuous 10.5-mile loop hike takes you to the summit of Gold Hill, at 12,711 feet the area's highest peak. This route also intersects Trail 57, running southwest along the area's dominant ridge toward 12,201-foot Lobo Peak. This route can be combined with trails intersecting from the south, west, and north to make shuttle hikes.

From the Columbine Campground, a popular hike is Trail 71. A pleasant and easy day hike heads south along Columbine Creek, where you will indeed find

Columbine–Hondo WSA

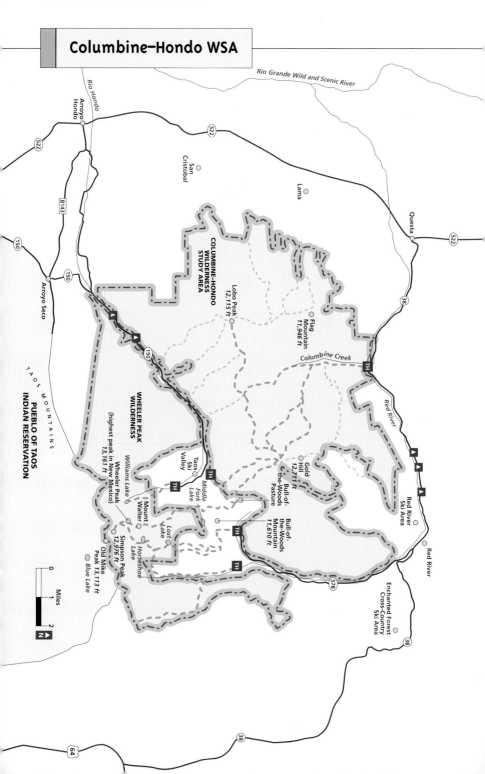

columbines. Continuing south, Trail 71 becomes steeper as it climbs out of the drainage to ascend the ridge where it connects with Trail 57. From here it's a relatively short downhill trek to the Red River and Highway 150. By continuing east along the ridge on Trail 57, you'll eventually get to the Twining Campground, near the Taos Ski Valley.

Another way to go from the Columbine Campground to the Twining Campground is over the Columbine Twining National Recreation Trail. This follows Trail 71 south from Columbine Campground until the junction with the Deer Creek Trail, No. 69, heading east. This ascends steeply before leveling out at grassy meadows —a good camping destination. Here Trail 69 intersects the Gold Hill Trail, No. 64, which runs south over Gold Hill's huge, rounded, bare summit before descending to the Twining Campground. The total distance is approximately 14 miles. You can also return to Columbine Campground with a loop hike via Trail 72 along the Placer Creek Fork of Columbine Creek (total distance 17 miles), or by heading southwest on Trail 57 to return via the upper section of Trail 71 along Columbine Creek (total distance 19.5 miles).

Eventually, the government will probably officially recognize that Columbine–Hondo is one of northern New Mexico's true and important wildernesses. When that happens, a few hikers will be able to say, "I knew it when. . . ."

OTHER RECREATIONAL OPPORTUNITIES

In the winter, the Columbine Creek Trail, No. 71, is available for non-motorized travel into the wilderness. The trail, located at the Columbine Campground four miles east of Questa on Highway 38, heads south. The first three miles are suitable for beginning and intermediate skiers; after that the terrain is more difficult.

From the south, the Long Canyon and Bull-of-the-Woods Trails enter the wilderness from the Taos Ski Valley and are also closed to snowmobiles. These trails are steep and suited for advanced skiers only. Avalanche hazards exist at the head of Long Canyon.

FOR MORE INFORMATION

Carson National Forest, Questa Ranger District, P.O. Box 110, Questa, NM 87556; (505) 586-0520.

Carson National Forest, Supervisor's Office, Forest Service Building, P.O. Box 558, 208 Cruz Alta Road, Taos, NM 87571; (505) 758-6200.

2 Cruces Basin Wilderness

Vast meadows, fringed with aspen groves and conifer forests, invite hikers to journey cross-country and explore the creeks, granite cliffs, ridges, and knolls within the basin that make up this remote and seldom-visited wilderness.

Amanita muscara mushroom in forest

LOCATION	In the Tusas Mountains just south of the Colorado border, between Tres Piedras and Tierra Amarilla
SIZE	18,902 acres
ELEVATION RANGE	8,525 to 10,840 feet
MILES OF TRAILS	No designated trails
ECOSYSTEMS	Spruce-fir, ponderosa pine, aspen, high-elevation grassland
ADMINISTRATION	Carson National Forest
TOPOGRAPHIC MAPS	Carson National Forest—Cruces Basin Wilderness
BEST SEASONS	Summer, fall
GETTING THERE	The Cruces Basin Wilderness is reached by going north on Highway 285 from the village of Tres Piedras to where dirt Forest Road 87 heads west just south of San Antonio Mountain. Drive on Forest Road 87 approximately 28 miles to the wilderness's boundary.
HIKING	The Cruces Basin Wilderness lacks developed trails and trailheads yet animal trails and unmarked human routes abound, and cross-country hiking is easy through the meadows.

I FIRST VISITED THE CRUCES BASIN WILDERNESS on a typical day in October, when the grassland was tawny as the fur on a puma and the aspens, just beginning to lose their leaves, seemed like translucent pewter. Leaves fluttered like a hillside choir in the faint breeze. Shallow snow lay puddled in hollows on the north slopes and beneath the great coats of spruce and fir, while in the meadows dandelions and even an occasional aster still bloomed in the lean warmth of the declining sun. Emerging from my tent at morning, I found my bootprints crystallized in frozen mud.

October, a transitional season, is a most appropriate time to visit an area that is itself a transition zone. The Cruces Basin Wilderness is New Mexico's northernmost wilderness, located just a mile south of the Colorado border. Here the semi-arid plains and forests of New Mexico—sagebrush and chamisa, piñon-juniper and ponderosa pine—gradually phase into the high-country parklands and spruce-fir and aspen forests of Colorado. It's also a transition area in that the current landscape resulted from a great fire in 1879 that cleared the old-growth forest, making room for the grasslands and welcoming back the pioneering aspen. The cycles of this transition zone are an enduring part of the southern Rockies ecology.

Although the terrain seems to reflect the stereotypic landscapes of both New Mexico and Colorado, political boundaries are as transitory as ecological ones. Not too long ago, this entire region was within the single entity created in 1598 when Don Juan de Oñate claimed this region for Spain and proclaimed himself "governor, captain general, and *adelantado* of *Nuevo Mejico* and all its kingdoms and provinces." When the great fire occurred in 1879, New Mexico had been part of the United States for only 33 years; statehood was still 33 years away. Among many of the region's Hispanic inhabitants, the old Spanish colony's cultural legacy persists today.

Certainly the place names reflect that Spanish heritage. The wilderness takes its name from Cruces Creek, meaning "crosses." Drainages in the basin include

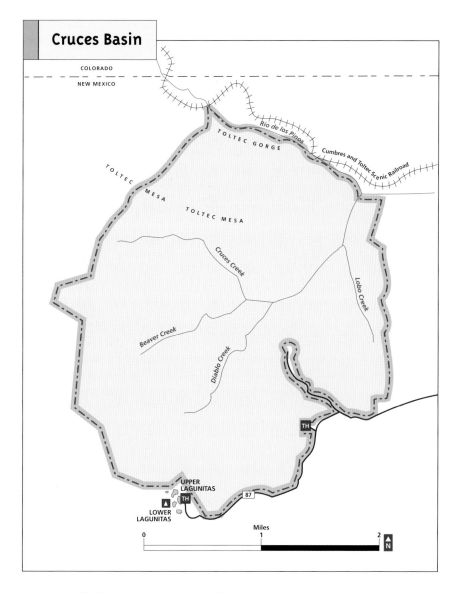

Escondido, "hidden"; Osha, the medicinal herb whose English common name is lovage; Lobo, "wolf"; and Diablo, "devil."

Forming the wilderness's northern boundary is the Rio de los Pinos, "river of the pines"; on the west is the Brazos Ridge, named for the Rio Brazos, river of many "arms" or tributaries; and to the east is the great volcanic landmark, San Antonio Mountain, named for the saint popular in the Spanish-speaking world.

Yet long before Spanish-speaking settlers arrived, this area was overlaid by still other human delineations. Natural features here marked the territories of the Native American tribes who hunted and foraged here: Utes, Jicarilla Apaches, Navajos, and

Indians from pueblos along the Rio Grande. Before these tribes, still other tribes were a part of this enduring cycle of flux and change.

The most recent significant human event in this cycle was the achievement of wilderness designation. In 1980 the Cruces Basin Wilderness was among several included in the federal legislation resulting from the RARE II process of identifying potential wildernesses. Actually, wilderness designation had little impact on this area. Livestock grazing, formerly sheep but now mostly cattle, was allowed to continue as a traditional use. While hikers may condemn the cow flops and contaminated water, there's no denying that grazing, along with fire, has contributed to the meadows and parks that give this area its unique character. Two grazing associations have allotments in the wilderness. Their separate pastures, marked by fences, are used from June through October on a rest-rotation basis that allows for vegetation recovery. Hikers wishing to avoid livestock can obtain a grazing schedule and map at the Ranger District office in Tres Piedras.

But aside from watering holes, fences, and livestock trails, human impact on this area has been slight. Remoteness has much to do with this. Taos, 60 air miles away and probably two hours by car, is the nearest population center and has more well-known wildernesses close at hand. Access to the Cruces Basin area's only maintained campground is over 28 miles of dirt road (informal campsites are somewhat closer). No obvious features like peaks, lakes, waterfalls, ghost towns, and so forth attract casual visitors, and there are no trails leading hikers into the wilderness (although game and livestock trails abound).

In the wilderness, hiking can be relatively easy as you stride over the gentle, grassy slopes—or devilishly difficult as you stumble over blowdowns in dense spruce-fir stands. Although the wilderness is centered on a basin, and the view is far reaching, the topography is nonetheless complex: map and compass are essential, and a GPS unit even more helpful. Attractive sites suitable for camping are abundant, yet established campsites, with fire rings and slashed trees, are refreshingly infrequent. Numerous streams provide water and, for the angler, brook trout. (But remember—livestock grazing means all water must be treated thoroughly.)

The Cruces Basin, with its patchwork of meadows, aspen groves, and forests, is rich habitat for wildlife, including elk, deer, black bears, coyotes—indeed all the animals associated with the southern Rocky Mountains. Because of this, the area is most heavily used during the fall hunting season. Veritable caravans of trucks and horse trailers raise clouds of dust as they head down the dirt road for hunting camps.

The Forest Service maintains two adjacent campgrounds: Upper and Lower Lagunitas, located on the wilderness's southwestern edge. It's a 28-mile drive over Forest Road 87 from Highway 285 north of Tres Piedras, just south of San Antonio Mountain. Numerous undesignated sites are also accessible from Forest Road 87 on the wilderness's southern and southwestern periphery. Regrettably, theft and vandalism of vehicles or tents left unattended—a problem throughout northern New Mexico—can occur even in this remote area.

There is no vehicular access to the wilderness area's northern portion, although you could plan an interesting expedition involving the Cumbres and Toltec Scenic Railroad that runs between Chama, New Mexico, and Antonito, Colorado. Disembark from the train in the Rio Grande National Forest in Colorado, then descend to the valley of the Rio de los Pinos to enter the wilderness from the north by crossing the river.

Much of the above would seem to discourage hikers from visiting the Cruces Basin Wilderness. The remote basin is the third smallest of all the state's wilderness areas and for the most part is overlooked by hikers and backpackers. Lacking the obvious attractions of other areas, the Cruces Basin Wilderness has simply its wildness to attract you.

DESTINATION HIKE: TOLTEC GORGE
One-way length: approximately 6 miles
Low and high elevations: 8,800 and 9,800 feet
Difficulty: moderate to strenuous

This hike begins at the end of Forest Road 572, on the southeastern edge of the wilderness. A well-worn trail follows Osha Creek into the basin and up to its confluence with Beaver and Cruces Creeks. From there the route follows Cruces Creek upstream, and climbs an unnamed drainage to reach Toltec Mesa. The trail then heads north by northwest and arrives at the cliffs flanking the Rio de los Pinos at Toltec Gorge. Careful map reading is essential for this trip; a GPS unit is recommended.

OTHER RECREATIONAL OPPORTUNITIES

The Forest Service roads here, including Forest Road 87, are great for mountain biking, with numerous good campsites along the way, as well as at Lagunitas, which has designated campgrounds. Lots of potential for cross-country skiing here, although in winter the area is generally inaccessible and most skiers seek comparable terrain closer to Highway 285.

FOR MORE INFORMATION

TRES PIEDRAS RANGER DISTRICT, P.O. Box 38, Tres Piedras, NM 87577; (505) 758-8678.

CARSON NATIONAL FOREST, Supervisor's Office, Forest Service Building, P.O. Box 558, 208 Cruz Alta Road, Taos, NM 87571; (505) 758-6200.

Latir Peak Wilderness

Relatively unknown and untraveled, the Latir Peak Wilderness is classic southern Rocky Mountain high country—emerald meadows; alpine grasslands and tundra; small, clear lakes; spruce-fir forest; and some of New Mexico's highest peaks.

Heart Lake in dawn light

LOCATION	In the Sangre de Cristo Mountains, northeast of Questa
SIZE	20,506 acres
ELEVATION RANGE	8,400 to 12,734 feet at Venado Peak
MILES OF TRAILS	24
ECOSYSTEMS	Spruce-fir, bristlecone pine, aspen, alpine tundra, and high-altitude grassland
ADMINISTRATION	Carson National Forest
TOPOGRAPHIC MAPS	Carson National Forest — Latir Peak and Wheeler Peak Wildernesses; Cerro, Questa, and Red River USGS 7.5-minute quadrangles
BEST SEASONS	Summer, early fall
GETTING THERE	Most people reach the Latir Peak Wilderness from the village of Questa by taking Highway 38 east briefly before taking Highway 563 northeast to packed dirt Forest Road 134, which parallels the wilderness's southern boundary.
HIKING	Several maintained and marked trails take hikers through the wilderness, with the sections above timberline especially appealing.

FROM LATIR PEAK'S ROUNDED SUMMIT, look north and you can see, hazy in the distance, the jagged fang of Colorado's 14,317-foot Blanca Peak; the view to the south reveals 13,161-foot Wheeler Peak, New Mexico's highest mountain. In the company of southern Rocky Mountain giants such as these, the grassy 12,000-foot mountains of the Latir Peak Wilderness might seem easy to overlook. Indeed, many people do, for this, the fifth-smallest New Mexico wilderness, attracts few visitors. Yet four of the state's 20 highest mountains—Venado Peak (12,734 feet), Latir Peak (12,708), Latir Mesa (12,692), and Virsylvia Peak (12,594)—are here.

The relatively small size of the Latir Peak Wilderness area has less to do with natural history than human history. Although the wilderness stretches almost seamlessly from Highway 38 in Red River Canyon north to the Colorado border, more than half this wildland is within the Sangre de Cristo Land Grant—over a million acres given in 1843 to Mexican citizens Narciso Beaubien and Stephen Louis Lee by the Mexican governor Manuel Armijo. This grant was among several northern New Mexico land grants that survived the somewhat turbulent transition from Mexican to American governance after 1848.

Of the other land grants in place at the time, most were later sold, dispersed, or eventually absorbed into the national forest system. Among the northern New Mexico Hispanic descendants of these land grant owners, feelings of betrayal and disenfranchisement persist, and Hispanic activists continue to press for the land-grant issue to be reopened by Congress and the courts. Whether this could affect the Latir Peak Wilderness, designated in 1980, is unknown, but at this time it's unlikely that the wilderness will be expanded northward. These northern lands are currently controlled by the Rio Costilla Co-op Livestock Associates (P.O. Box 111, Costilla, NM 87524; (505) 586-0542.) The association issues permits either at its office in Costilla or the self-service station at the park entrance in Amalia. Permits are not issued to enter its lands from the south because of difficulty controlling access.

The area's Hispanic presence is further revealed by the Spanish names in the wilderness: Venado, "deer"; Cabresto, "halter"; Pinabete, "spruce"; and Jaracito, "little willow." And Latir: while this name has been reported to be a French surname, more likely it's related to the Spanish verb, *latir*, meaning "to howl or bark," perhaps referring to wolf or coyote calls.

Although the wilderness has long been devoid of wolves, it remains rich wildlife habitat. As you hike above timberline, you quickly realize the trails here are trod less by humans than by elk; in the meadows below you're likely to see them grazing. Ptarmigan, marmots, and pikas live in the rocks at and above timberline. Black bears and mountain lions also live here, and boreal owls were recently discovered in the area.

Most hikers enter the wilderness from the southwest. From the village of Questa, take Highway 38 east a short distance. Then branch northeast on Highway 563, which is paved until it reaches the Carson National Forest boundary and becomes packed dirt at Forest Road 134. After 3.4 miles, Forest Road 134A branches left, climbing steeply two miles to Cabresto Lake. You'll need a high-clearance vehicle for 134A. At Cabresto Lake, the Lake Fork Trail, Number 82, traverses the lake's north side before entering the canyon to parallel the Lake Fork of Cabresto Creek. After

Latir Peak

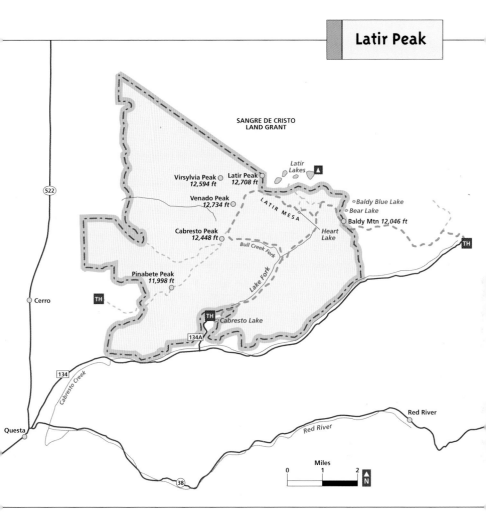

three miles, the trail meets Bull Creek and the Bull Creek Trail, Number 85. The main trail continues another 1.6 miles to scenic Heart Lake, the destination for most hikers.

Also from the southwest, a gravel road heads east from the village of Cerro to the head of Trail 167. This climbs steeply as it enters the wilderness before it runs along the ridge over 11,948-foot Pinabete Peak. The trail reaches the junction with the Bull Creek Trail after about 4.5 miles, just east of Cabresto Peak. Just west of Cabresto Peak, Trail 167 is joined from the northwest by the 2.5-mile trail that enters the wilderness via Rito Primero ("first creek").

The wilderness can be entered from the east via Baldy Mountain Trail, Number 81. To reach the trailhead, continue on Forest Road 134 approximately 12 miles past the forest's western boundary. After about 5.5 miles, the Baldy Mountain Trail joins the Lake Fork Trail just below Heart Lake.

From the north, you can enter the wilderness through the Sangre de Cristo Grant, but a permit is required from the Rio Costilla Co-op Livestock Association (see p. 48).

The canyons in the Latir Peak Wilderness are steep, narrow, and densely forested. The streams likewise are narrow and overhung with brush and tree limbs, making them difficult to fish—one reason the native Rio Grande cutthroat trout have survived here. The lakes, too, are small; many have no fish because of winterkill. Thus, most hikers are drawn primarily to the exhilarating expanses above timberline. From a base camp at Heart Lake, located near timberline, hikers can reach several of the wilderness's 12,000-foot summits in a day. None pose any technical difficulties; although, like elsewhere in the southern Rocky Mountains, the areas above timberline are exposed to sudden afternoon thundershowers and lightning during July and August.

Relatively few hikers explore the Latir Peak Wilderness; most head either into Colorado or to the higher, more readily accessible summits of the Wheeler Peak Wilderness to the south. But the clear consensus among hikers who have been here is that the Latir Peak region is one of New Mexico's wilderness jewels.

DAY HIKE: HEART LAKE
One-way length: 5 miles
Low and high elevations: 9,100 and 11,600 feet
Difficulty: moderate

This is the most popular hike in the Latir Peak Wilderness, and deservedly so. The journey is not only pleasant but also spectacular. Heart Lake is a lovely manmade lake surrounded by high peaks, making it a perfect base camp from which to climb and explore surrounding peaks. From Cabresto Lake, the Lake Fork Trail, Number 82, traverses around the lake's north side before entering the canyon to parallel the Lake Fork of Cabresto Creek. After three miles, the trail meets Bull Creek and the Bull Creek Trail, Number 85. The main trail continues another 1.6 miles to Heart Lake. At the lake's southwest side, a marked trail begins ascending around the lake and then switchbacks up the hillside to come out atop Latir Mesa. From here the trail is often obscure, but the route is marked by cairns and posts.

**LOOP HIKE: CABRESTO LAKE – HEART LAKE – LATIR PEAK –
VENADO PEAK – CABRESTO PEAK – BULL CREEK**
Round-trip length: 14 miles
Low and high elevations: 9,100 and 12,734 feet at Venado Peak
Difficulty: strenuous

Distance and elevation are what make this hike strenuous, as most slopes are fairly gentle. Venado and Cabresto Peaks are the steepest sections, and even these don't pose any serious difficulties. Follow cairns from Latir Mesa (see Heart Lake hike) to Latir Peak. Then return along the ridge, from which you'll see a trail leading along a narrow ridge to the lower slope of Venado Peak. Ascend this peak if your energy permits or continue west through a grassy valley, again watching for cairns and a faint track. Climbing Cabresto Peak from the junction at the Bull Creek Trail requires a sidetrip, returning to the Bull Creek Trail and following it downhill to the Lake Fork Trail to complete the loop. Coming down the Bull Creek Trail is much easier than going up.

SHUTTLE HIKE: BALDY MOUNTAIN TRAIL –
LAKE FORK CREEK TRAIL
One-way length: 11.1 miles
Low and high elevations: 9,100 and 12,046 feet at Baldy Mountain
Difficulty: moderate to strenuous

OTHER RECREATIONAL OPPORTUNITIES

Cross-country skiing and snowmobiling are allowed on the two miles of Forest Road 134A leading from Cabresto Canyon uphill to Cabresto Lake. From here only cross-country skiing is allowed on the Lake Fork Trail as it parallels Lake Fork Creek in the wilderness and eventually arrives at Heart Lake.

FOR MORE INFORMATION

CARSON NATIONAL FOREST, Questa Ranger District, P.O. Box 110, Questa, NM 87556; (505) 586-0520.

CARSON NATIONAL FOREST, Supervisor's Office, Forest Service Building, P.O. Box 558, 208 Cruz Alta Road, Taos, NM 87571; (505) 758-6200.

4 Pecos Wilderness

The Pecos Wilderness area is the second largest in New Mexico and arguably the most well-known. Its extensive trail network is famous for leading to some of the state's most spectacular mountain scenery.

Santa Fe Baldy Peak

LOCATION	In the Sangre de Cristo Mountains, northeast of Santa Fe
SIZE	222,673 acres
ELEVATION RANGE	8,400 to 13,102 feet at Truchas Peak
MILES OF TRAILS	445
ECOSYSTEMS	Diverse riparian, ponderosa pine, Engelmann spruce, Douglas fir, and alpine tundra
ADMINISTRATION	Carson National Forest, Santa Fe National Forest
TOPOGRAPHIC MAPS	Santa Fe National Forest—Pecos Wilderness Map; topographic map included with Pecos Wilderness Trail Guide
BEST SEASONS	Summer, early fall
GETTING THERE	The large size and central location of the Pecos Wilderness mean it is reached from several points, with major trailheads readily accessible from Santa Fe, Española, and Las Vegas. Highway 63 along the Pecos River from the village of Pecos to the locality of Cowles provides the best access to the wilderness's heart.
HIKING	The Pecos Wilderness has an extensive system of well-marked, well-maintained trails, allowing for hikes ranging from short excursions to extended backpack trips. New Mexico's longest trail, the 50-mile Skyline Trail, is here.

THE PECOS IS THE QUINTESSENTIAL NEW MEXICO mountain wilderness—
high, wide, and beautiful, a wonderland of wildflower-filled meadows, alpine lakes,
dark conifer forests, shimmering aspen groves, many of the state's highest mountains,
and abundant wildlife. Yet this seemingly pristine wilderness has suffered a sobering
number of changes and environmental indignities. As the New Mexico outdoor writer
Kay Matthews put it, "Perhaps the most remarkable aspect of the Pecos is the fact that
there is a Pecos Wilderness at all."

For centuries, the Pecos high country had been a resource for Native American
peoples, a place to hunt, fish, cut fuelwood and timber, and gather medicinal and edible
plants. On the west lived Tewa and Keresan Puebloan peoples; on the north lived Tiwa
Pueblos and nomadic mountain peoples such as the Utes; on the east Plains Indians
roamed; and on the south Towa Indians inhabited the pueblo the Spaniards called
Pecos, from a Keresan word meaning "place where there is water." From the pueblo
the name spread to the nearby river, thence to the headwaters in the mountains.
When the Spaniards arrived in 1540, they established villages around the periphery
of the wilderness and used the wilderness much as the Indians had.

But even when grazing commenced in the wilderness possibly as early as
1825, its impact on the land was relatively small. That changed, however, when
English-speaking settlers arrived after the American annexation of New Mexico in
1846, bringing with them new and vastly more powerful technologies and a philosophy that combined market rather than subsistence economics with an impetus to
"conquer" the West.

Because the Pecos area was relatively free of valuable minerals, and perhaps
because of the region's remoteness, Pecos was spared the worst ravages of mining.
(Nevertheless, mine dumps persist at Terrero, and the Jacks Creek Trailhead recently
underwent a lengthy closure to remove toxic soil from the parking area.) But the
wilderness's vastness could not protect its wildlife. By 1888 elk had been exterminated
in the Pecos Country. By 1900 they were gone from the rest of the state. Rocky Mountain
bighorn sheep had disappeared by 1900. The last grizzly in the Pecos Wilderness was
killed in 1923. Perhaps the most telling example of the wildlife devastation is that during
the 1915 hunting season on the one million acres of the Carson National Forest (which
includes much of the Pecos Wilderness), only eight deer were taken.

But even as this wildlife holocaust occurred, conservationists were acting to
protect the area and its resources. In 1892 President Harrison proclaimed the upper
Pecos watershed a timberland reserve for watershed protection (a proclamation not
implemented until 1898). The area was set aside and withdrawn from every use
including logging, grazing, and mining, and it was closed completely to the public.
The Pecos Primitive Area of 133,640 acres was established by the Chief of the Forest
Service in 1933. It was declared a Forest Service wilderness in 1955 and became
part of the National Wilderness Preservation System on September 3, 1964, when
President Johnson signed the Wilderness Act. In 1980, the New Mexico Wilderness
Act added 55,000 acres to include more lands with wilderness character.

Concurrent with wilderness preservation was wildlife restoration. In the Pecos
Wilderness much of this resulted from the leadership of Elliott Barker, who had grown
up on a ranch near the wilderness. Other changes were occurring. In 1911, when Barker

was a young assistant forest ranger, fewer than 300 people visited the high country solely for recreation during the year. By 1970, based upon wilderness travel permits (now no longer required), the total exceeded 20,000 a year, and the Pecos was among the top five most heavily used wilderness areas in the Forest Service system.

The nature of the use was also changing. In 1948 two young men attempted something novel: they would spend two weeks camping and fishing in the wilderness on foot! Previously, almost all travel in the wilderness was by horse and pack animals. Their backpacking was so unusual that *New Mexico Magazine* ran a feature article about the trip. By 1960, backpackers outnumbered horse riders in the wilderness.

But while portions of the Pecos Wilderness receive very heavy use, 85 percent of the hikers use 15 percent of the wilderness—other areas seldom receive visitors. I recall a trip to Pecos Falls, at the height of the summer hiking season, during which my friend and I spent a day hiking the headwaters of the Pecos River and didn't encounter another hiker. The most frequently traveled trails are those leading to Beattys, Puerto Nambe, Hermits Peak, the high peaks, the lake basins, and even Pecos Falls. But after Labor Day, visits to these areas decline precipitously, and early fall in the Pecos is magnificent and tranquil.

Because of its elevation, the Pecos Country is cooler than surrounding areas. Summer daytime temperatures average 70 degrees Fahrenheit, with nighttime averages in the 30s. Average annual precipitation is 35 to 40 inches, half from summer rain, half from winter snow. May and June generally are dry months, but heavy snowpack in the high country and on north slopes can impede travel into June. From mid-July through August, daily thundershowers are often heavy. September and October typically are dry, although snow can come to the high country during these months.

Only above timberline do hikers have to be concerned about availability of water, but because cattle grazing continues in the Pecos Wilderness, all water must be treated. Unfortunately, each year the wilderness is ravaged by mountain man wannabes convinced their outdoor experience won't be complete unless they've used their hatchets to hack down a few trees to make a lean-to, a huge fire, or whatever. Trails in the Pecos Wilderness are generally well-marked and easy to follow. Several excellent guidebooks for the area are available.

The southern Sangre de Cristo Mountains within the Pecos Wilderness are the southern end of the great Rocky Mountain chain whose northern end stretches to Alaska. Certainly, the wilderness more closely fits the image of the Rocky Mountains than the desert Southwest. The dominant trees here are Engelmann spruce; at lower elevations blue spruce, corkbark fir, and aspen thrive, while lower still live Douglas fir, white fir, limber pine, and ponderosa pine. The Pecos Wilderness is the southern limit of the long-lived bristlecone pine.

The wilderness also marks the southern limit of the pine marten. While you're not likely to observe a pine marten, on any trip in the Pecos of two days or more your chances of seeing elk are excellent, as are your chances of seeing Rocky Mountain bighorn sheep near the Truchas Peaks. (I remember stalking a herd of bighorn sheep on Truchas Peak so I could get photos before they fled. When they finally saw me, they began moving toward me so they could share my lunch!)

ELLIOTT BARKER

All hikers in the Pecos Wilderness should stop at least once on their trip to commemorate Elliott Barker—especially if they see a herd of elk. The

story of the Pecos Wilderness—in fact New Mexico wilderness in general—is intertwined with the story of Elliott Barker. In the 101 years that he lived, Barker witnessed dramatic changes in New Mexico's wild-lands, and he was a major agent of those changes.

Barker, born in 1886, came to New Mexico at the age of three when his family arrived from Texas in a covered wagon. They settled on a ranch on the south-east side of the Pecos Country, and there he grew up, hunting, fishing, cutting firewood, and absorbing the principles of waste-not. As a child he once caught far more trout than the family could eat, but his father nonetheless made him clean and process them all any-way to teach him a lesson. It was one he never forgot.

Barker was 12 in 1898 when President Harrison's 1892 order creating the Pecos River Forest Reserve was finally implemented. By this time he was familiar with forest fires, overgrazing, and scarce wildlife. In 1909 he became a ranger in the Forest Service headed by Gifford Pinchot, whose writings and philosophy he readily absorbed. He served 10 months near Cuba, New Mexico, before he was transferred back to his beloved Pecos Country.

The emphasis then was on forest fire prevention and, through it, water-shed protection. But Barker quickly recognized that livestock overgrazing was also a serious threat. "Reduction of cattle and sheep numbers without hurting the permittees' economic status was exceedingly difficult," he wrote. "That was a serious conservation problem to solve." He was sensitive to the permittees because, after all, his family and their friends and neighbors were among them. Especially devastating, he observed, was sheep grazing on high elevation slopes. Today, cattle still graze in the Pecos Wilderness but not sheep, thanks in large part to Barker.

In 1912 and 1913, an important association helped the fledgling conser-vationist's career: Barker worked in the Carson National Forest where the forest supervisor was Aldo Leopold. Barker once said of Leopold, "In the

continued on page 56

brief period of my service under him he gave me effective inspiration in the field of conservation, especially in conservation and management of wildlife. I have always considered it a great privilege to have worked under, and later associated with, that wonderful man who later became Dr. Aldo Leopold, America's greatest authority on wildlife management." It was only the beginning of their long association.

Barker himself soon became forest supervisor, but, in 1919, he resigned to buy the family ranch. When the Depression hit, ranching was doomed. He served for a year as wildlife manager at the Vermejo Park property, managed as a hunting preserve for wealthy visitors from the East. Barker, from childhood an avid hunter, was a product of his times: like Aldo Leopold early in his career, Barker was a fervent advocate of predator control to increase game populations. During his year at Vermejo Park, he killed 16 lions, 46 coyotes, and 39 bobcats.

In 1931, Barker was appointed state game warden, a position the family ranch had forced him to refuse five years earlier, despite the urging of Aldo Leopold. Barker remained state game warden until his retirement in 1953. During those 22 years, he changed the face of the New Mexico wilderness. He was especially active in restoration and protection of wildlife. He attempted reintroduction of Rocky Mountain bighorn sheep into the Sangre de Cristo Mountains (those attempts didn't succeed until 1967), as well as other former habitats such as the Sandia Mountains. He reintroduced beavers into the Pecos Country. He restocked elk in areas where they'd been exterminated. Barker established numerous fisheries and worked for watershed protection. He was instrumental in the public acquisition of key land in Cimarron Canyon, property along the Pecos River, and the Heart Bar Ranch at the confluence of the West Fork and Middle Fork of the Gila River, now an important wildlife area. Better game protection and management laws were the results of his lobbying efforts. He helped organize the National Wildlife Federation. Barker was even instrumental in Smokey the Bear becoming the national fire prevention symbol.

But, perhaps above all, he was an effective advocate for wilderness—speaking loudly, clearly, and with authority and credibility. He could connect with ranchers, because he'd been one. Hunters and fishermen listened because he was one of them, too. He was a plainspoken but effective writer, and in books such as *Beatty's Cabin* he presented his thoughts, observations, and experiences. Where others had studied the wilderness, he lived it.

Elliott Barker lived the Pecos Wilderness. In 1964, when he was testifying in favor of the act creating the national wilderness system, he stated: *I have been using wilderness areas ever since I was a little kid. Fifty-two years ago I took my young bride on a week-long camping trip in the Pecos Wilderness. We went again last year. And in between we have gone scores of times. We will go again come spring and take along some of our grand-children. I have ridden wilderness trails with many hundreds of others through the years on camping, picture-taking, hunting, and fishing trips. As a result, my honest appraisal is that such trips into the unspoiled, pristine backcountry are not only enjoyable, but are most beneficial for recreation and relaxation of mind and body.*

He once estimated he'd ridden 120,000 wilderness miles in his life; he took his last trail ride in the Pecos when he was 89. He died in 1987 at the age of 101. An inconspicuous mountain just west of Elk Mountain in the southern Pecos Country was later named for him and other family members, but his real memorial is the Pecos Wilderness itself. Take a moment and remember him.

The Pecos Wilderness is a true wilderness jewel. Trite though the metaphor may seem, it will feel appropriate when you're actually in the Pecos High Country, perhaps on a ridge looking down upon the river's headwaters where emerald meadows intermingle with crystalline ponds. On the grass a herd of elk are lying, absorbing the warmth of a sunset in a turquoise New Mexico sky. Looking around at the mountains and the valley extending to the horizon, you realize that in this supposedly crowded wilderness you haven't seen another person all day. A wilderness jewel—yes, indeed!

SHORT HIKE: MORA FLATS
One-way length: 3 miles
Low and high elevations: 9,350 and 9,800 feet
Difficulty: easy to moderate

This hike is among the most popular in the southern Pecos Wilderness, especially for families or parties with children. The trail is short, the hiking easy, the scenery beautiful, and the campsites, should you choose to spend the night, appealing. You can reach the trailhead at the Iron Gate Campground by driving Highway 63 north from the village of Pecos for 18.5 miles to where a dirt road branches right and heads 4.4 miles to the campground. The trailhead for Mora Flats is at the campground's northeast end. You'll start by hiking Trail 249, which goes to Hamilton

Pecos

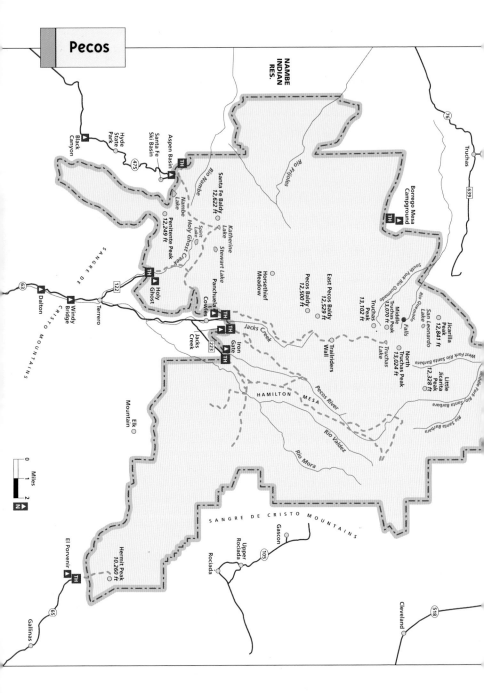

NAMBE INDIAN RES.

Black Canyon

Hyde State Park

Santa Fe Ski Basin

475

Aspen Basin

TH

Rio Nambe

Nambe Lake

Santa Fe Baldy 12,622 ft

Penitente Peak 12,249 ft

Spirit Lake

Holy Ghost Creek

Katherine Lake

Stewart Lake

Rio Frijoles

76

639

Truchas

Borrego Mesa Campground

TH

South Fork Rio Quemado

Rio Quemado Falls

San Leonardo Lake

Jicarilla Peak 12,841 ft

SANGRE DE

63

Dalton

Windy Bridge

Terrero

122

TH

Holy Ghost

Panchuela

Cowles

Horsethief Meadow

East Pecos Baldy 12,529 ft

Pecos Baldy 12,500 ft

Middle Truchas Peak 13,070 ft

Truchas Peak 13,102 ft

West Fork Rio Quemado

North Truchas Peak 13,024 ft

Little Jicarilla Peak 12,328 ft

CRISTO MOUNTAINS

Jacks Creek

TH

TH

Iron Gate

223

Jacks Creek

Trailriders Wall

Truchas Lake

Rio Santa Barbara

East Fork Rio Santa Barbara

HAMILTON MESA

Pecos River

Elk Mountain

Rio Valdez

Rio Mora

Miles
0
1
2

N

SANGRE DE CRISTO MOUNTAINS

El Porvenir

Hermit Peak 10,260 ft

TH

Rociada

Upper Rociada

Gascon

105

518

Cleveland

65

Gallinas

Mesa, although Mora Flats is also marked by a sign here. Trail 249 moves gently uphill through pleasant spruce-fir forest for 0.25 mile until it reaches a ridge overlooking the canyon of the Rio Mora far below. After another 0.75 mile or less, you reach the intersection with Trail 250, branching right and leading downhill to Mora Flats, an area of meadows along the Rio Mora. (The Spanish word *mora* means "mulberry.") The campsites might be occupied during summer, so plan ahead, although after Labor Day visitation declines dramatically.

> **DAY HIKE: HAMILTON MESA**
> One-way length: 3.5 miles
> Low and high elevations: 9,400 and 10,200 feet
> Difficulty: easy to moderate

This is a magnificent day hike, and I like it so much I've done it twice as an easy, laid-back overnighter. To begin, follow the directions for the Mora Flats hike, but at the trail junction continue on Trail 249 toward Pecos Falls. The trail climbs gradually through forest until you pass through a gated fence and enter the meadows; hence Hamilton Mesa. The views are spectacular and the meadows are a delight; wild irises grow in abundance here, as well as other wildflowers. At 3.5 miles is the junction with the trail leading downhill to Beattys. Trail 249 continues on toward Pecos Falls. I usually continue a little farther and begin looking for campsites. You'll find springs along the route, but they're likely to have been fouled by cattle.

> **DESTINATION HIKE: WINSOR TRAIL – PUERTO NAMBE**
> One-way length: 4 miles
> Low and high elevations: 10,280 and 11,000 feet
> Difficulty: moderate

The Winsor Trail is among the most popular in the Pecos Wilderness, perhaps because it's so easy to access from Santa Fe. The trail, 254, starts on the southwest side of the parking area at the Santa Fe Ski Area and is marked by a sign. It begins with a steady climb for 0.5 miles to the Pecos Wilderness Boundary at a saddle marked by a fence, a good spot to break and adjust equipment. From the saddle, the Winsor Trail slopes downhill for 1.1 miles to Nambe Creek. If you were to follow the creek uphill 1.5 miles, you'd come to the basin containing shallow Nambe Lake, but this ascent is very steep. From the creek, the Winsor Trail climbs gently 2.4 miles through pleasant aspen-spruce-fir forest and meadows to reach La Vega, "the meadow," at Puerto Nambe. To the north is 12,622-foot Santa Fe Baldy, while 12,409-foot Lake Peak and 12,249-foot Penitente Peak are to the south. The broad, open slopes and meadows of Puerto Nambe are a very popular camping destination.

DESTINATION HIKE: EAST PECOS BALDY

One-way length: 8.5 miles to East Pecos Baldy,
7.5 miles to Pecos Baldy Lake
Low and high elevations: 8,850 and 12,529 feet at East Pecos Baldy
Difficulty: strenuous

This classic hike of the Pecos Wilderness begins at the Jacks Creek Campground, which you can reach via Highway 63 from Pecos to Cowles. The first mile climbs through pine forest to the wilderness boundary, and soon you'll reach a pleasant meadow view of the high country. After about 2.5 miles from the start, you reach a trail junction; take Trail 251 to the left. Continue through meadows and aspen groves until you cross Jacks Creek. Soon after you ford the creek, you'll continue left at another trail junction. About 2 miles from the Jacks Creek crossing, you'll emerge from the forest to enter the timberline zone. A last steep climb brings you to another trail junction and Pecos Baldy Lake just ahead. A series of switchbacks takes you to the top of 12,529-foot East Pecos Baldy, rising 1,100 feet in one mile. The climb is worth it, if you have the time and energy, but don't be tempted to go if storms threaten. This long day hike also makes an excellent overnighter. Camping is not allowed around Pecos Baldy Lake, but you can find sites elsewhere.

DESTINATION HIKE: HERMIT PEAK

One-way length: 4 miles
Low and high elevations: 7,510 and 10,250 feet at Hermit Peak
Difficulty: strenuous

Local Spanish-speaking people once called this peak *El Cerro del Tecolote*, "the hill of the owl," but that was before Juan Maria de Agostini arrived here. Agostini walked over the Santa Fe Trail and set up residence as a hermit and holy man in a cave 250 feet below the rim of this monolith. He traded carved crucifixes and religious emblems for food, and local people made pilgrimages for healing and blessings. In 1867 he left this cave for another in the Organ Mountains outside Las Cruces; he was found murdered there in 1869. But local pilgrimages continued as late as 1965 to this peak, now called *El Solitario*, or Hermit Peak.

This hike begins at the El Porvenir Campground accessible via Highway 65 from Las Vegas. Trail 223 is well-marked and well-worn. At about two miles, you reach a series of steep switchbacks that seem interminable but actually last 1.5 miles before ending at a ridge. The last half-mile to the summit is relatively easy. A sign near the rim marks the short hike to Hermits Cave.

DESTINATION HIKE: TRUCHAS PEAK
One-way length: 13.5 miles
Low and high elevations: 9,040 and 13,102 feet at Truchas Peak
Difficulty: strenuous

This hike is an extension of the East Pecos Baldy hike. From Pecos Baldy Lake, Trail 251 goes north, passing through the long, level meadows atop the ridge known as Trailriders Wall. At 7.1 miles, Trail 251 ends at the Truchas Lakes, nestled on the east slopes of Truchas Peak. Camping is not allowed around the lakes, although you can find other spots nearby. From the lakes, a faint trail winds steeply up the talus slopes to the west to reach a saddle on the ridge. From here both Middle Truchas Peak, 13,070 feet, and Truchas Peak (sometimes called South Truchas Peak) are relatively easy to reach. North Truchas, 13,024 feet, requires some scrambling. This is a rather spare description of a multiday trip that some people have called the best hike in New Mexico. This classic hike of the Pecos deserves its reputation.

BOB JULYAN'S FAVORITE HIKE
HEADWATERS OF THE PECOS
One-way length: 8 miles
Low and high elevations: 10,450 and 12,130 feet
Difficulty: strenuous

After you hike eight miles over Trail 249 from Iron Gate Campground to Pecos Falls, Trail 249 continues along the Pecos River. It leaves the river 1.5 miles from the falls and ascends to the ridge on the east. The vegetation here is lush, and keeping the trail is not easy, so you may be bushwhacking. Atop the ridge, you find yourself above timberline, with breathtaking scenery. Here you join Trail 251, which goes northwest along the ridge to the major trail junction south of Barbara Peak. From the ridge you look down into the headwaters of the Pecos, with lush, green meadows, ponds, forests, and—with any luck—elk. From the trail junction, Trail 24 returns you to Pecos Falls.

OTHER RECREATIONAL OPPORTUNITIES

Traditionally, people have explored the Pecos Wilderness not on foot but on horses, and today pack animals, whether horses or llamas, are still used extensively. Several stables and outfitters specifically offer trips into the Pecos Country.

Mountain biking in the Pecos Wilderness vicinity is focused on the Osha Mountain—Elk Mountain area, at the upper end of Cow Creek, which you can reach by taking Highway 223 and then Forest Road 86 from the village of Pecos. Here is an extensive network of old roads that take mountain bikers into the high country, including 11,659-foot Elk Mountain. Mountain biking is also popular in the Johnson Mesa area (take Highway 283 southwest from Las Vegas to Mineral Hill, then follow Forest Road 18).

You can find several places for cross-country skiing and snowshoeing in the Pecos Wilderness. From the west, the most popular areas include the Winsor Trail, whose trailhead is at the Santa Fe Ski Basin east of Santa Fe (see Puerto Nambe above). From the south, skiers and snowshoers drive on paved Highway 63 to its end at Cowles. To access the trails, follow unplowed roads leading to the Jacks Creek and Panchuela Campgrounds. The most popular trail goes from Jacks Creek Campground to Beattys. Another popular route from Highway 63 is the unplowed road leading to the Holy Ghost Campground.

You'll find the main cross-country ski and snowshoe access to the wilderness from the north at the Santa Barbara Campground. The road is kept open in the winter until about 3.5 miles from the campground, at which point the road becomes a snowmobile and ski/snowshoe route. From the trailhead just below the campground, only nonmotorized travelers may enter the wilderness. Once inside the wilderness, trails diverge, following the East Fork, Middle Fork, and West Fork of the Rio Santa Barbara, the initial gentle gradients becoming steeper after the first four to five miles.

FOR MORE INFORMATION

CARSON NATIONAL FOREST, Supervisor's Office, Forest Service Building, P.O. Box 558, 208 Cruz Alta Road, Taos, NM 87571; (505) 758-6200.

CAMINO REAL RANGER DISTRICT, P.O. Box 68, Peñasco, NM 87553; (505) 587-2255.

SANTA FE NATIONAL FOREST, Supervisor's Office, P.O. Box 1869, 1220 St. Francis Drive, Santa Fe, NM 87504; (505) 438-7840.

PECOS RANGER DISTRICT, P.O. Box 429, Pecos, NM 87552; (505) 757-6121.

ESPAÑOLA RANGER DISTRICT, P.O. Box 1346, Española, NM 87532; (505) 753-7331.

LAS VEGAS RANGER STATION, 1926 Seventh Street, Las Vegas, NM 87701; (505) 425-3535.

Rio Chama
Wilderness Study Area

Adjacent to the Chama River Canyon Wilderness,
Rio Chama features rolling plains bisected by the
900-foot-deep Rio Chama Canyon.

LOCATION	South of El Vado Reservoir, along the Rio Chama
SIZE	11,985 acres Size recommended by the NM Wilderness Alliance: 5,918 acres
ELEVATION RANGE	6,530 to 7,530 feet
MILES OF TRAILS	No marked or maintained trails
ECOSYSTEMS	Grassland, sagebrush, ponderosa pine and Douglas fir, riparian
ADMINISTRATION	BLM
TOPOGRAPHIC MAPS	El Vado and Pounds Mesa USGS 7.5-minute quadrangles
BEST SEASONS	Spring, summer, fall
GETTING THERE	Boaters on the Rio Chama probably have the best access to this WSA. To access the western portion, drive through the Santa Fe National Forest via Highway 112. You can access the eastern portion by routes branching from BLM Road 1023, which leaves Highway 84 two miles south of Cebolla.
HIKING	This WSA is not so much a hikers' wilderness as a boaters' because the primary purpose of wilderness designation is to protect the river and the lands along it. This section of the Rio Chama is well-known among boaters and complements the stretch of river in the adjacent Chama River Canyon Wilderness.

6 Rio Grande Wilderness Inventory Unit

This area was dropped by the BLM because of range alterations affecting the wilderness. The NM Wilderness Alliance adjusted the boundaries of this unit in its proposal to avoid these conflicts and also to highlight scenic and wildlife values.

LOCATION	Adjacent to and west of the Rio Grande Wild and Scenic River, near the Colorado border.
SIZE	9,447 acres Size recommended by the NM Wilderness Alliance: 16,100 acres
ELEVATION RANGE	7,300 to 7,700 feet
MILES OF TRAILS	No marked or maintained trails
ECOSYSTEMS	Sagebrush, Great Basin grassland
ADMINISTRATION	BLM
TOPOGRAPHIC MAPS	Ute Mountain USGS 7.5-minute quadrangle
BEST SEASONS	Spring, summer, fall
GETTING THERE	The area is accessible by boat on the Rio Grande and by several roads best avoided in wet weather.
HIKING	At present seldom used for hiking, although the portion along the Rio Grande Gorge is popular among boaters, anglers, and photographers.

Sabinoso
Wilderness Study Area

*The Sabinoso Wilderness Study Area features rugged
mesas and canyons, including the Canadian River Gorge.*

Cañon del Muerto

New Mexico Wilderness Alliance

LOCATION	Northeast of Las Vegas, northwest of Highway 419, west of the Canadian River, south of Cañon Largo
SIZE	Size: 15,760 acres Size recommended by the NM Wilderness Alliance: 17,600 acres
ELEVATION RANGE	4,500 to 6,000 feet
MILES OF TRAILS	No marked or maintained trails
ECOSYSTEMS	Piñon-juniper, grassland, ponderosa pine, scrub oak
ADMINISTRATION	BLM
TOPOGRAPHIC MAPS	Sabinoso USGS 7.5-minute quadrangle
BEST SEASONS	Spring, fall
GETTING THERE	All current routes cross private land and have locked gates. The BLM is hoping that acquisition of private land will provide public access. The isolated hamlet of Sabinoso is across the Canadian River from the WSA's northeast end, but the bridge across the river is no longer passable.
HIKING	Limited by remoteness and lack of legal access, this area has no delineated routes. But you can travel cross-country without too much difficulty, and the area is certainly interesting and scenic.

San Antonio Wilderness Study Area

8

San Antonio features rolling grassland, a scenic stream with steep lava walls, and a dramatic view of San Antonio Mountain looming to the south.

LOCATION	Northwest of Taos, on the north side of San Antonio Mountain, near the Colorado border
SIZE	7,050 acres Size recommended by the NM Wilderness Alliance: 25,100 acres
ELEVATION RANGE	7,900 to 8,800 feet
MILES OF TRAILS	No marked or maintained trails
ECOSYSTEMS	Great Basin grassland, sagebrush, ponderosa pine, quaking aspen and Douglas fir communities, as well as cold temperate deciduous forest
ADMINISTRATION	BLM
TOPOGRAPHIC MAPS	Los Pinos 7.5-minute USGS quadrangle
BEST SEASONS	Spring, summer, fall
GETTING THERE	You can reach the WSA's southern edge from Highway 285 by taking BLM Road 1016 (north of San Antonio Mountain) for 3 miles to a dirt trail leading north to the eastern side of Rio San Antonio Canyon.
HIKING	Hiking here has been limited by lack of trails and obvious destinations.

PEOPLE OFTEN ASSUME from its name that this wilderness study area includes 10,908-foot San Antonio Mountain, the dramatic long-extinct volcanic cone that is a familiar landmark in this part of New Mexico, but in fact the WSA encompasses the rolling grasslands to the north and west, including a portion of the Rio San Antonio. For wildlife viewers, this is advantageous because the open terrain provides more visibility than you'll find in adjacent forested lands. Species found here include elk, mule deer, pronghorn, black bear, mountain lions, coyotes, prairie dogs, wild turkey, and raptors including bald eagles and peregrine falcons. While you won't find designated trails here, the terrain can withstand cross-country hiking, and you can access the area on foot from parking areas around San Antonio Mountain.

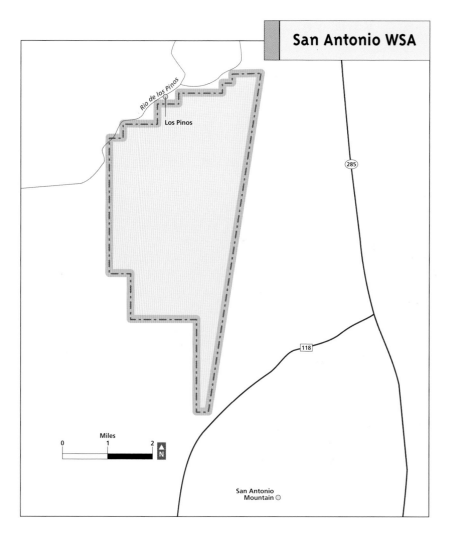

San Antonio WSA

9 Valle Vidal Unit Natural Area

You'll discover that the high mountains, lush meadows, clear streams, and sparkling lakes of the Cimarron Range make Valle Vidal one of New Mexico's finest wildlife habitats.

Martin Frentzel

A serene moment in Valle Vidal

LOCATION	Northeast of Red River Village, northeast of Bobcat Pass
SIZE	100,000 acres
ELEVATION RANGE	7,700 to 12,583 feet at Little Costilla Peak in the Cimarron Range
MILES OF TRAILS	Undetermined
ECOSYSTEMS	Mixed conifer and aspen, meadow grassland, alpine tundra
ADMINISTRATION	Carson National Forest
TOPOGRAPHIC MAPS	Abreu Canyon, Ash Mountain, Van Bremmer Park, Red River Pass, Comanche Point, and Baldy Mountain 7.5-minute USGS quadrangles
BEST SEASONS	Summer, fall
GETTING THERE	Most people access the Valle Vidal via Forest Road 1950, a packed dirt road that traverses the area and links its campgrounds and trailheads. The road goes between Highway 64 northeast of Cimarron and the village of Amalia, southeast of the village of Costilla, just south of the Colorado border on Highway 522.
HIKING	Marked and maintained trails are relatively few in this area, though logging and former ranch roads provide hiking routes, and the area is suitable for cross-country travel.

THE VALLE VIDAL UNIT OF THE CARSON NATIONAL FOREST has not formally been declared wilderness and likely never will be, but for most people who use and love it that's okay: they regard it as a model of public lands management.

The manager in this case is the Carson National Forest, but that's only been since 1982. Before then, the lands, now known as the Valle Vidal Unit, were part of the much larger 492,560-acre Vermejo Park Ranch. This, in turn, had been part of the still larger 1,714,765-acre tract known as the Maxwell Land Grant, at the time the largest single landholding in the Western Hemisphere. It was granted in 1841 by Mexican Governor Manuel Armijo to Carlos Beaubien, a trapper of French descent, and Guadalupe Miranda of Taos. In 1849, Lucien Bonaparte Maxwell arrived in New Mexico from Kansas. He married Beaubien's daughter, Luz, and after Beaubien's death in 1864 he bought out the other land-grant heirs for $3,000 and became a land baron. Later, he sold his vast holdings to foreign investors and moved out of the area. Eventually the property, or what was left of it, came to be owned by Pennzoil Corporation. In 1982, in exchange for tax credits, Pennzoil ceded 100,000 acres to the Forest Service. The U.S. Secretary of Agriculture at the time, John Block, said it was the largest and most valuable donation of private land ever made to the Forest Service. (As for the remaining Vermejo Park lands, much of those were acquired, in 1997, by media magnate Ted Turner, who has two other gargantuan properties in New Mexico.)

Pennzoil attached certain conditions to its gift, including: 1) allowing timber sales of 3 to 4 million board feet annually; 2) allowing the Kaiser Steel Corporation to retain rights to coal on 60,000 acres; 3) emphasizing wildlife management; and 4) providing the caveat that "the area will not qualify for wilderness designation due to past management practices and commitment to the timber resource." But while humans may quibble over designations, the wildlife care only about thousands of acres of streams, meadows, and forests, with few or no humans. Deer, black bear, turkey, bobcat, coyote, squirrel, beaver, mountain lion, and elk combine for a species total of 60 mammals. The area also includes 200 species of birds, 33 species of reptiles and amphibians, and 15 kinds of fish, including a rare pure strain of the Rio Grande cutthroat trout that is an invaluable genetic reservoir for restocking New Mexico's state fish. Bison occasionally wander into the area from Ted Turner's Vermejo Park property to the east.

You can attribute much of the wildlife abundance to the unseen hand of management. Everything is managed and limited in the Valle Vidal Unit—hunting, fishing, and camping. The only road access is via Forest Road 1950 (closed during elk calving season—January 1 to March 31). This graded dirt road extends northwest from Highway 64 near Cimarron to the village of Costilla near the Colorado border. The area has three designated campgrounds: McCrystal Creek, Shuree, and Cimarron. Primitive camping is permitted if away from roads and water sources. Trails are few in the Valle Vidal Unit, and due to the area's reputation for wildlife, hunters and anglers far outnumber hikers, especially during the fall deer and elk season. All water should be treated, as livestock grazing continues in the area.

The history of the former Maxwell Land Grant is still being written. Perhaps, in time, other portions of the vast Vermejo Park Ranch will pass into public ownership. In the meantime, the public should feel grateful that at least some of this wilderness—

Valle Vidal Unit Natural Area

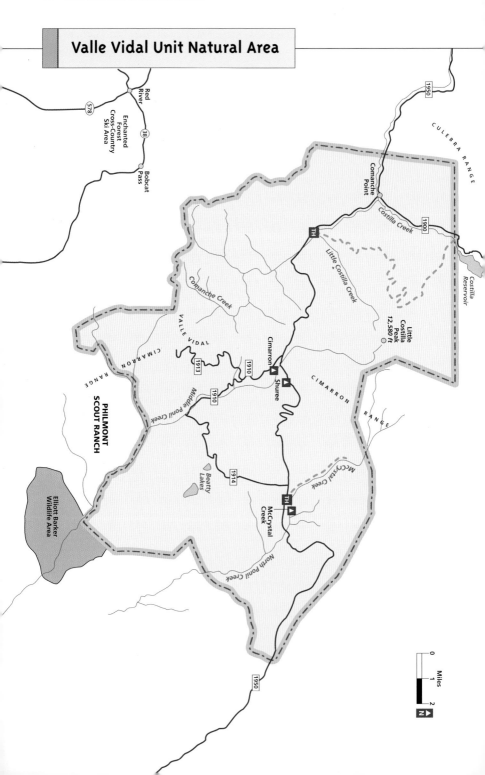

designated or not—has been preserved in a manner that would not disappoint former mountain men like Lucien Maxwell and Carlos Beaubien.

DAY HIKE: McCRYSTAL RANCH SITE
One-way length: 3.5 miles
Low and high elevations: 8,100 and 8,700 feet
Difficulty: easy

From the McCrystal Creek Campground, reached by Forest Road 1950, walk west along the road 0.25 mile to a dirt road heading northwest, which parallels the campground road. Bearing right, you pass through a gate. Then hike about a mile to McCrystal Creek, which the trail now follows, going by the ruins of a sawmill. At about 2.6 miles, the trail heads west along Can Creek, crossing it after 0.25 mile and then descending to the ruins of the McCrystal Homestead, which John McCrystal established in the late 1800s.

OTHER RECREATIONAL OPPORTUNITIES

The Carson National Forest has designated cross-country skiing areas on the Valle Vidal Unit's western side; these areas may be closed seasonally to avoid conflicts with elk migrations to the unit's east side, which is closed to all off-road use in the winter. Check with the Questa Ranger District. Also, the 10-mile Powderhouse – Little Costilla Peak Trail is specifically for cross-country skiing; it connects the trailhead located about 3 miles south of Comanche Point on Forest Road 1950 with the trailhead north of Comanche Point on Forest Road 1900, the Valle Vidal border. The trail follows old logging roads, and because these often fork, the Ash Mountain 7.5-minute USGS quadrangle would be helpful. Views of 12,580-foot Little Costilla Peak and the 12,000-foot summits of the Latir Peaks area are spectacular.

Mountain biking along the gravel Forest Road takes you through spectacular scenery, an excellent way to experience this large area.

FOR MORE INFORMATION

CARSON NATIONAL FOREST–QUESTA RANGER DISTRICT, P.O. Box 110, Questa, NM 87556; (505) 586-0520.

CARSON NATIONAL FOREST, Supervisor's Office, Forest Service Building, P.O. Box 558, 208 Cruz Alta Road, Taos, NM 87571; (505) 758-6200.

Wheeler Peak Wilderness

10

Wheeler Peak, New Mexico's highest summit, dominates the Sangre de Cristo Mountains in this area, which is characterized by steep slopes, alpine lakes, expanses of tundra, and dense spruce-fir forest.

Horseshoe Lake

LOCATION	In the northern Sangre de Cristo Mountains, northeast of Taos, south of the Rio Hondo, and southwest of Red River Village
SIZE	19,150 acres
ELEVATION RANGE	8,000 to 13,161 feet at Wheeler Peak
MILES OF TRAILS	37
ECOSYSTEMS	Engelmann spruce, subalpine fir, alpine tundra
ADMINISTRATION	Carson National Forest—Questa Ranger District
TOPOGRAPHIC MAPS	Carson National Forest—Latir Peak and Wheeler Peak Wildernesses
BEST SEASONS	Summer, early fall
GETTING THERE	The Wheeler Peak Wilderness is reached either from Taos via Highway 150 leading to the Taos Ski Valley or from the village of Red River via Highway 578.
HIKING	Numerous marked and maintained trails connect the major summits, lakes, and other features of the Wheeler Peak Wilderness. During the summer, the trails often receive heavy use. Hikes range from day excursions to backpack trips.

WHEELER PEAK

It may seem simply appropriate that New Mexico's highest summit wears the regal cloak of a Wilderness, yet the story of Wheeler Peak and the Wilderness named for it is anything but simple.

In fact, only recently was Wheeler Peak even recognized as the state's highest mountain. United States Army Major George M. Wheeler, for whom the peak was named, directed surveys west of the 100th Meridian between 1871 and 1878 and mapped much of New Mexico. He certainly made no such pronouncement. Prior to 1948, the Truchas Peaks farther south in the Sangre de Cristo Mountains earned the title of highest. In 1948, however, Harold D. Walter, a Santa Fe accountant whose passions were mountains and photography, borrowed some surveying equipment, photographed

Bob Julyan

Wheeler Peak, and then announced that his readings showed Wheeler edging out the Truchas summits. Subsequent surveys confirmed his conclusion. (After Walter's death in 1958, a previously unnamed prominence just north of Wheeler Peak was officially named Mount Walter, a name Walter himself had begun using for the mountain. A plaque on the summit commemorates Walter, "who loved these mountains.")

Furthermore, when Wheeler Peak Wilderness was first established, a protracted conflict with the Indians of Taos Pueblo ensued. At issue was Blue Lake southeast of Wheeler Peak. The lake is the pueblo's most sacred site and the scene of annual religious rituals. Blue Lake and the surrounding mountains had been incorporated into the Carson National Forest in 1906 over the Indians' vehement protests. The issue reached a crisis in the 1960s. The area had been declared the Wheeler Peak Wild Area in 1960; it became the Wheeler Peak Wilderness with passage of the 1964 Wilderness Act. Soon, more hikers and recreationists began visiting the lake. With many non-Indian New Mexicans supporting them, the Taos Indians took their case to Congress, to the courts, and to the Departments of Agriculture and the Interior. Finally, in 1970, Blue Lake and 48,000 surrounding acres were returned to the pueblo. Author William de Buys captured the moment's significance when he wrote: "The celebration that followed was the celebration of a people who had survived a cultural apocalypse." In 1997, the nearby area known as the Bottleneck, between Old Mike and Simpson Peak, was also transferred back to the pueblo.

TODAY, HIKERS AND RECREATIONISTS in ever-increasing numbers converge on the Wheeler Peak Wilderness. Most seek to stand atop New Mexico's highest mountain. It's a worthy goal, for while summiting Wheeler Peak requires no mountaineering skills, it does require commitment and stamina. There are three primary approaches to Wheeler Peak and to the Wheeler Peak Wilderness. The shortest and fastest route to the top is from Williams Lake at the peak's west base. Here an unmarked and unmaintained but fairly clear route climbs very steeply up the western slopes, then runs south along the summit ridge to the top. (The Forest Service may soon put in a real trail to curtail erosion.) This route allows day hikers to make the climb and return before late summer afternoon thundershowers strike.

The most popular route is the trail that goes over Bull of the Woods Mountain, Frazer Mountain, and on to Wheeler Peak. You'll reach both of these routes from the Taos Ski Valley (once the site of the mining boomtown of Twining).

The third route leads to the top from the village of Red River by going south to where the Middle Fork of Red River joins the West Fork. Here a trail continues south to enter the wilderness just before Middle Fork Lake. This leads to Horseshoe Lake and eventually reaches Wheeler Peak from the south. This route, which includes lakes and pleasant campsites, is a backpackers' favorite.

Snow can linger in the high country until mid-June, and the season from mid-July through August is New Mexico's wettest with thunderstorms almost daily. Late June and September are usually the best hiking months. The area receives 35 to 40 inches of precipitation a year, so water is usually available, although ridges above timberline often are dry.

Whatever route you take to the top, once on the summit you behold a vision of New Mexico far removed from that of people who regard the state only as desert: dense forests extending to the horizon; high, treeless summits carpeted with tundra; and sapphire lakes set in green meadows. Of the wilderness's 19,150 acres, 6,029 are above timberline. Here alpine fescue grass and several species of sedges form dense, tough mats that are wind-blasted in winter, yet bloom in summer with beguiling beauty and delicacy. Repeated freezing and thawing have heaved up rocks from the thin soil, and among these rocks live pikas (also called coneys), which are shy, appealing animals not unlike guinea pigs. Their high bark alerts you to their presence. You'll also see yellow-bellied marmots, which are large, brown rodents; the ones at Wheeler's summit have turned to panhandling.

Below the alpine zone, dense conifer forests thrive, including stands of bristlecone pines—although avalanches have slashed away the trees in certain areas. In these forests, as well as above timberline, mule deer mingle with elk, Rocky Mountain bighorn sheep, black bears and mountain lions—esteemed symbols of wilderness to all who love the outdoors. It's easy to see why Harold Walter loved these mountains.

Yet the person who has been most associated with the mountains here was Kit Carson. Taos was among his many homes. The Kit Carson Home and Historical Museum in Taos has his rifle, and Carson is buried in the Taos cemetery. He was drawn to this area because it was still the frontier, which he loved. He attended mountain man rendezvous along with Plains Indians, Pueblo Indians, Hispanics, and anyone else who sought to join in. Although Wheeler Peak isn't visible from Taos (it's hidden by other peaks often confused with Wheeler), rendezvous participants likely would have been familiar with it.

It's interesting to speculate by what name Carson called the mountain. Perhaps he'd have called it by an Indian name, for he was acquainted with several Indian languages. It was likely that he used a Spanish name that hasn't been recorded; Spanish was the language spoken in the Carson home. He wouldn't have called it Wheeler Peak, for Major George M. Wheeler hadn't made his surveys yet.

Equally interesting is the question of what name he'd have called the range encompassing Wheeler Peak. Perhaps he used the name Sangre de Cristo, for that name had attained some currency, but just as likely he'd have used the older Spanish name, *La Sierra Madre*, "the mother range." Perhaps he used the name English-speaking mountain men called it—The Snowies.

Today, hikers atop Wheeler Peak look out upon a mountain wilderness not greatly altered from what Carson beheld. To be sure, a host of political and administrative changes have occurred since then. Wildlife species he'd have taken for granted—grizzlies, Merriams elk, wolves—have vanished. Other species, such as American elk and Rocky Mountain bighorn sheep, became extinct and have since returned due to restocking.

Also, many of the Indian tribes he'd have expected to encounter in these mountains—Utes, Jicarilla Apaches, Comanches, and Kiowas from the Plains—long ago left their traditional hunting and trading territories.

I sometimes wonder what Carson would think of today's hordes of hikers, with modern equipment, on the trail simply so they might stand on the state's highest summit. Certainly we, with our highly evolved, polycolored techno-gear, our bodies honed in fitness classes, our freeze-dried trail food, our detailed maps, compasses, and GPS units, and our regulations, are a far cry from the wilderness he knew. Would he understand that to us such remnants of wilderness are all the more precious to us for their rarity? Would he understand that on trails laid out by the Forest Service we still seek the challenge and adventure that lured him onto ancient Indian trails? Were we to tell him the Indian wars are over, the terrifying grizzlies are gone, no unexplored places are left on any maps—would he look out over the Wheeler Peak Wilderness and say, "Well, at least you saved this?"

DESTINATION HIKE: LOST LAKE – HORSESHOE LAKE
One-way length: 13.5 miles
Low and high elevations: 9,400 and 11,950 feet
Difficulty: strenuous

This is classic New Mexico high country: small alpine lakes nestled in a basin beneath the state's highest peak. The hike is long but not otherwise difficult. And unlike Williams Lake on the west side of Wheeler Peak, these lakes have trout.

You can reach the trailhead from the village of Red River by taking Highway 578 south slightly more than six miles to where it splits. The left road, Forest Road 58A, parallels the East Fork of the Red River as it goes by summer homes for one mile to the East Fork Trailhead. Here the Horseshoe Lake Trail, No. 56, follows an old road until Sawmill Creek crosses it at mile 1.7. The trail continues along the East Fork until it leaves the drainage to cross a divide to drop into the basin and meet the trail from Middle Fork Lake, No. 91. By going north on Trail 91, you reach Lost Lake. By going south 0.7 mile, you come to Horseshoe Lake.

Camping is forbidden within 300 feet of each lake, but you shouldn't have trouble finding suitable campsites. From Horseshoe Lake it's an easy shot to summit Wheeler Peak. By returning on the Middle Fork Trail, No. 91, you could make a loop hike, but the lower two miles of this are open to off-road vehicles and at the height of tourist season these two miles are not pleasant for hikers.

DESTINATION HIKE: WHEELER PEAK – BULL OF THE WOODS TRAIL
One-way length: 7.2 miles
Low and high elevations: 9,400 and 13,161 feet
Difficulty: strenuous

This is the most popular route to New Mexico's highest summit, with relatively gentle gradients and magnificent scenery. Still, it's a long day at high altitude with considerable elevation gain.

Bull of the Woods Trail, No. 90, begins near Taos Ski Valley. At the Forest Service Twining Campground, from the northeast corner of the parking lot, follow a dirt road a short ways to the trailhead. You'll reach Bull of the Woods Pasture after 1.8 miles, passing private land and numerous intersecting trails on the way. This portion can be very confusing and is probably the most difficult part of the hike.

At 4.3 miles you'll come to a sign for the Bear Lake Trail. At 5.1 miles, heading south above timberline, you'll cross a small stream before dropping into forested La Cal Basin (where you'll find plenty of good campsites). Many hikers prefer not to lose elevation in the basin and instead leave the trail to follow the basin's contours and rejoin the trail later. By the time you reach 13,141-foot Mount Walter you're almost there; Wheeler's summit is just 0.3 mile farther. Be alert for panhandling marmots.

DESTINATION HIKE: WILLIAMS LAKE
One-way length: 3.5 miles
Low and high elevations: 9,960 and 11,040 feet
Difficulty: moderate

Williams Lake is a small, shallow, but nonetheless scenic remnant of the glaciers that carved the high peaks here. To reach the trailhead from Taos, drive three miles north on U.S. 64 to Highway 150, where signs indicate that the Taos Ski Valley

Rose crown on high slopes, Wheeler Peak Wilderness

Wheeler Peak

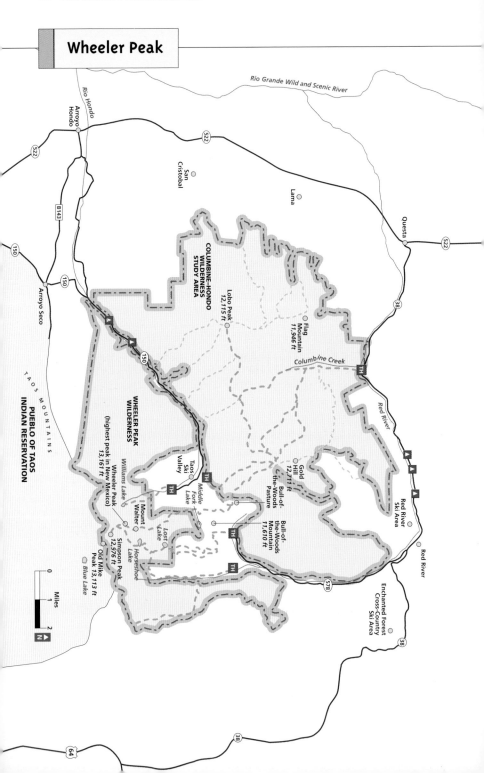

Rio Grande Wild and Scenic River

Rio Hondo

Arroyo Hondo

522

522

B143

150

150

Arroyo Seco

San Cristobal

Lama

Questa

522

38

Red River Ski Area

COLUMBINE-HONDO WILDERNESS STUDY AREA

Lobo Peak 12,115 ft

Flag Mountain 11,946 ft

Columbine Creek

Red River

WHEELER PEAK WILDERNESS

Gold Hill 12,711 ft

Bull-of-the-Woods Pasture

Bull-of-the-Woods Mountain 11,610 ft

Williams Lake

Wheeler Peak (highest peak in New Mexico) 13,161 ft

Taos Ski Valley

Middle Fork Lake

Mount Walter

Lost Lake

Simpson Peak 12,976 ft

Horseshoe Lake

Old Mike Peak 13,113 ft

Blue Lake

578

Red River

Enchanted Forest Cross-Country Ski Area

T A O S   M O U N T A I N S

PUEBLO OF TAOS INDIAN RESERVATION

38

64

0 Miles 1 2

N

is 15 miles away. As you enter the ski area, look to your left, opposite the resort complex, for a parking lot where a Forest Service sign indicates the Wheeler Peak Wilderness Area access. Just a few yards away is the dirt Twining Road. Drive on this 0.5 mile, then turn left on the dirt road labeled Phoenix Switchback. Drive on this approximately 1.1 miles to a sign reading "Hikers Parking." Park here and walk on the road, which is closed to public vehicular traffic, past the Phoenix Restaurant and ski lift area to signs indicating the route to Williams Lake. (The Forest Service plans to reroute the trail just past the Phoenix Restaurant around 1999.)

Continue following a rough dirt road on the east side of Lake Fork Creek, until at approximately 0.25 mile from the restaurant the main road crosses the creek. Keep left, and soon you'll encounter a Carson National Forest sign indicating Williams Lake Trail No. 62, Williams Lake two miles. The trail gradually but persistently ascends the valley through spruce-fir forest before reaching the glacial cirque and the little lake. Don't bring your fishing rods!

OTHER RECREATIONAL OPPORTUNITIES

The primary cross-country skiing route in the Wheeler Peak Wilderness is the East Fork – Ditch Cabin – Sawmill Park Trail. You'll reach this from the village of Red River by taking Highway 578 south from the village's east end, approximately 6.5 miles, until the pavement ends. The trail, No. 56, parallels the East Fork of the Red River to the area known as Ditch Cabin. Snowmobilers and cross-country skiers share the trail to this point, but Trail 55, which branches left and follows Sawmill Park Creek to Sawmill Park, is for cross-country skiers only.

You can also access the wilderness by taking the trail to Middle Fork Lake near the wilderness boundary. To get to the trailhead, take Highway 578 to Forest Road 487, which goes along the Middle Fork of the Red River.

While you won't be in the wilderness, you'll find excellent cross-country skiing near Red River at the privately operated Enchanted Forest Cross-Country Ski Area. Downhill skiing is available at Red River and Taos Ski Valley. The most popular cross-country skiing and snowshoeing route from Taos Ski Valley is to Williams Lake; however, the steep slopes above the valley and lake pose hazardous avalanche potential.

FOR MORE INFORMATION

CARSON NATIONAL FOREST–QUESTA RANGER DISTRICT, P.O. Box 110, Questa, NM 87556; (505) 586-0520.

CARSON NATIONAL FOREST, Supervisor's Office, Forest Service Building, P.O. Box 558, 208 Cruz Alta Road, Taos, NM 87571; (505) 758-6200.

The Jemez Mountains

While physiographers include the Jemez Mountains within the Rocky Mountain region of New Mexico, all that these mountains really share with the Sangre de Cristo Mountains to the east and across the Rio Grande is proximity and a distant link to the region's general geological instability. The Jemez Mountains (pronounced HAY-mehz) are 273 million years younger than the Sangre de Cristos, and unlike them were not created by gradual uplift but rather by cataclysmic volcanic eruptions and the ensuing ash fall and lava flows. The Sangre de Cristos are comprised of light-colored granite, but the Jemez Mountains contain black basaltic lava and compressed volcanic ash which erodes easily. This juxtaposition of resistant basaltic pillars and soft, porous tuff give the Jemez Mountains a conspicuously distinctive character.

On a large-scale shaded-relief map, the entire volcanic structure of the Jemez Mountains is readily seen—a circular depression with ridges and canyons radiating outward like the hub of a wheel. The best place to visualize the hub is on Highway 4 along the rim of the Valle Grande— a huge basin of meadows and forests, surrounded by summits often exceeding 10,000 feet. The Valle Grande is merely a part of the larger Valles Caldera, created when the Jemez volcano collapsed in upon itself after eruptions emptied its magma chamber of lava and ash. This occurred about one million years ago, almost yesterday in geological terms, and throughout the Jemez Mountains residual geothermal heat feeds several hot springs. People soaking in these natural pools beneath towering ponderosa pines and the exquisite New Mexico blue sky probably don't think of the warm water as geological evidence, but in fact it is.

Beyond this hub, volcanic deposits that are hundreds of feet thick have weathered into a pattern of long, flat-topped mesas—the spokes of the wheel, so to speak—which are flanked by cliffs colored red, yellow, ochre, tan, and black. These formations are displayed dramatically as long finger-mesas at Bandelier National Monument and the adjacent Dome Wilderness. These canyons, with their precipitous walls breached by only a few ancient Indian trails, are a major challenge for backcountry hikers, but the compensations are exceptional scenery and unexpected delights.

Foremost among these delights are reminders of the long and continuing Indian presence in the Jemez Mountains: potsherds, flint flakes, rock art, and remains of dwellings, including cliff dwellings in the soft, volcanic tuff. Throughout the region such reminders are ubiquitous. Finding arti-

Martin Frentzel

The Valle Grande

facts is always exciting, but even more exciting is the consideration that these are not simply relics from a long-vanished prehistoric culture but rather part of a living cultural continuum. Even the mountains' name is part of this: *Jemez* is the early Spanish approximation of the Jemez Pueblo Indians' name for themselves. Although their pueblo now stands in the Jemez River Valley, their settlements once included pueblos on mesa tops, now regarded simply as ruins. Similarly, people visiting the cliff dwellings in Bandelier National Monument and Puye can visit the modern pueblos of Santa Clara, Cochiti, and others to meet descendants of the cliff dwellers. The Jemez Mountains' highest summit, Chicoma, has a shrine on top, and while the shrine is no longer used, the Indians who built it still view the mountain as sacred. Understanding the cultures and history associated with the Jemez Mountains, and realizing that we too are part of that history, adds a special significance to this wild area.

Abutting the Jemez Mountains' northwestern edge is a small north-south linear range, the Sierra Nacimiento, geologically separate from the Jemez

Mountains in that it has a granite core. Here on the high plateau is the San Pedro Parks Wilderness, a lush, green upland of meadows, forests, and streams.

Also technically outside the Jemez Mountains, but included within the region, is the gorge of the Rio Chama and the Chama River Canyon Wilderness. The Chama, which rises in Colorado and joins the Rio Grande near the northeastern foothills of the Jemez Mountains, is among New Mexico's major drainages. Usually more attractive to boaters than hikers, this canyon deserves consideration—the colorful sandstone formations carved by the Rio Chama are among the most scenic in the state.

The startling beauty of the Jemez Mountains region is plentiful. At higher elevations, in the mountains' core, clear streams meander through green, grassy valleys, flanked by unusual volcanic rock formations. Mule deer and elk are abundant here—so much so that mountain lion sightings have increased dramatically. Black bears are also common. Add to this hot springs, great mountain-biking, trout fishing, and numerous picnic areas, and you'll understand the region's popularity. More significantly, however, the Jemez Mountains are readily accessible from New Mexico's largest population centers—Albuquerque and Santa Fe.

The Jemez Mountains receive heavy use. In the summer campgrounds are usually full, often with large groups having parties. Attractions such as hot springs, waterfalls, wading pools, and lakes are often crowded. Sunday evening vehicle traffic on Highway 4, the main paved route through the mountains, is heavy. Finding solitude in the Jemez Mountains, especially in the summer, often requires creativity and flexibility. Except in the Bandelier Backcountry, the Jemez Mountains don't lend themselves to extended, long-distance backpack trips.

This is partly because forest roads and private inholding have allowed wilderness designation for relatively little of the region. But if a current legislative initiative succeeds in purchasing the 95,000-acre Valles Caldera at the heart of the Jemez Mountains, the wilderness landscape will change dramatically. Presently, the Jemez region wildernesses are on the region's periphery; the Valles Caldera, however, is at the region's very heart. And while the region's popularity has resulted in heavy use, it has also engendered popular support for preservation. Proposals to open specific areas for pumice mining have provoked public outcries blocking the proposals. When stonewashed jeans were in vogue, wearing them drew censure among New Mexico environmentalists because the washing stones were pumice.

Frijoles Canyon in spring, Bandelier National Monument

Bandelier National Monument

Bandelier National Monument is famous for high mesas of piñon-juniper, and ponderosa pine cut by narrow, vertical-sided canyons. Numerous ruins and other remnants of the ancient Indians who once lived here abound.

Kiva at Ceremonial Cave

LOCATION	In the Jemez Mountains, northwest of Santa Fe, south of Los Alamos
SIZE	32,727 acres
ELEVATION RANGE	5,326 to 8,670 feet
MILES OF TRAILS	70-plus
ECOSYSTEMS	Canyon bottom riparian, piñon-juniper, ponderosa pine, mixed conifer
ADMINISTRATION	National Park Service
TOPOGRAPHIC MAPS	Trails Illustrated Bandelier National Monument
BEST SEASONS	Spring, fall
GETTING THERE	The official entrance to Bandelier National Monument is at the monument's east side, off Highway 4 south of the village of White Rock. From the visitor facilities in Cañon de los Frijoles is access to the extensive network of backcountry trails.
HIKING	A well-developed, well-marked system of scenic, interesting, and often challenging trails exists in the backcountry of Bandelier National Monument. Permits, issued free, are required for backcountry camping, and sensitive archaeological and ecological areas are closed to camping. The area can be very exposed and hot, so hikers must be sure to carry adequate water, as natural sources are not always available in the backcountry.

The Pajarito Plateau of Bandelier National Monument is like an amphitheater of the past echoing former peoples and events. The name *Pajarito*, for example, is Spanish and means "little bird," but it was given to this sprawling land of tufaceous volcanic mesas by the early American archaeologist Edgar Lee Hewett (a contemporary of Adolph Bandelier, for whom the monument was named). Pajarito, Hewett explained, was inspired by the ruins of a large, prehistoric pueblo nearby, which descendants call in the Tewa language *Tshirege*, "place of the bird people." But Tshirege is only one of many major Puebloan sites on the Pajarito Plateau. Created primarily to preserve the dramatic ruins and cliff dwellings in Cañon de los Frijoles, the monument bears evidence of still other cultures, Spanish-speaking and English-speaking. Only very recently has the Bandelier Wilderness been a landscape where people are only visitors.

The area's human past is visible everywhere, but so is its geologic past. However you choose to approach Bandelier National Monument (but especially as you drive down into the canyon housing the monument's visitor center), towering, tan-colored cliffs greet you. The light-colored stone is tuff, or compressed volcanic ash, and it contrasts with layers of black basalt. Elsewhere in New Mexico, Indians term this congealed lava "giant's blood."

The metaphor is appropriate, for the volcanic activity that created the Jemez Mountains and the Pajarito Plateau was indeed gigantic. First, volcanism created the Jemez Mountains about 13 million years ago. Then approximately 3 million years ago, lava spewed forth from vents formed by the spreading of the Rio Grande Rift, resulting in basalt layers at the monument's eastern edge. Finally, in two periods of cataclysmic explosions occurring 1.4 million years ago and then again 1.1 million years ago, a magma chamber beneath the layers erupted, ejecting enormous volumes of ash that today form the Pajarito Plateau. (Scientists at Los Alamos National Laboratory have detected a magma chamber still existing beneath the plateau.) Then, its core ejected, the entire structure collapsed, creating what space satellite photos show clearly to be a gigantic caldera. The numerous hot springs in the Jemez Mountains are reminders of this latent volcanism. One of the great delights of hiking in the Jemez Mountains is soaking in an isolated hot spring beneath towering ponderosa pines, watching fluffy white clouds float by in a turquoise sky. There are no hot springs in the Bandelier Back-country, but they're close enough to make a perfect end to your backcountry hike.

In the Bandelier Backcountry, the solidified ash flows form a plateau sloping gently to the southeast, a plateau carved by small, often intermittent streams into a series of *potreros*, a Spanish term referring here to mesas radiating outward like fingers from a palm.

Separating these finger mesas are dramatic canyons: Alamo Canyon is 500 feet deep and scarcely a quarter-mile wide. The trails here often coincide with ancient Indian trails. One November I was camping on a backcountry mesa when I was overtaken by a serious rainstorm. Because a forest fire years earlier had removed the vegetative cover, the water quickly flowed into the canyons where it became an impassable torrent. To my dismay, I was completely cut off from the visitor center (where my vehicle was), and the only way to get out was by a very long and difficult hike in the opposite direction.

The deep canyons—Lummis, Alamo, Capulin, and Sanchez—contain the only water you'll find, except for the Rio Grande tracing the southern boundary of the wilderness. Even as early as May, the mesas can be fiercely hot. Because of the cramped space and fragile ecosystem, camping in the canyons is often prohibited.

These canyons, with their streams and lush vegetation including cottonwoods, box elders, ponderosa pines, and chokecherries, were what first attracted the prehistoric Indians. (However, the area also boasts stinging nettle and poison ivy, which are not so attractive.)

Campsite remains show that hunter-gatherers visited the area as early as 1750 B.C., but it was the arrival of agricultural Puebloan peoples about 1075 A.D. that resulted in the well-known ruins. Where they came from is obscured in part by two surviving Pueblo groups—speaking widely divergent languages—both stating their ancestors once lived on the Pajarito Plateau. Doubtless both groups are correct. The Keres-speaking people of Cochiti, Santo Domingo, and San Felipe Pueblos to the south have traditions involving carved stone lions, similar to the ones at the shrine above Capulin Canyon in the wilderness, while the Tewa-speaking people of San Ildefonso and Santa Clara Pueblos have intimate knowledge of former residency at ruins such as Tsankawi and Puye. Perhaps in acknowledgment of this dual occupancy, Tyuonyi, the ruined pueblo in Cañon de los Frijoles, has a Keresan name that Adolph Bandelier claimed meant "place of the treaty," which might have established boundaries between the two peoples.

By A.D. 1200, Indians on the Pajarito Plateau, like prehistoric Puebloans elsewhere, had entered what is called the Classic Phase of their civilization, characterized by large, multi-storied, multi-roomed communal villages. One of the largest of these was Yapashi, whose ruins are a 5.5-mile hike from the visitor center. The present inhabitants of Cochiti Pueblo say Yapashi was one of their ancient homes; in the Keres language the name means "sacred enclosure," referring to the Shrine of the Stone Lions just 0.5 mile farther. Although the lions' figures, carved from soft stone, are badly eroded, their shapes are still recognizable, and it's not uncommon to find fresh offerings of plants and grain. (Not all the offerings are by Indians, a fact that annoys them.)

Indians were living on the Pajarito Plateau when the Spaniards arrived in New Mexico with the Coronado expedition of 1540. They were still on the plateau when Don Juan de Oñate led colonists up the Rio Grande in 1598. The Indians must have been bewildered by the strangely attired, bearded strangers who rode unworldly terrible beasts. But the Spaniards were oblivious to the Indians' presence on the Pajarito Plateau: no contemporary accounts mention them, and by 1600 the Indians had departed to the lower-elevation settlements where their descendants live today.

Later, in the eighteenth and nineteenth centuries, Spanish-speaking settlers intermittently occupied the area, although in 1811 Spanish authorities ordered the area vacated because it had become a haven for outlaws. Late in the nineteenth century, the area was "discovered" by American archaeologists Adolph Bandelier, Charles Lummis, and Edgar Lee Hewett, among others. Bandelier, an ethnologist, wrote a novel called *The Delight Makers* about prehistoric life in the area. Between 1908

Upper Frijoles Falls, Bandelier National Monument

and 1912, Hewett directed excavations of the major sites in Cañon de los Frijoles. In 1916 President Theodore Roosevelt established by proclamation Bandelier National Monument; in 1935 administration was transferred from the U.S. Forest Service to the National Park Service. The roadless areas of the backcountry became part of the National Wilderness Preservation System in 1976.

Today, the Bandelier Wilderness is as beguiling for hikers and backpackers as it was for the explorer archaeologists. Yet while literally thousands of people arrive at the visitor center in Frijoles Canyon each year, relatively few ever venture into the backcountry. That's probably due in part to the mesas being torridly hot in summer, since almost all backcountry hikes involve climbing onto the mesas. The staccato pattern of high, dry mesas and deep, steep canyons also means intermittently difficult hiking. Many people probably conclude it's not worth the effort because the short, easy, and partially paved trails near the visitor center lead to the monument's most impressive ruins.

What these visitor center trails don't lead to is wilderness. Nor do the visitor center ruins give you the same excitement of discovery that you'll find in backcountry ruins. Thousands of prehistoric sites have been identified in the wilderness, and while you have to be alert to detect many of them, the thrill of discovery can be exhilarating when you notice, for example, that the earthen mounds around you are actually the remains of masonry walls. No, to truly appreciate the sense of time, rich and deep, that is the essence of Bandelier National Monument, you need the wilderness.

DAY HIKE: YAPASHI RUINS
One-way length: 5.5 miles
Low and high elevations: 6,066 and 6,625 feet
Difficulty: strenuous

This is perhaps the most interesting and scenic trail in the Bandelier Backcountry. It's not extraordinarily difficult, but it's not for the woefully out-of-shape. The Yapashi Ruins Trail begins at the visitor center and immediately ascends the mesa to the southwest, where it meanders through open grassy parkland studded with ponderosas. It dips into Lummis Canyon and onto another mesa before reaching Alamo Canyon—500 feet deep at its midsection.

Here you'll find the most difficult hiking in the monument. Approximately 600 stone steps—on each side—retrace an ancient Indian route traversing the narrow canyon. The steps have been improved, although nothing can be done about their number. The canyon bottom itself is a pleasant contrast with the mesas above: bright green cottonwoods, box elder, New Mexico locust, chokecherry, willows, and other plants survive with the help of a tiny stream.

The trail climbs back onto the mesa, then down into another, smaller canyon, then up on the mesa again, where it's only a short distance to Yapashi Ruins. The Cochiti Indians regard these ruins as one of their ancestral homes. The name means "sacred enclosure," and refers to the Stone Lions Shrine 0.5 mile farther. If you visit the shrine, please respect it, as it still is venerated by local Indians.

DESTINATION HIKE: FRIJOLES FALLS
One-way length: 2 miles
Low and high elevations: 5,600 and 6,066 feet
Difficulty: easy

While not within the wilderness, this makes a good short hike for anyone at the monument's visitor center. From the visitor center, cross the small stream, the Rito de los Frijoles, then turn left and walk downhill through parking and picnic areas, paralleling the stream, to where signs mark the trailhead. The trail parallels the tranquil little stream, or *rito*, until suddenly the stream leaps from a basalt ledge to dive 70 feet in a graceful, beautiful waterfall. A half mile farther is Lower Frijoles Falls, not quite as scenic as the upper falls but still worth the hike. If you were to continue 0.75 mile past the lower fall, on the steep, rocky trail, you'd come to the Rio Grande.

SHUTTLE HIKE: PONDEROSA CAMPGROUND –
VISITOR CENTER
One-way length: 7.3 miles
Low and high elevations: 6,066 and 7,600 feet
Difficulty: moderate

Ponderosa Campground is just east of the junction of Highways 4 and 501, south of Los Alamos. The trail begins with a gradual descent through ponderosa forest before going down some steep switchbacks to reach the trail junction known as Upper Crossing after 1.7 miles. Here at Upper Crossing, you join the Rito de los Frijoles, which you'll follow downstream for the rest of the hike. Camping is not allowed at Upper Crossing; signs along the trail inform you where camping is allowed. Some of the meadows about halfway down are especially appealing. The narrow canyon bottom, with its perennial stream and lush vegetation, is a welcome contrast to the arid mesas far above. But be careful, especially if you're hiking or camping with children: the vegetation includes a lot of poison ivy and stinging nettle. About 1.25 miles from the visitor center you arrive at Ceremonial Cave and the numerous people who've made the easy hike to see it. After climbing up to see Ceremonial Cave yourself, follow the broad, well-traveled path to the visitor center, perhaps finishing by taking the Ruins Trail, which branches from the main path.

BACKPACK HIKE: VISITOR CENTER – YAPASHI RUINS –
CAPULIN CANYON – PAINTED CAVE –
FRIJOLES FALLS
One-way length: approximately 19 miles
Low and high elevations: 5,475 and 6,625 feet
Difficulty: strenuous

Although you can do this hike in two days, your trip will be easier and more enjoyable if you allow three. The first part is the same as the hike to Yapashi Ruins described above. From Yapashi Ruins you hike 0.5 mile past the Stone Lions Shrine, then another mile that ends with a steep descent into Capulin ("chokecherry") Canyon. Overnight camping is not allowed in upper Capulin Canyon near the ranger cabin. Check at the visitor center to see what areas are open to camping.

When you reach Capulin Canyon, it's 3.5 miles of pleasant, easy hiking downstream to Painted Cave, a grotto in the cliffs with designs and figures painted by prehistoric and historic peoples. No camping is allowed here. From Painted Cave, continue down the canyon about a mile, then leave the canyon and make a steep, dry hike over a divide to drop into the mouth of Alamo Canyon. From here it's 6.4 miles back to the visitor center.

OTHER RECREATIONAL OPPORTUNITIES

Surrounding Bandelier National Monument are numerous Forest Service roads in the Jemez Mountains; along Highway 4 west of Los Alamos are several Forest Service campgrounds. In the winter, these same roads are outstanding cross-country skiing routes. This is beautiful country, and the Bandelier Backcountry is just part of it.

FOR MORE INFORMATION

BANDELIER NATIONAL MONUMENT, Los Alamos, NM 87544; (505) 672-3861.

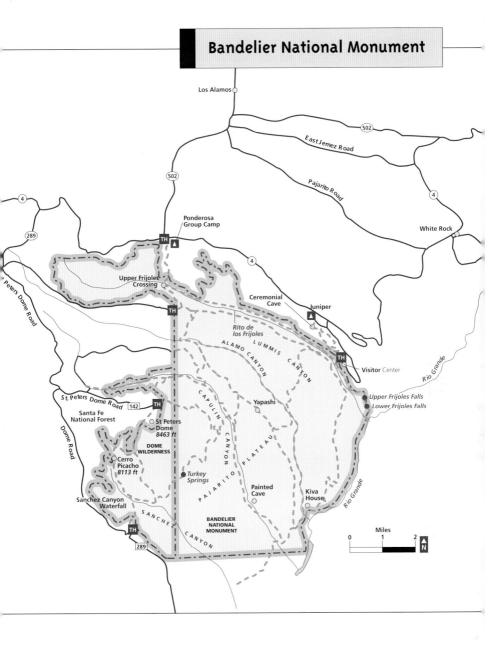

Bandelier National Monument

Los Alamos

502

East Jemez Road

502

Pajarito Road

4

4

White Rock

289

Ponderosa
Group Camp

TH

Peters Dome Road

Upper Frijoles
Crossing

Ceremonial
Cave

Juniper

TH

Rito de
los Frijoles

LUMMIS CANYON

ALAMO CANYON

Visitor Center

St. Peters Dome Road

142

TH

Santa Fe
National Forest

St Peters
Dome
8463 ft

CAPULIN CANYON

Yapashi

Upper Frijoles Falls

Lower Frijoles Falls

Rio Grande

Dome Road

DOME
WILDERNESS

Cerro
Picacho
8113 ft

Turkey
Springs

PAJARITO PLATEAU

Painted
Cave

Kiva
House

Rio Grande

Sanchez Canyon
Waterfall

SANCHEZ CANYON

TH

289

BANDELIER
NATIONAL
MONUMENT

Miles

0   1   2

N

12 Chama River Canyon Wilderness

This linear wilderness along the Rio Chama offers colorful mesas and cliffs, as well as a broad floodplain of meadows and cottonwoods.

Morning on the Chama River

LOCATION	On both sides of the Rio Chama, between El Vado Reservoir and Abiquiu Reservoir, north of Abiquiu
SIZE	50,300 acres
ELEVATION RANGE	6,200 to 8,600 feet
MILES OF TRAILS	12
ECOSYSTEMS	Piñon-juniper, ponderosa pine, floodplain meadows, riparian deciduous
ADMINISTRATION	Santa Fe National Forest, Carson National Forest, BLM Taos Resource Area
TOPOGRAPHIC MAPS	Laguna Peak, Echo Amphitheater, Navajo Peak, Llaves, French Mesa, Youngsville, and Arroyo del Agua USGS 7.5-minute quadrangles; Abiquiu 1:100K USGS quadrangle
BEST SEASONS	Spring, summer, fall
GETTING THERE	The only vehicular access to the Chama River Canyon Wilderness is via packed dirt Forest Road 151, which heads west from Highway 84 about a mile north of the Ghost Ranch Living Museum.
HIKING	This wilderness centers on the river, and consequently hiking is rather limited with only one marked trail, the Ojitos Trail. If you are willing to walk cross-country or along roads, however, the endeavor is well worthwhile. The Continental Divide National Scenic Trail coincides with the Ojitos Trail and Forest Road 151.

IT WAS A LATE OCTOBER MORNING, clear and cold, when I walked north along the road from the Forest Service's Rio Chama Campground where I'd spent the night. The south-leaning sun was beginning to warm the air. A down-canyon breeze rustled the golden cottonwood leaves, and shadows were evaporating from the russet and buff-colored cliffs flanking the river valley. Looking at the dramatic sandstone formations, I realized a human was perched atop a boulder high above. Not a hiker, not a climber, but rather a resident at the Christ in the Desert Monastery just down the road, sitting, like me, watching the valley wilderness awaken.

If ever there were a wilderness to remind us that the wild represents human values beyond what we term "outdoor recreation," it is the Chama River Canyon Wilderness.

This wilderness owes its existence, physically and officially, to the Rio Chama, second only to the Rio Grande as north-central New Mexico's most important river. Like the Rio Grande, the Chama rises in Colorado and runs south. It goes through the village of Chama, past Abiquiu, to join the Rio Grande just north of Española. In 1598, at a Tewa Indian pueblo near this confluence, Spanish colonizer Don Juan de Oñate established the first European capital in what is now the United States. (The Spanish capital moved to Santa Fe in 1609.) The name "Chama," from the Tewa language, refers either to a pueblo that existed north of the present village of Abiquiu, or, more likely, is a corruption of the Tewa word *tzama*, "red," the color of the river as it carries silt from the reddish rocks and soil of northern New Mexico.

Like the Colorado River, whose red-color name the Chama echoes, the Chama on its journey south has carved a dramatic gorge out of the surrounding sandstone. Flanking and protecting the Rio Chama Wild and Scenic River (designated in 1988), this gorge comprises the Chama River Canyon Wilderness (also designated in 1988). The 50,300-acre wilderness and the 24.6-mile stretch of river running between El Vado Reservoir and Abiquiu Reservoir are two components of a collage of public lands collectively called the Rio Chama Corridor. This area is administered by several federal agencies including the Santa Fe and Carson National Forests, the Bureau of Land Management, and the U.S. Army Corps of Engineers. Adjacent to the northern boundary of the Chama River Canyon Wilderness is the 11,985-acre Rio Chama Wilderness Study Area, administered as wilderness by the BLM.

Very few people come to the wilderness to hike or backpack; for most visitors, the river is the main attraction. But then the Chama River Canyon Wilderness isn't really a hikers' or backpackers' wilderness. For the adrenaline-pumping, character-testing qualities we usually associate with wilderness, get on the Rio Chama Wild and Scenic River in the spring. The river bustles with whitewater enthusiasts riding the wild water of the Colorado snowmelt, putting in, taking out, shuttling back and forth, and setting up camps at the numerous sites along the river. (Boating on the river is controlled through permits issued by the BLM's Taos Resource District Office, address below.) But the boaters come here for the river's wildness, not the scenery. For most of the year the river is rather quiet and serene, meandering through its broad floodplain of meadows and cottonwood groves.

The entire wilderness has only one hiking trail, a relatively easy six-miler that ascends the western mesa from the river. This is ironic—with more than 50,000 acres, the Chama River Canyon Wilderness is the fifth largest of New Mexico's 24 designated

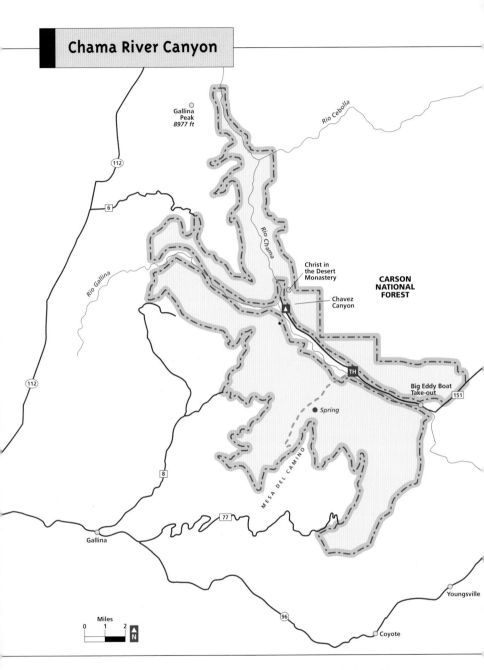

Chama River Canyon

Gallina
Peak
8977 ft

Rio Cebolla

112

6

Rio Chama

Rio Gallina

Christ in
the Desert
Monastery

Chavez
Canyon

**CARSON
NATIONAL
FOREST**

112

TH

Big Eddy Boat
Take-out

151

8

• Spring

M E S A   D E L   C A M I N O

Gallina

77

Youngsville

Miles
0   1   2

N

96

Coyote

wildernesses. The scenic 2.3-mile Rim Vista Trail lies just outside the wilderness;
the 0.8-mile Chavez Canyon Trail, located south of the monastery, was closed as of
this writing.

This unusual "linear" wilderness requires further elaboration. For example, a
dirt road runs through it and from this road you can look up and see the boundaries

of the wilderness. No sense of unexplored vastness here. Also, at the road's end is a tiny human settlement with the brothers and sisters associated with the Christ in the Desert Monastery. So, if you're looking for a place for solitary backcountry trekking, the Rio Chama Canyon Wilderness isn't for you.

But then, as the monastery reminds us, wilderness isn't just about excitement, adventure, and testing ourselves and our equipment. (The Wyoming poet C.L. Rawlins once quipped that "We now go outside mostly to screw around with stuff we just bought.") If we accept that we can experience wilderness in other ways than simply hiking through it, then the Chama River Canyon Wilderness deserves a second look.

> **DAY HIKE: CHAVEZ CANYON**
> One-way length: 0.8 mile
> Low and high elevations: 6,560 and 6,800 feet
> Difficulty: easy

This short but interesting trail was closed for resource recovery in the fall of 1997, but if it's open it's worth an hour or two. The trailhead is on the east side of Forest Road 151 less than 0.5 mile south of the entrance to the Christ in the Desert Monastery. The trail heads through piñon-juniper forest into the canyon, which narrows dramatically, becoming almost a slot canyon. Soon you encounter pour-offs in the slots, where you can decide to turn back or scramble onward. Chavez Canyon offers great views of the surrounding sandstone cliffs.

> **DAY HIKE – BACKPACK HIKE: OJITOS TRAIL**
> One-way length: 6 miles
> Low and high elevations: 6,360 and 8,100 feet
> Difficulty: moderate

The only official trail in the wilderness, the Ojitos Trail is excellent either as a long day hike or as an overnighter, with good campsites and running water. From the Big Eddy parking area, drive 2.8 miles north on Forest Road 151 to Skull Bridge. Park here and walk across the bridge to the trailhead. The trail follows an old road west, then north. Then another road branches south, which the trail follows, marked by marker posts. South of a log pass-through are the *ojitos*, "little springs," to which the canyon owes its name. Nearby is a fork; take the north branch. After about 5 miles, the gentle gradients end as the trail leaves the canyon bottom and begins switchbacking up the side of Mesa del Camino ("mesa of the road") where the trail ends at a road on a ledge below the mesa's top.

> **DESTINATION HIKE: RIM VISTA TRAIL**
> One-way length: 2.3 miles
> Low and high elevations: 6,600 and 7,380 feet
> Difficulty: easy to moderate

While not quite within the wilderness, this wild trail offers a magnificent view of northern New Mexico. To reach the trail, take Forest Road 151 west 0.7 mile from its junction with Highway 84 to where a sign reading Trail 15 marks a two-track running north. After 0.5 mile, you'll reach a rough parking area and a trail sign. The easy-to-follow trail, marked by blue diamonds on trees, ascends gradually but persistently through piñon-juniper forest. At about 1.75 miles, the trail swings northeast to slab beneath the mesa's rim before a final short but steep dash to Vista Rim, the inspiration of the name being obvious. To the southeast are the polychrome cliffs and canyons of Ghost Ranch; to the south is Abiquiu Reservoir and surrounding plains; to the southwest are the high northern peaks of the Jemez Mountains, dominated by chisel-shaped Cerro Pedernal. Forest Road 131A ends at the rim, but motorists miss the hike.

SHUTTLE HIKE: BIG EDDY – CHRIST IN THE DESERT MONASTERY
One-way length: 8 miles
Low and high elevations: 6,400 feet throughout
Difficulty: moderate (due to length)

This "hike" is actually a walk along dirt Forest Road 151 from the Big Eddy boat take-out to the Christ in the Desert Monastery, but unless you go during the peak of boating season, traffic along the road will likely be light. The scenery along the road is magnificent, and you'll encounter numerous campsites along the river that make attractive places to break. At the monastery, you can visit the gift shop and chapel.

OTHER RECREATIONAL OPPORTUNITIES

As indicated above, the main recreation activity here is boating on the river, which is regulated by the Bureau of Land Management Taos Resource District. Also, Forest Road 151, with its gently rolling hills and little net elevation gain, is excellent for mountain biking. You'll find numerous campgrounds along the Rio Chama.

FOR MORE INFORMATION

SANTA FE NATIONAL FOREST—COYOTE RANGER DISTRICT, P.O. Box 160, Coyote, NM 87012; (505) 638-5526.

CARSON NATIONAL FOREST, Supervisor's Office, Forest Service Building, P.O. Box 558, 208 Cruz Alta Road, Taos, NM 87571; (505) 758-6200.

BUREAU OF LAND MANAGEMENT, Taos Field Office, 226 Cruz Alta Road, Taos, NM 87571; (505) 758-8851.

GHOST RANCH LIVING MUSEUM, Carson National Forest, Highway 84, Abiquiu, NM 87510; (505) 685-4312.

EL VADO RANCH, P.O. Box 129, Tierra Amarilla, NM 87575; (505) 588-7354.

WILD RIVERS RECREATION AREA, Bureau of Land Management, Taos Field Office, 226 Cruz Alta Road, Taos, NM 87571; (505) 770-1600.

Dome Wilderness | 13

The Dome Wilderness features peaks with expansive views; deep, narrow canyons; archaeological sites; and interesting geology.

Sunflowers in burned forest

LOCATION	On the southwest border of Bandelier National Monument Wilderness
SIZE	5,200 acres
ELEVATION RANGE	5,900 to 8,463 feet
MILES OF TRAILS	6
ECOSYSTEMS	Canyon bottom riparian, piñon-juniper, ponderosa pine
ADMINISTRATION	Santa Fe National Forest
TOPOGRAPHIC MAPS	Trails Illustrated Bandelier National Monument
BEST SEASONS	Spring, summer, fall
GETTING THERE	Vehicular access to the Dome Wilderness is via packed dirt Forest Road 289, which connects with Highway 4 on the north and Forest Road 286 on the south. From Forest Road 289, Forest Road 142 leads to St. Peters Dome.
HIKING	Though the number of marked and maintained trails here is small, they can be linked with trails in the surrounding Santa Fe National Forest and Bandelier National Monument backcountry for much more extensive hiking.

LOS ALAMOS HISTORIAN, naturalist, and hiker Dorothy Hoard was instrumental in the designation of the Dome Wilderness, an area she describes as "a nice little wilderness."

Little?

From the top of 8,113-foot Cerro Picacho, you can see mountains and mesas stretching for miles in all directions, every view untarnished by roads or other human intrusions. Yet at 5,200 acres, Dome is the smallest Forest Service wilderness in the Southwest, barely exceeding the 5,000-acre minimum in the federal guidelines. But to judge Dome solely by its diminutive size is inappropriate, for it abuts the 32,727-acre Bandelier National Monument Wilderness, and together they comprise a unit exemplifying the wilderness system's best characteristics: a large, contiguous natural area; unique cultural and natural features; valuable wildlife habitat; natural beauty; and solitude.

The Bandelier Wilderness was designated in 1976, but wilderness advocates, including Hoard, said, "Why get Bandelier without getting Dome? They're part of the same viewshed. You want wilderness to be a unit." Congress agreed and in 1980 designated the Dome Wilderness, named for the region's most prominent feature, 8,463-foot St. Peters Dome. The wilderness is characterized by rounded, pine-forested summits, deep canyons, and relatively flat mesas. Saint Peters Dome is the main summit of the small mountain chain called the San Miguel Mountains, which includes 8,165-foot Boundary Peak, located on the boundary of Bandelier National Monument. About a mile to the southwest is the other prominent summit of the Dome Wilderness, 8,113-foot Cerro Picacho, whose Spanish name is a curious double-generic, "hill peak."

The other major topographic feature of the Dome Wilderness is Sanchez Canyon, running from northwest to southeast through the wilderness. It's one of many canyons ranging from 300 to 500 feet deep in this region, all created by erosion of the soft volcanic tuff (compressed volcanic ash) that makes up the Pajarito Plateau. This tuff characteristically weathers into vertical walls, and throughout the Dome Wilderness and adjacent Bandelier Backcountry hikers must confront the problem of crossing the chasms, for often what appears from the top to be a passable route down suddenly ends at the brink of a hundred-foot cliff. That's why many modern hiking routes coincide with trails used by the ancient Indians of the Pajarito Plateau.

On the mesa east of where the Dome Trail crosses Sanchez Canyon are several small, inconspicuous ruins, perhaps shelters used by Pueblo Indians who grew seasonal crops here. Scattered on the ground are pottery shards and flakes of obsidian, the black, volcanic glass that was traded throughout the Southwest and used for making skinning tools and projectile points.

About the time the Spaniards arrived in New Mexico in 1540, Indians left the Pajarito Plateau, moving to settlements closer to the Rio Grande where they continue to live today. They did not forget their former homeland, however-the Keres-speaking Indians of Cochiti Pueblo still know Sanchez Canyon by a name meaning "canyon of the waterfall," referring to a small but lovely waterfall at the crossing of the Dome Trail. The Indians were succeeded on the plateau by Spanish-speaking pastoralists. Sanchez Canyon's full Spanish name is Cañon de José Sánchez, recalling a man who once owned land here.

The ruggedness of the Dome Wilderness and the diversity of habitat—dry piñon-juniper mesas, moist ponderosa-lined canyons, uplands with Gambel oak, locust, and mountain mahogany—have made it a refuge for wildlife. Among the mammals here are mountain lions, black bears, bobcats, foxes, coyotes, elk, and mule deer. The Dome Wilderness is also designated range for wild burros. Once a scourge to the Pajarito Plateau ecosystem, the numbers of these feral burros have been significantly reduced. Despite their small population, the burros survive; you can still see burro droppings on the plateau.

The small size and proximity to the better-known Bandelier Backcountry means that most Dome Wilderness hikers are either en route elsewhere or simply choose day trips. But the area features several campsites for overnight stays in upper Sanchez Canyon (the only reliable water source in the wilderness area). Because the wilderness generally has a south-facing aspect, spring and fall are the best hiking seasons.

During a severe drought in the spring of 1996, a forest fire ravaged 3,092 acres of the total 5,200-acre area, affecting conditions for years to come. The fire exposed hundreds of the archaeological sites in the wilderness, and while the fire itself didn't harm the sites, subsequent erosion on unprotected soil may indeed damage them. The area lost some of its appeal for hikers.

To enter the wilderness from the south, drive to the village of Cochiti Lake. From small Lake Plaza shopping center, drive 2.8 miles north to where Forest Road 289 heads east. After 3.4 miles on this rough dirt road, you'll reach a parking area to the right at the site of the abandoned Eagle Canyon pumice mines. From this parking area, Dome Trail, No. 118, heads into the wilderness. After 1.5 miles, this trail crosses Sanchez Canyon, from which it ascends to the mesa where it branches: one fork heads east to Turkey Springs in Bandelier National Monument, and the other heads north past Cerro Picacho to St. Peters Dome.

From the north, drive on New Mexico 501 west from Los Alamos to Highway 4. Proceed south on Forest Road 289 to Forest Road 142, leading to the Dome Lookout. Here also are trails leading into Capulin Canyon in Bandelier National Monument. The Dome Wilderness is small; its very existence is little known. It's not a "collectible" wilderness like the Gila or Pecos, and it's very rugged with few and inconspicuous trailheads. Relatively few hikers (just a few hundred) visit the wilderness, whereas thousands visit adjacent Bandelier National Monument. And of those hundreds, most simply traverse the Dome Wilderness en route to better-known Bandelier; few hikers linger in the Dome Wilderness itself. Yet the hikers who do explore here experience a private wilderness that they come to regard as special.

DAY HIKE: SANCHEZ CANYON
One-way length: 1.5 miles
Low and high elevations: 6,400 and 6,720 feet
Difficulty: moderate

The short hike to Sanchez Canyon from the Eagle Canyon pumice mines (see access directions above) makes for a pleasant day in the southern Jemez Mountains, with several possible interesting side trips. From the parking area, the Dome Trail, No. 118, heads northeast, crossing Eagle Canyon before descending into Sanchez Canyon with its lovely little waterfall. The hike from here up Sanchez Canyon is interesting and easy. By continuing east on the trail out of Sanchez Canyon for one mile, you come to the junction with the St. Peters Dome Trail. Near this junction, sharp eyes can find evidence of the ancient Indian inhabitants of the Pajarito Plateau.

LOOP HIKE: CERRO PICACHO – SANCHEZ CANYON
Round-trip length: 6.5 miles
Low and high elevations: 6,400 and 8,113 feet
Difficulty: strenuous

Starting at the Eagle Canyon pumice mines (see access directions above), hike on the Dome Trail, No. 118, 1.5 miles northeast into Sanchez Canyon. Then hike another mile to the junction with the St. Peters Dome – Picacho Trail. This trail ascends gradually for 1.5 miles to a saddle at 7,400 feet on the southeast of Cerro Picacho. From here, bushwhack steeply up to the summit. More bushwhacking follows when finding a route down into the bottom of Sanchez Canyon; this descent can be difficult and tricky. Once in the canyon, the hiking becomes easier as you follow the canyon downstream to the junction with the Dome Trail, which you take back to the parking area.

SHUTTLE HIKE: PICACHO TRAIL
One-way length: 5.5 miles
Low and high elevations: 6,400 and 8,320 feet
Difficulty: moderate to strenuous

By starting this at the Forest Service picnic area northwest of St. Peters Dome (see access directions above), you'll hike mostly downhill, but you'll still have to traverse 300-foot-deep Sanchez Canyon. Making a 600-foot climb to the summit of 8,113-foot Cerro Picacho takes this hike from moderate to strenuous, particularly considering the fact that no clearly marked trail leads to the summit. For those with the energy, however, this sidetrip is worth it. Hikers wishing to turn this trip into a backpack hike will find water and campsites either in Sanchez Canyon or at Turkey Spring in Bandelier National Monument (accessible via the Capulin Trail). Linger at Sanchez Canyon to view the waterfall there, and as you ascend, pause to appreciate the views behind you. The hike ends at the abandoned pumice mines near Eagle Canyon. Forest Road 289 will eventually return you to your vehicle in the north.

OTHER RECREATIONAL OPPORTUNITIES

Although the Dome Wilderness and the Bandelier National Monument Wilderness are administered by separate agencies, they comprise a single wilderness unit. You can design several hikes and backpack trips that cross the boundary between the two areas.

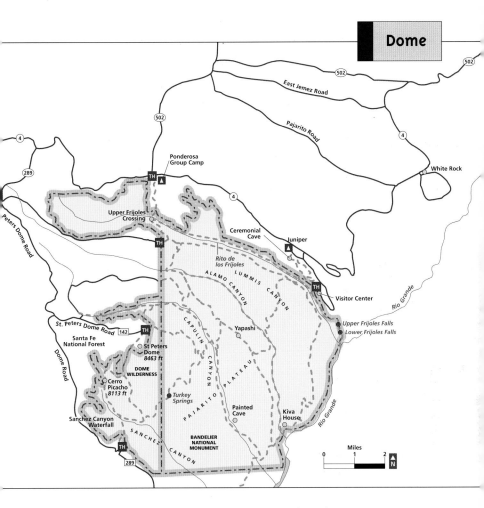

The numerous trails and forest roads throughout the Jemez Mountains make for outstanding mountain biking. During the winter, these same roads and trails are popular with cross-country skiers, although south-facing slopes at lower elevations often lack sufficient snow.

If you approach the Dome Wilderness from the south in the fall, you'll surely want to join the many New Mexicans making the ritual journey to the Dixon Apple Orchards (look for apple signs past the village of Cochiti Lake). The red and yellow varieties are famous throughout the state.

FOR MORE INFORMATION

BANDELIER NATIONAL MONUMENT, Los Alamos, NM 87544; (505) 672-3861.

SANTA FE NATIONAL FOREST, Supervisor's Office, 1220 St. Francis Drive, Santa Fe, NM 87504; (505) 438-7840.

14 San Pedro Parks Wilderness

With an average elevation of 10,000 feet, the San Pedro Parks Wilderness is an emerald-colored archipelago of low hills surrounded by an ocean of meadows, aspen groves, and spruce-fir forests.

Sneezeweed in a meadow

LOCATION	In the western Jemez Mountains, northeast of Cuba
SIZE	41,132 acres
ELEVATION RANGE	8,400 to 10,605 feet
MILES OF TRAILS	60
ECOSYSTEMS	Spruce-fir, ponderosa pine, scrub oak, aspen
ADMINISTRATION	Santa Fe National Forest—Cuba Ranger District; Carson National Forest—Coyote Ranger District
TOPOGRAPHIC MAPS	Forest Service San Pedro Parks Wilderness
BEST SEASONS	Summer, fall
GETTING THERE	While trailheads are reached via forest roads from the north, west, and east, most people access the San Pedro Parks Wilderness from the south by taking Highway 126 east from the village of Cuba, then taking Forest Road 70 to the campground near Gregorio Lake.
HIKING	An extensive network of well-marked and well-maintained trails exists throughout the San Pedro Parks Wilderness, with numerous trailheads around the wilderness's periphery.

THIS AREA IS GENTLE AND WELCOMING, lush with verdant marshes, tiny streams, and rolling meadows punctuated by aspen groves and conifer forests. All this velvety prose accurately describes the San Pedro Parks Wilderness, but to enjoy this pleasant area, one must first reach it.

Park, in the geographic lexicon of the American West, refers to open grassland in a setting of mountains and forest, and that indeed describes the San Pedro Parks. But here the broad, high upland (average elevation 10,000 feet) with its distinctive and inviting *vegas*, "meadows," is guarded on all sides by ramparts of varying steepness, for the wilderness sits atop the Sierra Nacimiento, an igneous uplift that abuts but is geologically different from the volcanic Jemez Mountains. This uplift is most obvious from Highway 44 and Highway 96, west and north of Cuba, where the Sierra Nacimiento rises abruptly from the mesas and plains to the west, a wall cut by canyons only slightly less steep than the ridges separating them. Before reaching the lush forests and meadows, hikers must climb through a fringe of scrub oak growing on rocky, arid soil. The approaches from the east are less daunting, but only from the south, from the trailhead at Gregorio Lake, hikers can enter the wilderness without a significant climb (see Vacas Trail on p. 105).

Once in the parks, however, the hiking becomes dramatically easier. At the center of the wilderness are the San Pedro Peaks, but they resemble hills more than peaks, their contours rounded and gentle. One doesn't come to this wilderness for peak-bagging.

No, the main attraction is the complex matrix of meadows and marshes. Where the volcanic rocks of the nearby Jemez Mountains are generally soft and permeable, the Sierra Nacimiento is an uplift along a fault of very ancient Precambrian granite, overlain on the west by Triassic and Jurassic sedimentary layers in which you can find marine fossils. Because the 10,000-foot Sierra Nacimiento is the first upland that storms encounter coming across the Colorado Plateau, the wilderness receives 35 inches of precipitation annually—not bad for New Mexico. At least 20 named streams have their headwaters here, as well as numerous unnamed drainages. The named streams include four of northern New Mexico's "rivers": the Rio Puerco, Rio Capulin, Rio Gallina, and Rio de las Vacas. (It takes non–New Mexicans a while to get used to the term *rio*, or river, referring to a stream you often can leap across.) Indeed, the Spanish name Sierra Nacimiento, "birth range," refers to the uplands being the birthplace of the Rio Puerco.

The area's human history has been dominated by rural Spanish-speaking people, evidenced by other stream names in the wilderness: Rio Puerco, "muddy river," referring to conditions outside the wilderness; La Jara Creek, "the willow"; Corralitos Creek, "little corrals"; Agua Sarca, "blue water"; Rito de las Palomas, "creek of the doves"; José Miguel Creek; Rito de los Pinos, "creek of the pines"; and many more.

So for hikers and campers here, the availability of water is not an issue. What is an issue is the water's potability. The 1964 Wilderness Act allowed certain traditional uses for the land, including livestock grazing. Consequently, you will find cattle in many, if not most, New Mexico wildernesses, but probably nowhere as plentiful as in the San Pedro Parks Wilderness. Lucky are the cows who spend their summers here in this lush region, but unlucky are the hikers who drink the foul water. Despite its clarity and natural setting, all water in the San Pedro Parks is suspect and

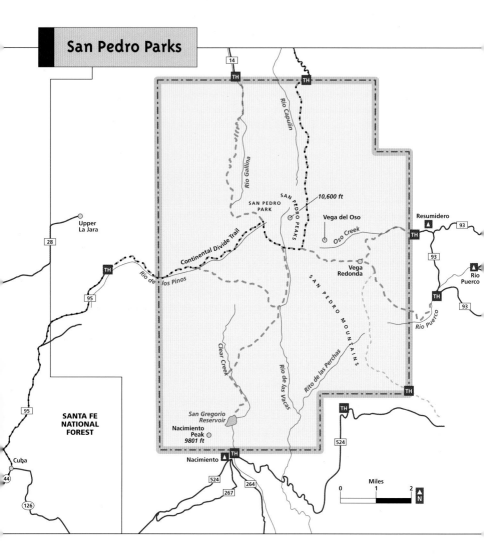

must be treated thoroughly. (I learned this the hard way on my first trip into the parks; after drinking from a crystalline stream, I rounded a bend to see a herd of cattle standing in the stream I had just drunk from and two days later my intestines confirmed my worst suspicions.) These streams support trout, including populations of the native cutthroat, cattle notwithstanding.

But while cows are the largest mammals you're most likely to see here, they're not alone in this rich habitat. Elk, deer, black bears, coyotes, foxes, bobcats, mountain lions, blue grouse, squirrels, beavers, and others also live here, and one of the pleasures of camping in the parks is sitting quietly at the edge of a meadow, at dawn or dusk, to see what emerges from the forest.

Wilderness preservation in the San Pedro Parks began in 1931 when the area was designated a primitive area by the Chief of the Forest Service. In 1941 the Secretary of Agriculture reclassified it as a Wild Area, with 41,132 acres. It became a formal wilderness in 1964, with the passage of the Wilderness Act.

The San Pedro Parks Wilderness has a reputation of being little known, even though the area has been recognized for more than thirty years as having outstanding wilderness attributes. Travel within the parks is conspicuously easy, relative to other wildernesses. Trails in the wilderness are generally clear and well marked, though the absence of conspicuous landmarks means it's easy to become confused if you stray from the trail. Furthermore, the trailheads are but a three hour drive from either Albuquerque or Santa Fe. The campgrounds surrounding the wilderness are heavily used, especially by local people.

High elevation and northern latitude (for New Mexico) mean snow lingers late in the San Pedro Parks, at least into May. Trails with poorly drained soils will be boggy even after that. But by late June and certainly early July, the abundant wildflowers will begin to appear. By mid-August, afternoon showers douse visitors almost daily. Still, the parks' patchwork of forests and aspen groves offer numerous campsites sheltered by trees, and there are worse places to wait out a rainstorm.

By early September, the monsoon rains subside and the long, mild, and generally dry New Mexico fall begins. In the San Pedro Parks Wilderness, the vibrant greens are augmented by the shimmering gold of aspen leaves and the russet and auburn colors of grass preparing for winter. Nights are chilly, but not bone-cracking cold, and the days can be comfortably warm. At times such as these, it's easy to understand the San Pedro Parks' reputation as New Mexico's gentle wilderness.

DAY HIKE: VACAS TRAIL
One-way length: 5.5 miles
Low and high elevations: 9,200 and 10,040 feet
Difficulty: easy to moderate

This is the route by which most hikers enter the San Pedro Parks Wilderness. It's readily accessible and scenic, and avoids the steep climbs of other entry routes. You can reach the trailhead from Highway 44 at Cuba (the Santa Fe National Forest Cuba Ranger District offices are at the village's south end). Go approximately 6.5 miles east on Highway 126 to where the pavement ends. Near here Forest Road 70 goes north and after 2.6 miles arrives at Nacimiento Campground. From the campground, the Vacas Trail, No. 51, heads north and after slightly less than a mile of gentle ascent through spruce-fir and aspen forest comes to Gregorio Lake, a manmade reservoir very popular with local anglers. The Vacas Trail continues north around the east side of the lake, then bends east to join Clear Creek. It parallels the stream, soon entering an area of aspen groves and meadows. This is a natural place to break, turn around, or camp.

Almost two miles from the lake, the Vacas Trail leaves Clear Creek to pass through more forest, aspens groves, and meadows, ultimately arriving 4.3 miles from the lake at the Rio de las Vacas ("river of the cows") and the intersection with the Las Palomas Trail, No. 50. Just 0.2 mile farther is the terminus of the Anastacio Trail, No. 345.

DESTINATION HIKE: VEGA REDONDA
One-way length: 3.5 miles
Low and high elevations: 8,980 and 10,070 feet
Difficulty: moderate

Vega Redonda ("round meadow") is a beautiful place for a picnic. The Vega Redonda Trail, No. 43, begins near the Resumidero campground. You can reach the campground from Highway 96 by taking Forest Road 103, accessed either near Gallina or Coyote, to Forest Road 93, arriving after two miles at the campground. Both roads are good gravel. The trail follows an old dirt road 0.75 mile to the fenced wilderness boundary. From here the trail meanders gradually upward through conifer and aspen forest, heading generally southwest until it turns due south at a large meadow with several beaver ponds. Although numerous livestock trails often obscure the main trail, keep heading south and watch for route-marker stakes until you reach the grassy basin of Vega Redonda. You can complete a loop can by returning on the Rio Puerco Trail, No. 385, to Forest Road 93 and then walking back to the campground.

SHUTTLE HIKE: CONTINENTAL DIVIDE TRAIL
One-way length: 12.3 miles
Low and high elevations: 8,050 and 10,440 feet
Difficulty: strenuous

The Continental Divide Trail (CDT) is perhaps the nation's most significant long-distance hiking trail, and at 3,100 miles certainly the longest. While the trail in some parts of New Mexico is still crude and undefined, the stretch through the San Pedro Parks Wilderness is well-marked and ready to hike. If you're hiking the CDT south to north, you'll enter the wilderness from the west. At the northwest end of the village of Cuba on Highway 44, Forest Road 95 branches right and goes northeast 6.7 miles until the road ends at a trail sign for the Los Pinos Trail, No. 46. You begin with a gentle gradient, but soon you're climbing steadily up the Sierra Nacimiento Escarpment. At 1.9 miles you reach the wilderness boundary. At 3.1 miles you finally top out at the junction with the Anastacio Trail, No. 435. The meadows and aspen groves of the San Pedro Parks stretch before you. At 10,000 feet, your climbing is essentially over, and the scenery is beautiful.

The CDT continues following Trail No. 46 as it parallels the pleasant Rito de los Pinos until it ends at its headwaters in a marshy area in San Pedro Park. The surrounding meadows are what makes this area famous. Here the CDT briefly joins the Vacas ("cows") Trail, No. 51, before joining Trail 32, a short link to Trail 31. Trail 31 heads north, across perhaps the largest meadow in the wilderness, before beginning its steep descent down the northern slopes. You'll find a parking area at the northern wilderness boundary. If you drive here from the north, follow Highway 96 to Forest Road 76. Then follow the road south to Forest Road 171 and take a sharp right turn onto Forest Road 1160, which ends at the wilderness boundary.

BOB JULYAN'S FAVORITE HIKE: RESUMIDERO – VEGA REDONDA – VEGA DEL OSO – SAN PEDRO PARKS
One-way length: 5.5 miles
Low and high elevations: 8,980 and 10,200 feet
Difficulty: moderate to strenuous

This hike takes you through the essence of the San Pedro Parks Wilderness, and while the total distance makes for tired feet at day's end, the hiking is relatively easy after the initial ascent. The Vega Redonda Trail, No. 43, begins at the spacious Resumidero Campground. It ascends through conifer forest to Vega Redonda (see Vega Redonda hike). Here it joins the Rio Puerco Trail, No. 385, following it west (check your map and compass). With little elevation gain through conifer forest, you'll ultimately cross tiny Oso Creek to Vega del Oso ("meadow of the bear"), an appendix of the large park area surrounding the San Pedro Peaks. As you hike along the southern edge of Vega del Oso, you'll meet the Peñas Negras Trail, No. 32. Just 0.25 mile farther, you'll reach the junction with the Capulin Trail, No. 31, and part of the Continental Divide National Scenic Trail, which runs north. Continue farther west to the Rio de las Vacas and a junction with the Vacas Trail, No. 51. All of these trails sometimes become obscure in the meadows, so look for the route to be marked by stakes. Return the way you came.

OTHER RECREATIONAL OPPORTUNITIES

Most cross-country skiers who visit the San Pedro Parks head for the southern end. By driving Highway 126 east from the southern end of Cuba, you'll come first to Forest Road 98, about three miles from the Santa Fe National Forest boundary. This forest road goes south and provides access to Bluebird Mesa. Although it is not in the wilderness itself, this area is nonetheless very popular with cross-country skiers because it's relatively flat, has a network of old logging roads, and offers several scenic overlooks. By going about a half mile farther on Highway 126 you come to Forest Road 70, which heads north toward Gregorio Lake and provides access to the wilderness via the Vacas Trail, described above.

The wilderness's northern side also has an extensive network of forest roads, which you can access from the Gallina area. However, the steepness and distance make getting into the wilderness itself more difficult. All the above Forest Roads are also excellent for mountain biking.

Because of the summer lushness of its meadows and the relative gentleness of its trails, the San Pedro Parks Wilderness is ideally suited for pack animals, especially low-impact ones like llamas.

FOR MORE INFORMATION

Cuba Ranger District, P.O. Box 130, Cuba, NM 87103; (505) 289-3264; local Santa Fe (505) 988-6997.

Santa Fe National Forest–Coyote Ranger District, P.O. Box 160, Coyote, NM 87012; (505) 638-5526.

Santa Fe National Forest, Supervisor's Office, 1220 St. Francis Drive, Santa Fe, NM 87504; (505) 438-7840.

The Central Rio Grande

Few areas in New Mexico are as ecologically diverse as the Central Rio Grande region. Mountain ecosystems above 10,000 feet, characterized by spruce-fir forest and aspen forest, range downward to the Chihuahuan Desert with its creosote bush, ocotillo, and soaptree yucca. This diversity is reflected in the wildlands here: long linear mountain ranges, small compact mountain ranges, upland mesas and canyons, arid flatlands, and lush riparian areas.

This region is defined by the Rio Grande, which in turn is defined by the Rio Grande Rift. The river didn't cause or contribute to the rift: it simply flows over the subsidence zone. While the earth in the rift is sinking, the land on its flanks is rising, creating the linear north-south fault-blocks border flank the Rio Grande on its journey south to Mexico. The same limestone layers that appear at 10,000 feet atop the Sandia Mountains lie beneath 10,000 feet of sediment underneath the city of Albuquerque. The mountains are fault-blocks, uplifted like sidewalk blocks by a sprouting tree. Their gentle slopes rise to a linear crest and then plunge precipitously down an escarpment facing the rift.

This is readily seen in the Sandia and Manzano Mountains, the ranges that include the region's two designated wildernesses. In both ranges a core of Precambrian granite underlies a layer of sedimentary limestone, dramatically displayed on the ranges' western faces. Here steep ridges and canyons climb to a 10,000-foot north-south ridge, passing through several life zones in just a few miles: the Upper Sonoran, with its yucca, scrub oak, and piñon-juniper forest; the transition zone of ponderosa pines; and finally the northern coniferous spruce-fir forest.

But while the two ranges are similar in origin and ecology, their wildernesses are very different in use. The Sandia Mountain Wilderness has been described as an "urban wilderness," and while wildness and solitude can be found in the 28-mile-long range, the mountains are unalterably adjacent to Albuquerque, New Mexico's largest city, and ringed on all sides with residential and recreational development. Although wilderness trails are numerous, easy access means that some trails are heavily used by day hikers. Most local hikers use the wilderness only for day hikes and overlook backpacking possibilities.

Rio Grande Gorge

By contrast, the Manzano Mountain Wilderness, while relatively near Albuquerque in air miles, is buffered on the north by military, Indian, and private lands, and access to the few trailheads in the south requires a long drive. No downhill ski areas attract visitors and cross-country ski routes are few. All of this results in the Manzano Mountains being far less visited than their sister range to the north, and hence far wilder. Day hikers tend to concentrate on a few well-known trails, and backpackers, for the most part, ignore the Manzanos. The Manzano Mountain Wilderness will never will upstage the Pecos Wilderness, but hikers who take the trouble to really explore the Manzanos will not be disappointed.

Neither range has much surface water. Springs and small, intermittent streams exist, allowing extended trips by hikers who plan carefully, but from neither range flows a stream that survives on the surface past the mountains' foothills.

The only other designated mountain wildland in this region is the Sierra Ladrones Wilderness Study Area. This small, isolated mountain complex southwest of Albuquerque is steep, extremely rugged, accessible only via long dirt roads, lacking in trails, and usually without water—great wilderness! A few day hikers come here to explore, and sight-reading a route to the 9,210-foot summit is locally considered a minor hiking coup. But for the most part, the Sierra Ladrones are left to mule deer, desert bighorn sheep, mountain lions, and other wildlife that thrive best where humans seldom go.

Northwest of Albuquerque, along the Rio Puerco Valley, is a cluster of BLM wilderness study areas of high scenic and cultural interest. Known as the Boca del Oso Complex, it includes the Chamisa, Empedrado, Ignacio Chavez, and La Leña WSAs; the Cabezon WSA is also here, and the Ojito WSA, while further away, is related in general location and character. In this area, the New Mexico Wilderness Alliance has proposed adding other areas for wilderness consideration: the Forest Service roadless area called the Banco Breaks and the BLM areas called San Luis, Cerro de Guadalupe, and Cerro Cuate.

Throughout this area the terrain is complex—highly eroded sandstone mesas and canyons, punctuated by stark, dramatic volcanic plugs often likened to fire-blackened, weathered tree stumps. No trails exist here, springs are few, and even the Rio Puerco, "muddy river," often lacks water. Moreover, much of the land is privately held, and the landowners aren't always welcoming to hikers. But the area can be beautiful, and scattered here and there—in canyons and atop mesas—are echoes of prehistoric and historic peoples, who lived here. Few people hike here; even fewer backpack. To those who do come, the area imparts a strong sense of remoteness, both in distance and in time—yet Albuquerque is just over the horizon, a mere two-hour drive away.

Similar in appeal is the cluster of BLM wilderness study areas southwest of Albuquerque and east of the Rio Grande: Veranito, Las Cañas, Presilla, Stallion, Jornada del Muerto, Big Yucca, and Antelope. From a distance, these low, barren hills and eroded plains looks conspicuously unappealing. But during the right season (not summer), these wildlands reveal a surprising array of interesting landforms, plants, and animals, as well as archaeological sites. And when other areas are locked in winter, these wildlands, readily accessible from Albuquerque, are still hikeable. Again, this isn't backpacking country, although a warm night spent under the stars here would be delightful, and you certainly wouldn't have to worry about all the good camping sites being taken. Rather, this is poking-around country, a good place to trust to serendipity as you

follow a ridge or an arroyo simply because it looks interesting, even when you can't say precisely why.

Big Arsenic Spring

Antelope Wilderness Study Area

15

This expanse of rolling grassland complements adjacent and nearby wilderness and proposed wilderness areas. It is a good antelope habitat seldom visited by the public.

LOCATION
Between the Little San Pascual Wilderness of the Bosque del Apache National Wildlife Refuge, on the west, and White Sands Missile Range, on the east

SIZE
20,710 acres
Size recommended by the NM Wilderness Alliance: 18,109 acres

ELEVATION RANGE
4,725 to 4,790 feet

MILES OF TRAILS
No marked or maintained trails

ECOSYSTEMS
Rolling Chihuahuan Desert grassland and scrub

ADMINISTRATION
BLM

TOPOGRAPHIC MAPS
Little San Pascual Mountain USGS 7.5-minute quadrangle

BEST SEASONS
Fall, winter, spring

GETTING THERE
From Highway 380 six miles east of San Antonio take County Roads A153 and A250 south for access to the WSA's eastern boundary

HIKING
Understated terrain and lack of trails have kept the number of visitors to the Antelope WSA low.

Big Yucca
Wilderness Inventory Unit

16

This area of desert flats and large sand dunes earned its name from the soaptree yuccas that stand up to 30 feet high.

LOCATION	34 miles south of Socorro, east of the Rio Grande, just north of the Jornada del Muerto Wilderness Study Area
SIZE	5,460 acres Size recommended by the NM Wilderness Alliance: 5,200 acres
ELEVATION RANGE	Approximately 4,750 feet throughout
MILES OF TRAILS	No marked or maintained trails
ECOSYSTEMS	Chihuahuan Desert scrub
ADMINISTRATION	BLM
TOPOGRAPHIC MAPS	Harriet Ranch and Little San Pascual Mountain USGS 7.5-minute quadrangles
BEST SEASONS	Fall, winter, spring
GETTING THERE	Take County Road A153 south from Highway 380 east of San Antonio, then take County Road 250. A dirt road running west forms the boundary between this unit and the Jornada del Muerto WSA to the south.
HIKING	Hiking here is limited by lack of trails, scant public awareness, difficult access, and a landscape remarkable for little except its soaptree yuccas.

THIS AREA WAS DROPPED by the BLM inventory because of its small size, although it meets the 5,000-acre minimum criterion. Big Yucca is separated only by a road from the Jornada del Muerto WSA, but the New Mexico Wilderness Alliance believes that the distinctive soaptree yuccas found here make it deserving of wilderness protection in its own right.

Boca del Oso Wilderness Study Area Complex

17

Located along the Rio Puerco Valley, this complex consists of four roughly contiguous WSAs separated only by infrequently traveled dirt roads. The four areas include: Ignacio Chavez (33,264 acres), Chamisa (13,692 acres), Empedrado (9,007 acres), and La Leña (10,438 acres). Collectively they are referred to as the Boca del Oso ("mouth of the bear") Wilderness, and collectively they have very high scenic, wildlife, archaeological, and recreational value. But these areas receive relatively few visitors.

Volcanic plugs

LOCATION	Northwest of Albuquerque, southwest of Cuba, along the upper Rio Puerco watershed
SIZE	66,401 acres combined Size recommended by the NM Wilderness Alliance: 107,692 acres combined
ELEVATION RANGE	5,600 to 7,500 feet
MILES OF TRAILS	No marked or maintained trails
ECOSYSTEMS	Douglas fir, ponderosa pine, piñon-juniper, scrub, and grasslands
ADMINISTRATION	BLM
TOPOGRAPHIC MAPS	Chaco Mesa USGS 1:100k quadrangle
BEST SEASONS	Spring, fall
GETTING THERE	To reach this complex of WSAs, drive 19 miles northwest from the village of San Ysidro on Highway 44—you'll see Cabezon Peak to the west—to a sign indicating San Luis is west via an all-weather dirt road, County Road 39. Past the village of San Luis, the road divides: County Road 42 heads southeast, and County Road 19 heads northwest. Despite the abundance of public land in this area, you'll also find considerable private land. Trespassers are often unwelcome; please respect signs and fences.
HIKING	While this area lacks marked or maintained trails, the network of old roads, cattle trails, and drainages offers numerous routes for anyone wishing to explore this scenic and fascinating area.

IN THE NINETEENTH CENTURY, the Rio Puerco Valley was an important agricultural area, with at least four small villages and a stage route connecting Santa Fe and Fort Wingate. But railroads meant the end of stages. Erosion, probably resulting from overgrazing, created huge arroyos that lowered the water table. People began leaving the area for better opportunities in growing cities like Albuquerque. Villages, ranches, and homesteads were abandoned, and the Rio Puerco Valley was forgotten except by a few tenacious residents and ranchers.

But a small cadre of hikers have not forgotten this place. Looking from the top of Cabezon Peak, hikers behold a beautiful, seemingly uninhabited valley pierced by volcanic formations. On the sandstone walls of deep canyons, prehistoric Indians carved petroglyphs. Mesa Chivato sprawls beyond. For those who knew about it, the Rio Puerco area had become a special, private wilderness just a short drive from Albuquerque.

Today, the Boca del Oso Complex is slightly better known, but still relatively undiscovered by recreationists. That is likely to change. For one thing, the BLM has routed the Continental Divide Trail through here, although the route is mostly on dirt roads. Also, mountain bikers are discovering these dirt roads, and the area is outstanding for horseback riders, as well.

Relatively easy access also increases traffic. Dirt roads, of varying roughness, lead into most areas, although these roads can be treacherous after thunderstorms.

Boca del Oso WSA Complex

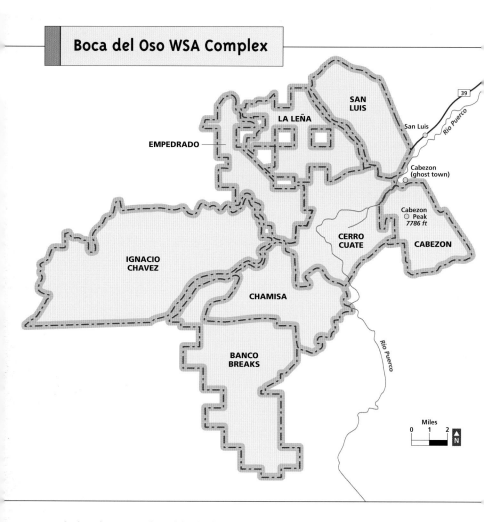

Marked trails are rare, but old vehicle routes and cattle paths help guide hikers. Water is sporadic at best, and ubiquitous cattle mean all water must be treated.

The canyons and mesas are the most obvious destinations for hikers, although climbers and scramblers often get into "plug-bagging"—getting to the top of the valley's numerous volcanic formations. Archaeological sites are not uncommon. You'll also see Hispanic homesteads, most of which are still owned and visited by the descendants of homesteaders. And rising more than 1,500 feet above the Rio Puerco Valley is Mesa Chivato, a forested and relatively flat, rich wildlife habitat. At the mesa's northeast end is the pinnacle called Boca del Oso, for which the complex is named.

In addition to the four designated WSAs in this complex, the NM Wilderness Alliance has proposed other areas for wilderness consideration, including the former Forest Service roadless area called Banco Breaks; San Luis, an extension of the San Luis WSA; Cerro de Guadalupe, an extension of the Cabezon WSA; and Cerro Cuate, an entirely new area. See also Cabezon WSA.

Cabezon Wilderness Study Area

18

Surrounded by the mesas and grasslands in the Valley of the Rio Puerco, this dramatic volcanic neck lies northwest of Albuquerque.

Cabezon Peak

LOCATION	Northwest of Albuquerque, in the Rio Puerco drainage, west of Highway 44
SIZE	8,159 acres. Size recommended by the NM Wilderness Alliance: See Boca del Oso Wilderness Study Area Complex
ELEVATION RANGE	5,980 to 7,786 feet at Cabezon Peak
MILES OF TRAILS	No marked or maintained trails, though several user trails go around Cabezon Peak
ECOSYSTEMS	Mixed grassland steppe, open piñon-juniper forest
ADMINISTRATION	BLM
TOPOGRAPHIC MAPS	Cabezon Peak USGS 7.5-minute quadrangle
BEST SEASONS	All
GETTING THERE	To reach Cabezon Peak, the area's dominant feature, drive 19 miles northwest from the village of San Ysidro on Highway 44. You'll see Cabezon Peak—to the west—and a sign indicating that San Luis lies to the west via an all-weather dirt road, County Road 39. After 3.8 miles a road branches left to go around the south side of the WSA, but if you're after the peak, keep to the right and go through San Luis. Twelve miles from Highway 44, when you're north of the peak, take the left, south fork in the road, cross a bridge, and then continue until a rough dirt road. At this point you might consider walking east one mile to the peak.
HIKING	Trails in the Cabezon WSA, like those around Cabezon Peak, are unmarked and unmaintained. The open terrain, however, readily allows cross-country hiking and ridges and drainages provide natural routes.

THE SPANISH NAME EL CABEZÓN, "the big head," accurately describes this volcanic formation, but it hardly does justice to the largest, most well-known, and arguably most dramatic of many volcanic plugs in the Mount Taylor volcanic field, which began erupting about 25 million years ago. To many people, Cabezon resembles Wyoming's more famous volcanic neck, Devils Tower. It has the same swarthy, basaltic appearance, the same black columns rising vertically to a rounded top. And it, too, is beloved by climbers. Indeed, only one non-technical route leads to the summit, a steep and exposed route on the plug's southeast side.

Navajos, whose reservation is to the northwest, call the peak by a name meaning simply "black rock." But in their myth of the Twin War Gods, the foreboding formation is the head of a slain giant whose blood is the congealed lava near Grants. To early Hispanic settlers, Cabezon would have been an obvious landmark, especially to those rural people who once grazed livestock and farmed in ranches and villages along the Rio Puerco, including the ghost town named Cabezon at the peak's base. This village, now closed to visitors, was a stop on the stage line that ran during the 1800s between Santa Fe and Fort Wingate. Today, overgrazing, arroyo cutting, dropping water tables, and greater opportunities elsewhere have resulted in the area being depopulated, yet Cabezon Peak remains a conspicuous landmark for travelers on Highway 44.

Most people visiting this WSA are interested in climbing the peak. From the vehicular directions above, a crude, unmarked trail heads south then southeast to the summit route. Still unmarked, this ascends a steep talus slope, then climbs a chute onto a ledge, then scrambles over rocks—eventually reaching the summit. No technical climbing is required, but beware of loose rock, test your holds, don't hike when snow and ice are present, and look for indications that you're on the standard route. Don't climb anything you can't climb down. Avoid this area if thunderstorms threaten.

Although Cabezon Peak dominates the WSA, the surrounding area is also interesting, especially the southeast portion where mesas, grassy steppes, and piñon-juniper woodlands provide outstanding views of other volcanic features along the Rio Puerco Valley.

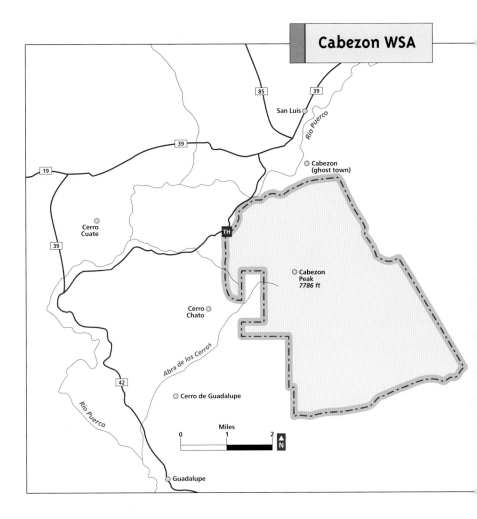

Cabezon WSA

19 Jornada del Muerto Wilderness Study Area

Located along the desolate route called the Jornada del Muerto, "journey of the dead man," this WSA features an old lava flow and its associated cinder cone. Early Spanish settlers and traders traveled this rugged and isolated region.

LOCATION	10 miles south of Bosque del Apache National Wildlife Refuge, on the east side of the Rio Grande
SIZE	31,147 acres Size recommended by the NM Wilderness Alliance: 36,847 acres
ELEVATION RANGE	4,700 to 4,900 feet
MILES OF TRAILS	No marked or maintained trails
ECOSYSTEMS	Chihuahuan Desert scrub, semidesert grassland, soaptree yucca
ADMINISTRATION	BLM
TOPOGRAPHIC MAPS	Pope, Harriet Ranch, Tucson Spring, and Fuller Ranch USGS 7.5-minute quadrangles
BEST SEASONS	Spring, fall, winter
GETTING THERE	From Highway 380 east of San Antonio County Roads 2268 and 2322, head south to the WSA, where a dirt access road runs along the northern boundary.
HIKING	Very limited. This area is isolated with poor access and inhospitable terrain, although hiking cross-country through the grassland is not too difficult, and exploring the features associated with a large lava flow—lava tubes, sink holes, pressure ridges, etc.—would be interesting.

Little San Pascual, Chupadera, and Indian Wells Wildernesses

20

These small swatches of the upper Chihuahuan Desert make for three wild, and generally inaccessible, wilderness areas.

LOCATION	Flanking the wetlands of Bosque del Apache National Wildlife Refuge, on both sides of the Rio Grande, south of the village of San Antonio
SIZE	30,287 acres (combined)
ELEVATION RANGE	4,610 to 5,912 feet in the Chupadera Wilderness
MILES OF TRAILS	2.2
ECOSYSTEMS	Chihuahuan Desert scrub and grassland
ADMINISTRATION	U.S. Fish and Wildlife Service
TOPOGRAPHIC MAPS	Indian Wells Wilderness and Little San Pascual Mountain USGS 7.5-minute quadrangles
BEST SEASONS	Fall, winter, spring
GETTING THERE	These areas would be accessed from Bosque del Apache National Wildlife Refuge, located on Highway 1 south of San Antonito.
HIKING	Except for the short nature trail described below, these areas lack marked or maintained trails, and cross-country hiking is discouraged because of very poor public access.

THESE THREE SMALL WILDERNESS AREAS complement the natural wetlands of Bosque del Apache National Wildlife Refuge. Most visitors to the refuge would be surprised to learn about these wildernesses, and in any case they would wonder why a visitor would neglect the lush marshlands, with their abundant wildlife, for hot, arid scrubland. They have a point; the wilderness areas weren't really established with visitors in mind.

Of the three wildernesses, Little San Pascual is the largest. Located east of the Rio Grande, it encompasses the Little San Pascual Mountains, a tiny desert group. No trails lead into this area, and access is very difficult.

The Chupadera ("sinkhole") and Indian Wells Wildernesses are on the refuge's west side and extend west of I-25 into the Chupadera Mountains, another small desert range. The only access into this area is a short nature trail that touches upon the wilderness before looping back to its start. My advice to Bosque del Apache visitors is to hike the nature trail (see below) for a good introduction to the Chihuahuan Desert ecosystem, but concentrate your time on the marshlands and go elsewhere, such as the Las Uvas Mountains or Robledo Mountains BLM Wilderness Study Areas, for a Chihuahuan Desert wilderness experience.

LOOP HIKE: CANYON TRAIL
Round-trip length: 2.2 miles
Low and high elevations: 4,540 and 4,808 feet
Difficulty: easy

The Canyon Trail is 1.6 miles south of the Bosque del Apache visitor center on the west side of Highway 1. The trail is marked with numbered posts keyed to interpretive notes in the trail guide, which is available at the trailhead. Scores of animal tracks in the soft sand are reminders that the desert, like the marshland, is home to a rich assembly of creatures. The trail ascends Solitude Canyon with perhaps New Mexico's smallest natural arch before ascending to the mesa top, where you can enjoy views of the marshlands and distant mountains that in the evening are spectacular.

OTHER RECREATIONAL OPPORTUNITIES

These three small wilderness areas are meant to complement the wildlife refuge at Bosque del Apache, and like the preserve, they offer excellent opportunities for wildlife observation and photography, especially as birds and animals often travel between the wilderness areas and the refuge.

FOR MORE INFORMATION

REFUGE MANAGER, Bosque del Apache National Wildlife Refuge, P.O. Box 1246, Socorro, NM 87801; (505) 835-0314.

Manzano Mountain Wilderness

21

Despite its proximity to the population centers of Albuquerque and the Rio Grande Valley, the Manzano Mountain Wilderness retains its wild and remote character.

Sloping maples

LOCATION	North-central New Mexico, east of the Rio Grande, southeast of Albuquerque
SIZE	36,970 acres
ELEVATION RANGE	6,000 to 10,098 feet at Manzano Peak
MILES OF TRAILS	100
ECOSYSTEMS	Piñon-juniper, ponderosa pine, spruce-fir, aspen, Chihuahuan Desert scrub
ADMINISTRATION	Cibola National Forest—Mountainair Ranger District
TOPOGRAPHIC MAPS	Cibola National Forest—Manzano Mountain Wilderness map
BEST SEASONS	Spring, summer, fall
GETTING THERE	Most access to the Manzano Mountain Wilderness is from east, from forest roads heading west from Highways 337 and 55. The mountains are reached from the south, via Forest Road 422 from Highway 60. From the west, only Forest Road 33 leads to the mountains, heading east from Highway 47.
HIKING	Somewhat poor access and competition with the nearby Sandia Mountains tend to limit hiking on the extensive network of trails in the Manzano Mountain Wilderness, which otherwise offer outstanding backcountry travel.

ASK PEOPLE IF THEY'VE HIKED IN THE MANZANO MOUNTAINS, and many will say yes. They've been to Fourth of July Canyon in the fall to see the foliage display, or perhaps they've been to John F. Kennedy Campground and hiked a portion of the Trigo Canyon Trail. But ask about Comanche Canyon, Manzano Peak, Pine Shadow Spring, or the Jacquez Trail—no, never been there, never even heard of it. The Manzano Mountains are the mountains everyone knows about and few people really know.

Much of that can be blamed on the Manzano Mountains' sister range to the north, the Sandia Mountains situated on the outskirts of Albuquerque. The Sandias are easily accessible from all directions, with a paved road to the summit, a ski area, an aerial tram, and abundant trails for hiking, mountain biking, and cross-country skiing. The Sandias readily absorb most of the outdoor recreationists in the Albuquerque area. The Manzanos, on the other hand, are difficult to get to know. For one thing, the entire northern part of the range is closed completely to the public because the land belongs to Isleta Pueblo or has been withdrawn by the U.S. Department of Defense for Kirtland Air Force Base. That leaves only the more remote, southern section open for public exploration. Even there, only one trailhead, at John F. Kennedy Campground, allows access to the dramatic western escarpment, and to get there you have to endure a long, traffic-congested drive from Albuquerque to Belen followed by a 19-mile drive over a sometimes-rough dirt road. Of the four trails accessed from the trailhead, only one, the Trigo Canyon Trail, is well-known to hikers. The others— Comanche Canyon Trail, Salas Trail, and Jacquez Trail—are long and difficult. On the east side, access is somewhat better, but even the closest wilderness trails involve a long drive from Albuquerque.

Furthermore, the Manzanos are more forbidding than the Sandias, bigger and wilder—40 miles long as opposed to the Sandias' 28 (with fewer roads and far fewer trails). Treasure hunters believe the mountains still guard the secret of a silver mine worked by early Spaniards and concealed by Indians following the Pueblo Revolt of 1680. Mountain lions and desert bighorn sheep find refuge in the mountains.

The inhabitants of Isleta Pueblo believe they originally lived at the mountains' base, to the east of their present pueblo on the Rio Grande. Spaniards in the 1600s found several inhabited Piro and Tiwa pueblos in the Manzanos' foothills; at these pueblos the Spaniards established missions whose ruins survive at the Abo and Quarai units of Salinas Pueblo Missions National Monument. Famine and persistent raids by nomadic Indians forced the missions and pueblos to be abandoned, even before the 1680 Pueblo Revolt. Following the reconquest in 1692, Hispanic villagers reoccupied many of the sites, and other rural Hispanic villages, which sprang up as land grants, were given to settlers who had the tenacity to occupy the harsh, dangerous Manzanos. These villages survive today in the mountains' eastern foothills, where their inhabitants pursue traditional uses of the land such as fuelwood gathering and hunting. Indeed, it was one of these villages, Manzano, that gave the mountains their name. Tradition says the village took its Spanish name from apples (*manzanas*) grown in ancient orchards here, and the name spread to the nearby range.

In the 1970s, members of the NM Wilderness Study Committee became involved in the Forest Service's Manzano Land Use Plan, with people such as Tom Green and Phil Tollefsrud checking boundaries and verifying wilderness conditions. The Wilderness Study Committee recommended setting aside 37,000 acres as wilderness (the present total is 36,970 acres). Although this proposal was included in the Endangered American Wilderness Act, introduced in 1976 into the 94th Congress, final enactment was delayed until the 95th Congress of 1978.

Today, the wildlands of the Manzano Mountain Wilderness exist as they have for centuries. Logging that once fed sawmills such as that in Kayser Mill Canyon ceased even before wilderness designation, and if you believe the legends, mining ceased in the 1600s. Local people still gather firewood and hunt deer and elk, but recreational development has remained minimal. The Manzano Mountain Wilderness requires determination to explore, but people willing to make that commitment will find true wilderness.

DAY HIKE: TRIGO CANYON
One-way length: 4 miles
Low and high elevations: 6,250 and 8,800 feet
Difficulty: moderate to strenuous

To reach the trailhead, drive south on Highway 47 from its intersection with Highway 309 east of Belen. At 5.8 miles, a Cibola National Forest sign on the right indicates that John F. Kennedy Campground is 19 miles away. Across the highway from the sign, a good dirt road, Forest Road 33, passes between two adobe pillars and heads east toward the Manzano Mountains. At 5.8 miles, at another sign, the dirt road bends north. Then at 12.2 miles, at still another sign, it bends east again. At 18.6 miles, you'll reach the National Forest boundary. At 19 miles you'll find the campground.

The Trigo Canyon Trail, No. 185, passes through an iron gate at the campground's east end, crosses the intermittent stream, and heads up the canyon through a forest with numerous large alligator junipers. At about 2.5 miles, the trail passes a shallow cave, a good place to break as just upstream are several small waterfalls and then a 25-foot waterfall (a mere trickle in dry seasons). Most parties go no farther because the trail becomes much steeper above the waterfall, switch-backing up the canyon's north side. Still, it's worth the effort to go beyond the waterfall to an overlook of the cliffs here. Above the waterfall, the trail still parallels a tiny stream, but instead of threading up a deep canyon it meanders up a pleasant forested valley. At about four miles the trail leaves the stream and passes briefly through dry ponderosa forest before topping out at a saddle and the junction with Crest Trail, Number 170. Just north along this trail is a pleasant knoll with beautiful views to the north. The summit in the foreground is Osha Peak, while in the distance are the towers of the Capilla Peak electronic site.

Manzano Mountain

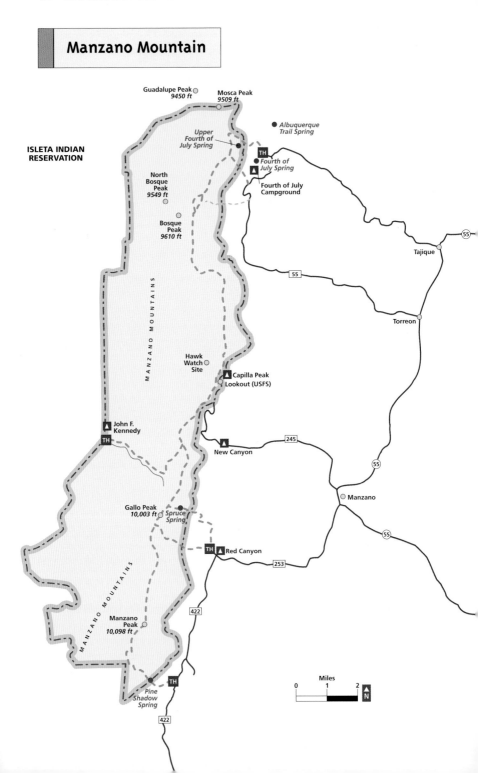

ISLETA INDIAN
RESERVATION

Guadalupe Peak
9450 ft

Mosca Peak
9509 ft

Albuquerque
Trail Spring

Upper
Fourth of
July Spring

TH

Fourth of
July Spring

Fourth of July
Campground

North
Bosque
Peak
9549 ft

Bosque
Peak
9610 ft

55

Tajique

MANZANO MOUNTAINS

55

Torreon

Hawk
Watch
Site

Capilla Peak
Lookout (USFS)

John F.
Kennedy

TH

New Canyon

245

55

Manzano

Gallo Peak
10,003 ft

Spruce
Spring

TH

Red Canyon

253

55

422

MANZANO MOUNTAINS

Manzano
Peak
10,098 ft

TH

Pine
Shadow
Spring

Miles

0   1   2

N

422

DESTINATION HIKE: MANZANO HAWK WATCH SITE
One-way length: 0.75 mile
Low and high elevations: 9,200 and 9,280 feet
Difficulty: easy

HawkWatch International, a not-for-profit raptor conservation program, has identified this site as a focal point for one of the West's major raptor migration routes, and it maintains a monitoring program here. (They've identified a similar site in the Sandia Mountains for the spring migrations; see Sandia Mountain Wilderness description.) The public is welcome to visit the Manzano site during the migrations, which typically occur from late September through late October, and HawkWatch staff members help identify and interpret the sometimes hundreds of eagles, hawks, falcons, kite, vultures, and other birds that often pass by on a single day.

To reach the site from I-40 east of Albuquerque, take the Tijeras exit and drive south on Highway 337 for 29.6 miles to Highway 55. Then go southwest on Highway 55 for 12.4 miles to the village of Manzano. Opposite the church, Forest Road 245 heads west. Follow signs to the New Canyon and Capilla Peak Campgrounds. After nine miles, you'll reach the second campground. Park before the fire tower, hike west across the meadow, and then follow the Gavilan ("hawk") Trail along the ridge to the site.

LOOP HIKE: FOURTH OF JULY CANYON – CERRO BLANCO
Round-trip length: 4.5 miles
Low and high elevations: 7,600 and 8,680 feet
Difficulty: easy to moderate

This hike is pleasant in the spring and summer, but for a brief time in the fall it's gorgeous. That's when the Rocky Mountain maples—rare elsewhere—create one of New Mexico's most spectacular natural displays. It's deservedly well-known and well-publicized, but hiking just a short distance leaves the crowds behind.

You can reach the picnic area by taking either I-40 or Highway 333 east from Albuquerque to Tijeras, and then driving 29.6 miles south on Highway 337 then west three miles on Highway 55 to the old Hispanic village of Tajique. At the village's south end, Forest Road 55 heads west 7.5 miles into the Manzano Mountains' foothills and the picnic area. At the back of the picnic area is the Fourth of July Trail, No. 173, which is marked by a sign. After 1.5 miles, the trail joins the Cerro Blanco Trail, No. 79. Follow this 0.5 mile north to the Manzano Crest Trail, No. 170. Continue north on this 0.25 mile to a saddle with a spectacular overlook where a sign directs you to the Ojito Trail, No. 171, just 140 feet away. Returning to the 173–79 junction and continuing on the Cerro Blanco Trail takes you past a panorama of the eastern Manzanos. The Cerro Blanco Trail then descends into a small canyon and soon puts you back on Forest Road 55. The

Fourth of July picnic area is about one mile down this road to the north; the walking is easy, and the maples here are as colorful as anywhere.

LOOP HIKE: SPRUCE SPRING – RED CANYON
One-way length: 3.4 miles
Low and high elevations: 7,960 and 9,160 feet
Difficulty: moderate

You can hike this loop in a day, but it's best as an easy overnighter, camping at a pleasant grassy meadow with a spring nearby and expansive views from the Manzano Crest of the Rio Grande Valley far below.

The trail begins at the Cibola National Forest Red Canyon Campground, which you can reach from Albuquerque by driving east on I-40 to the Tijeras exit and then taking Highway 337 south 29.6 miles to Highway 55. Go west on Highway 55 through the old Hispanic villages of Tajique and Torreon for 12.4 miles to the seventeenth-century village of Manzano. From the junction of Highway 55 and Highway 131, Red Canyon Campground is six miles away via Forest Road 253.

The Spruce Spring Trail, No. 189, heads north from the campground and is marked by a sign. It ascends gradually as it passes through a forest of piñons, ponderosas, and alligator junipers. The trail's gradient remains easy as it leads north and then west. Just 0.4 miles farther, Trail 189 reaches a saddle and the junction with the Manzano Crest Trail, No. 170. Immediately north of the junction you'll find several campsites.

From the saddle, follow the Manzano Crest Trail south 0.75 mile. Then take a side trip to climb 10,003-foot Gallo Peak. The route to the top is not obvious and will probably involve some trial and error, despite a faint trail, but the distance is not long—just about 0.5 mile—and the side trip is definitely worth it.

From the Gallo Peak side trip, hike another 0.25 mile farther south until the Manzano Crest Trail brings you to another saddle (with campsites) and the junction with Red Canyon Trail, No. 89. This leads downhill 2.7 miles to Red Canyon Campground, completing the loop.

BOB JULYAN'S FAVORITE HIKE
PINE SHADOW SPRING – MANZANO PEAK
One-way length: 5.5 miles
Low and high elevations: 7,240 and 10,098 feet
Difficulty: moderate to strenuous (due to length)

Manzano Peak is the highest point in the Manzano Mountains, but relatively few hikers reach its scenic summit because of the long drive and long hike required. Those who do make the effort will not be disappointed.

You can reach the trailhead from Highway 60, southeast of Belen, by driving 11 miles on a packed dirt road (Forest Road 422) to the parking-picnic area at Pine Shadow Spring. Be sure to take plenty of water. From here Trail 170A begins its long, gradual ascent, although the final mile—along a ridge—is almost level.

As you hike, watch the vegetation change with elevation—from piñon-junipers to ponderosas and eventually to Douglas fir, Mexican white pine, and aspen. And throughout, even on the summit, are numerous species of cacti. The rocks on the trail sparkle with the fine grains of Precambrian quartzite.

After 5.5 miles you'll reach the junction of Trail 170, where a spur trail leads 0.25 mile to the summit (and breathtaking views in all directions).

OTHER RECREATIONAL OPPORTUNITIES

Remoteness, problematic access, paucity of trails, difficult terrain, and unpredictable snowfall severely limit backcountry skiing in the Manzano Mountains. Snowshoers can explore the wilderness using the short, easy Albuquerque Trail in Tajique Canyon, near the Fourth of July Campground. A longer, more challenging snowshoe route is the Spruce Canyon – Red Canyon Loop, described above.

Outside the wilderness, mountain biking has become very popular in the northern part of the Manzanos, with an extensive network of trails around Cedro Peak and in the canyons west of Highway 337. Contact the Cibola National Forest Tijeras Ranger District in Tijeras for current maps and trail conditions.

The only road leading to the Manzano Mountains' crest is Forest Road 245—a good dirt road servicing the lookout tower and observatory atop 9,360-foot Capilla Peak. From here a short trail leads north to the Manzano Hawk Watch site (see Destination Hikes).

FOR MORE INFORMATION

CIBOLA NATIONAL FOREST, Mountainair Ranger District, P.O. Box 69, Mountainair, NM 87036; (505) 847-2990.

22 Ojito Wilderness Study Area

If you visit the Ojito Wilderness Study Area, expect the unexpected—geologically, archaeologically, and naturally. This interesting quasi-badland lacks trails but is endlessly fascinating.

Moonset over Mesa Cliffs

LOCATION	In the eroded, dissected country between the Rio Puerco and the Jemez River, 25 air miles northwest of Albuquerque
SIZE	10,903 acres Size recommended by the NM Wilderness Alliance: 11,703 acres
ELEVATION RANGE	5,650 to 6,261 feet
MILES OF TRAILS	No marked or maintained trails
ECOSYSTEMS	Piñon-juniper, four-wing saltbush, cholla, grassland
ADMINISTRATION	BLM
TOPOGRAPHIC MAPS	Ojito Spring, San Ysidro, Sky Village Northwest, and Sky Village Northeast USGS 7.5-minute quadrangles
BEST SEASONS	Spring, fall
GETTING THERE	Drive northwest from Bernalillo on Highway 44 northwest until a dirt road branches west 2 miles before San Ysidro—just before a wide turn crossing the Rio Salado. The dirt road soon forks at a Zia Pueblo sign; take the left fork. The public lands boundary is 3.9 miles from Highway 44. The BLM's Albuquerque office has a pamphlet about the Ojito WSA.
HIKING	Though the Ojito WSA lacks marked or maintained trails, the terrain allows for cross-country travel. Old roads and livestock trails, ridges, and drainages offer routes for exploration of the terrain as well.

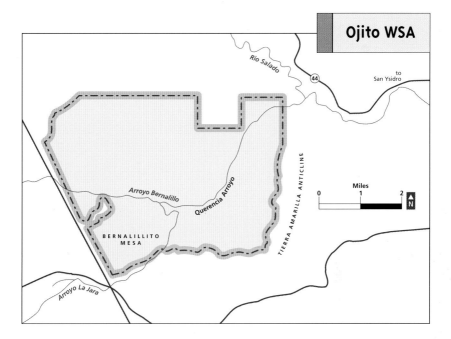

NAVIGATING THE OJITO WSA requires a topographic map—you won't find marked trailheads or trails. Even with a map the landscape here is often confusing— a maze of canyons, arroyos, draws, mesas, and bluffs. That's the appeal of this area: in this geologic thicket, serendipity works overtime. Rarely do hikers go more than a hundred yards without someone saying, "Look at this!" This area contains abandoned Hispanic homesteads, ruins of pre-Columbian Indian pueblos, pottery shards, water-worn pebbles, as smooth and polished as cabochons of semi-precious stones, and animal tracks in the sand and mud at the bottom of arroyos. And if you're very lucky, you'll find dinosaur bones. It was here that some Albuquerque hikers looked down at their feet one day and saw, protruding from the soil, fossilized bones that when later excavated proved to be those of Seismosaurus, then the largest dinosaur ever discovered. (These hikers are worthy role models: they recorded the location of their find, and then left it to be excavated by professionals.)

Water, for the most part, is lacking in the Ojito WSA, and temperatures in the summer can be torrid. And while the broad valleys would seem easy hiking, most are cut with deep arroyos (the result of overgrazing) that can be challenging to cross. Still, for a fascinating day hike or overnighter, the Ojito WSA is hard to beat.

Just outside the Ojito WSA, to the east about four miles from Highway 44 on the dirt road, is a geologic feature called the Tierra Amarilla ("yellow earth") Anticline. Long a favorite challenge for mountain bikers, it also offers a very interesting day hike as you explore precipitous ridges, abrupt valleys, and numerous springs with their associated travertine formations.

23 Presilla, Las Cañas, Veranito and Stallion Wilderness Study Areas

These areas feature low desert mountains, canyons, gullies, Upper Sonoran plants, and a few archaeological sites.

New Mexico Wilderness Alliance

Las Cañas Wilderness Study Area

LOCATION	East of the Rio Grande, northeast of Socorro
SIZE	40,962 acres (combined)
ELEVATION RANGE	4,600 to 7,100 feet
MILES OF TRAILS	No marked or maintained trails
ECOSYSTEMS	Upper Sonoran Desert scrub, scattered piñon-juniper forest
ADMINISTRATION	BLM
TOPOGRAPHIC MAPS	Loma de las Cañas, Mesa del Yeso, Bustos Well, and Sierra de la Cruz USGS 7.5-minute quadrangles
BEST SEASONS	Spring, fall
GETTING THERE	The easiest way to access these four areas is to take the BLM-designated Quebradas Backcountry Byway. To reach the Byway from I-25 north of Socorro, take the Escondida exit, head east, and then north. Then turn right, cross the Rio Grande, and proceed east through the community of Pueblitos. From there, turn south onto the road paralleling the Rio Grande. After about 0.6 mile, an all-weather dirt road turns sharply east. This is the Byway, which is marked by signs. After 24 miles, it arrives at Highway 380, 11 miles east of San Antonio.
HIKING	Though these WSAs lack marked or maintained trails, the terrain allows for cross-country travel. Old roads and livestock trails, ridges, and drainages offer routes for exploration of the terrain as well.

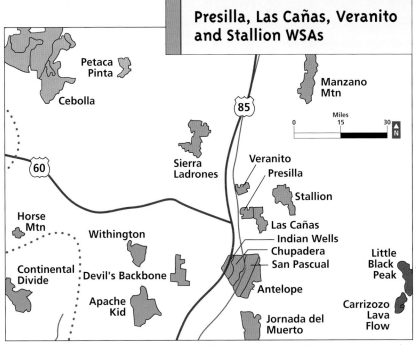

This map is a detail of map on pages 8 and 9.

I'VE ALWAYS REGARDED THESE AREAS as a paradigm of New Mexico itself. Viewed from I-25, the land might appear nondescript, even drab. But when explored on foot, it reveals a world of unexpected beauty and wonder.

These four areas are not all contiguous, but aside from general proximity they share the vegetation of the Upper Sonoran Life Zone—creosote bush, ocotillo, mesquite, desert grassland, and piñon-juniper woodland. They also share a landscape that erosion has shaped into arroyos, deep narrow canyons, broken badlands, and mesas, ridges, and low mountains. The areas just east of the Rio Grande are characterized by the Spanish term *quebradas*, meaning "breaks," referring here to the eroded bench lands above the Rio Grande floodplain. At one time the land may have been more hospitable, as several archaeological sites indicate that people lived here. These include the remains of a Piro Indian pueblo, a rare prehistoric painted panel, and several petroglyph sites.

You won't find hiking trails or trailheads here, so topographic maps are essential. (The BLM Quebradas Backcountry Byway and ancillary roads are great for mountain biking.) The terrain lends itself to cross-country walking, but water is generally lacking. As the area is cruelly hot in summer, spring, with its wildflowers, is probably the best season for visiting.

24 Sandia Mountain Wilderness

Next door to Albuquerque, the Sandia Mountain Wilderness is considered by many to be an "urban wilderness." It offers easily accessible and widely diverse outdoor recreation opportunities, including the experience of being in a true wilderness.

Cibola National Forest

LOCATION	Immediately east of Albuquerque, north of I-40
SIZE	37,232 acres
ELEVATION RANGE	6,000 to 10,678 feet
MILES OF TRAILS	112
ECOSYSTEMS	Upper Sonoran desert, piñon-juniper, ponderosa pine, spruce-fir
ADMINISTRATION	Cibola National Forest—Tijeras Ranger District
TOPOGRAPHIC MAPS	Cibola National Forest—Sandia Mountain Wilderness
BEST SEASONS	All
GETTING THERE	Located immediately east of Albuquerque and north of I-40, west of Highway 14 and south of Highway 44, the Sandia Mountain Wilderness is the most readily accessible wilderness in New Mexico.
HIKING	An extensive and well-maintained system of trails exists in the Sandia Mountain Wilderness. Most hikers go just for the day, but overnight trips are possible.

AT LEAST ONE-THIRD OF NEW MEXICO'S POPULATION, more than a half-million people, live within 20 miles of the Sandia Mountain Wilderness. The mountains look down upon two major interstate highways. The world's longest aerial tram ferries diners to the High Finance Restaurant on the mountains' crest, along with skiers headed for nearby slopes. At the mountains' highest point, visitors who drive up the paved road can shop for souvenirs at a gift shop or watch hang gliders launch themselves from the cliffs adjacent to the thicket of electronic transmission towers.

This is the setting for a wilderness?

Oddly enough, yes. From my home on the south side of the Sandias, I have hiked cross-country through terrain in which the only trails are those made by wild animals. I've made it to campsites where at night I can't see a single electric light. These areas are not large, but when the need arises in my urban-beleaguered soul, I know they are there.

The Sandia Mountain Wilderness is indeed a study in contrasts and compromises. The north-south trending range, approximately 30 miles long and less than 10 miles wide, has wilderness designation at both ends, but its middle is bisected by the tram as well as a road. On the west, the wilderness boundary is less than one mile from dense housing developments within the city limits of Albuquerque. Many trails heading into the wilderness receive heavy use by day hikers, but because most hikers perceive the Sandias as their backyard and suitable only for day use, backpackers are infrequent. Campers do, however, enjoy considerable solitude. Because the mountains are so close to Albuquerque and are so heavily used, hunting with guns is not allowed, thus protecting a diverse array of wildlife.

People have lived in the Sandia Mountains a long time. In Las Huertas Canyon, archaeologists discovered a cave with artifacts left by Paleo-Indians about 10,000 years ago. The Sandias have figured prominently in the worldview of Pueblo Indians living along the Rio Grande. Tiwa Indians, still living in the Rio Grande pueblos of Isleta and Sandia, know the mountains as a single unit, calling it Oku Pin—turtle mountain—because of its turtle-backed shape, or Bien Mur, meaning big mountain.

When the Spaniards arrived in 1540, they linked the Sandias with their sister range to the south, the Manzano Mountains, often labeling the two ranges as one on their maps. The name *Sandia* is Spanish for "watermelon." When viewed from the northwest where the first Spaniards camped, the mountains indeed resemble a watermelon section, especially when the evening light gives a pinkish hue to the mountains' granite core and the white limestone layers on top resemble a rind. This explanation has never been disproved, but more likely the name Sandia was given first to the Tiwa pueblo in which the Spaniards saw growing gourds that resembled watermelons, and the name then spread to the nearby mountains.

For generations, Hispanic peoples made little use of the Sandia Mountains. After all, the arable land along the river was separated from the mountains by several miles of scrub-covered mesa. The mountains held little these people wanted. The few mines that opened in the mountains were hugely disappointing. And finally, the mountains were dangerous, frequented by nomadic Indians.

This situation changed little after Americans arrived in the mid-1800s. Not until after 1900 did human activity in the Sandias substantially increase. Soon after 1920 the first road was hacked through the thick forest to the summit. By 1940 a road through Las Huertas Canyon allowed car travel completely around the mountains. Albuquerque boomed following World War II. The city began expanding eastward, over the mesa, and by the 1950s people were building houses in the foothills. At the same time, logging operations expanded on the northeast side of the mountains, especially around La Madera. In the 1950s and 1960s, the ski area expanded, along with parking at the Crest. Electronic antennae and transmitters increased to more than 200 units. The tram was constructed in the mid-1960s.

Around this time environmentalists began raising concerns. By 1966, government hunters and others had exterminated the area's bears and lions. In 1969 a plan was announced to run a major road from the Crest north to the village of Placitas. The plan was abandoned in 1971, but not before a wide swath of land was cleared, still visible from the Crest Road. In 1971, motorized trail bikes and four-wheel-drive vehicles spun their wheels for the first time to the Crest from the west side. Environmentalists sounded an alarm, and Sandia Ranger Jack Miller, backed by his supervisors, forbade vehicles.

Clearly, the time had come for more than just ad hoc protection. As a result of the Environmental Policy Act of 1969, the Forest Service issued a Land Use Plan in 1975. Then in 1976, U.S. Senators Frank Church of Idaho and Henry M. Jackson of Washington introduced a wilderness bill that included the Sandias into the 94th Congress. Congress adjourned before its enactment, but a similar bill was introduced into the 95th Congress, and in 1978 President Jimmy Carter signed the Endangered American Wilderness Act, which set aside as wilderness 30,981 acres of the Sandia Ranger District's 100,555 acres. Appropriately, Senator Church, supporter of the Sandia Mountain Wilderness, also was was among the drafters of the 1964 Wilderness Act. In 1972, at a hearing of his subcommittee on Public Lands, he stated: "Sights and sounds from outside the boundary do not invalidate a Wilderness designation or make buffer and threshold exclusions necessary, as a matter of law"—a remarkably prescient statement regarding the Sandias.

Today, the Sandia Mountain Wilderness comprises about 45 percent of the mountains' total area. Mountain lions and black bears have returned to the wilderness, although attempts to reintroduce bighorn sheep have been frustrated by endemic disease. Outside the wilderness, the pace of Albuquerque development has not abated. Usually only a fence separates dense housing developments from public lands. In 1981 Albuquerque purchased portions of the former Elena Gallegos Grant in the mountains' western foothills. When 6,251 acres of the Gallegos Grant were added to the Sandia Mountain Wilderness, the total wilderness acreage reached 37,232 while much of the rest was preserved as open space, providing some buffer between city and wilderness. In 1997, open space advocates finally succeeded in keeping Three Gun Spring Canyon, on the mountains' south side, out of development. In the East Mountain area, growth continues mushrooming.

Yet ironically, perhaps the greatest threat to the wilderness status of this area comes not from new interlopers but from the mountains' traditional owners—the

Indians of Sandia Pueblo. They say their tribal lands' correct boundary, designated by a colonial Spanish land grant, is the Sandia Crest, not farther west as it has been interpreted. Their long-standing claim is finally being argued before U.S. courts. If the court confirms their boundary interpretation, the Sandia Mountain Wilderness's northwestern portion would become Sandia Pueblo tribal lands. The Indians have said the public would be little affected by such a change, but the pueblo's governor has also stated that use would be regulated by fees and permits. The public is generally denied access to tribal lands already owned by the pueblo. Many environmentalists in New Mexico prefer that the wilderness remain within Cibola National Forest.

Most Sandia hiking trails connect with a central trail running spine-like along the crest. The northern terminus of the Crest Trail (Number 130) is at Tunnel Spring near the village of Placitas; its southern end is at Canyon Estates near the village of Tijeras. In its 28 miles it ascends through piñon-juniper forest into the ponderosa pine zone at about 8,000 feet, and finally reaches spruce-fir forest below the 10,678-foot summit.

The Sandias are fault-block mountains, the Precambrian granite slab's western end rising upward as the strata in the Rio Grande Rift subside. The Pennsylvania—limestone layers on the 10,000-foot crest are also found 10,000 feet beneath the river—represents a vertical displacement of about four miles. The mountains' fault-block nature has resulted in the forested eastern slopes rising gradually before reaching the cliffs of the steep, craggy western escarpment. From a distance, the western face seems vertical, but in fact numerous trails penetrate the mountains from the west, and it is there, adjacent to Albuquerque, where you'll find the best hiking trails. Only three maintained trails—Pino, Embudo-Embudito, and La Luz—lead to the crest from the west. Of these, La Luz is the most popular, not only because of its dramatic scenery but also because it ends at either the Crest House or the Sandia Tram. The Embudo and Embudito trails meet at Oso Pass and then ascend to the crest near South Peak, a beautiful area as remote as any in the Sandias. The Pino Trail goes from the popular Elena Gallegos Picnic Area to join the crest where the Cienega Trail joins it from the east, between South Peak and the tram.

The Sandias' mile of vertical relief means climate varies widely on the mountain. The foothills receive about 8 to 10 inches of precipitation a year; the mountains' upper regions receive 25 to 30 inches. While most drainages have small, intermittent streams, you can also find a few springs and other reliable water sources; all this water needs to be treated before drinking. In the summer, heat stroke and dehydration are very real hazards. Temperatures on the crest average 15 degrees cooler than in the foothills. Cross-country skiers and snowshoers traveling the crest in winter should be prepared for weather as severe as almost anywhere in the West, yet hikers can walk most foothills trails year-round. In July and August, New Mexico experiences daily afternoon thunderstorms accompanied by lightning and downpours sometimes so torrential that drainages are subject to flash-flooding. Poison ivy is common in localized wet areas. And the lower Sandias are a notorious reservoir for *Yersinia pseudotuberculosis. var. pestis*, the bacterium that causes plague (yes, that plague, as in Black Death). Avoid all contact with rodents, living or dead, including their burrows. If you develop suspicious flu-like symptoms after hiking, tell your physician you might have been exposed to plague.

Curiously, relatively few backpackers camp in the Sandias. A ranger once called the Sandia Mountain Wilderness a "training wilderness," and indeed people who do camp in the mountains seldom are more than a couple of hours' walking distance from civilization. Despite this, many people get lost in the mountains each year—some for several days.

Call it a training wilderness if you will, the Sandia Mountain Wilderness nonetheless offers all the natural beauty, solitude, and rejuvenation of more remote wildernesses even though the trailheads are but minutes from Albuquerque. On numerous late afternoons I've hiked into the wilderness from my home in the southern Sandias, set up camp before dark, eaten a backcountry meal, and watched for wildlife. I've slept beneath a sky sparkling with all the stars only a desert night can reveal. Awakening to a morning of peace and promise, I've enjoyed a backcountry breakfast, ventured out to look for animal tracks and wildflowers, and returned home less than 24 hours from my departure. On the yardstick of my soul, the Sandia Mountain Wilderness does indeed measure up as wilderness.

> **DAY HIKE: DOMINGO BACA CANYON**
> One-way length: 2.0 miles
> Low and high elevations: 6,200 and 7,500 feet
> Difficulty: easy

Among the most pleasant hikes in the Sandias, the Domingo Baca Canyon Trail refutes any notion that the mountains' west side is just steep, dry rock. The hike begins at the Elena Gallegos Picnic Area, maintained as open space by the city of Albuquerque and reached from Tramway Boulevard just north of Academy Road. You'll find water and rest rooms at the picnic area. The Domingo Baca Trail heads northeast from the parking area and is well marked by sign posts. The trail follows a rolling course past granite monoliths through the Upper Sonoran life zone, with piñons, junipers, mountain mahogany, beargrass, and Apache plume, as it heads toward the mountains' west face and the canyon immediately beneath the tram cables. At its mouth the canyon becomes constricted, the vegetation changing from desert scrub to willows, cottonwoods, and poison ivy along the tiny stream. At a point 0.25 mile into the canyon, the trail briefly leaves the stream, branching right and going up a short, steep bank. This junction is not marked and is difficult to find, but it's worth searching for because the trail soon becomes distinct again, and the little forested stream it leads to after 0.25 mile is delightful—lush and green with tiny waterfalls. From here, no one would suspect that a city of a half-million people is just two miles away.

> **DAY HIKE: PIEDRA LISA SPRING TRAIL**
> One-way length: 5 miles total (2 miles from the south
> end to the Rincon saddle)
> Low and high elevations: 6,120 and 8,200 feet
> Difficulty: moderate to strenuous

This route links two interesting and scenic valleys. Low elevations and southern exposures allow snow-free hiking for most of the year. Although my wife and I have a personal preference for going from east to west, the difficulty and views are similar going the other way. Starting at the Three Gun Spring Trailhead (see Hawk Watch Trail for vehicle directions), Trail 194 gradually ascends the broad valley until after 1.75 miles it arrives at the spur trail leading to Three Gun Spring (someone once carved the outlines of three pistols in a wooden trough here, hence the name). From here the trail ascends more steeply via switchbacks 0.75 mile to Post Pass and the junction with the Embudo Trail, No. 193. Here you'll find outstanding views of the southern Sandias. Descend via the Embudo Trail, but pause at the ridge separating the two canyons to enjoy more great views. The distance from Post Pass to the Embudo trailhead is three miles. (You can reach the Embudo Trailhead by driving to the east end of Indian School Road.) As you exit the valley, you'll pass through a rocky constriction from which the valley got its Spanish name (*embudo* means "funnel").

SHUTTLE HIKE: THREE GUN SPRING – EMBUDO CANYON
One-way length: 5.5 miles
Low and high elevations: 6,200 and 8,000 feet
Difficulty: moderate to strenuous

The southern part of this hike receives more visitors, partly because many more hikers live in Albuquerque than in Placitas, the village near the trail's north end, and also because the route to the Rincon from the north is much more difficult than from the south. Using the directions to the La Luz Trail, bypass the stone pillars and continue north on the dirt road until it ends at the parking area. About 0.5 mile from the parking area you cross a drainage; for an interesting diversion, follow this upstream 0.5 mile to the waterfall for which Waterfall Canyon was named. The Piedra Lisa Trail, No. 135, climbs persistently through piñon-juniper-ponderosa forest to the saddle known as the Rincon (the Spanish *rincón*, "box canyon," here refers to the ridge closing off the valley running south). This is a worthy destination, although many hikers may choose to scramble up the ridge to the northern base of the huge granite face called the Shield.

To hike from the north, drive from I-25 east on Highway 165 about three miles. About 0.25 mile past the west entrance to Forest Road 445 is the east entrance, where a dirt road branches south. After about two miles another dirt road heads east to Piedra Lisa "smooth rock" Spring and the trailhead. The trail is pleasant and scenic but often quite steep.

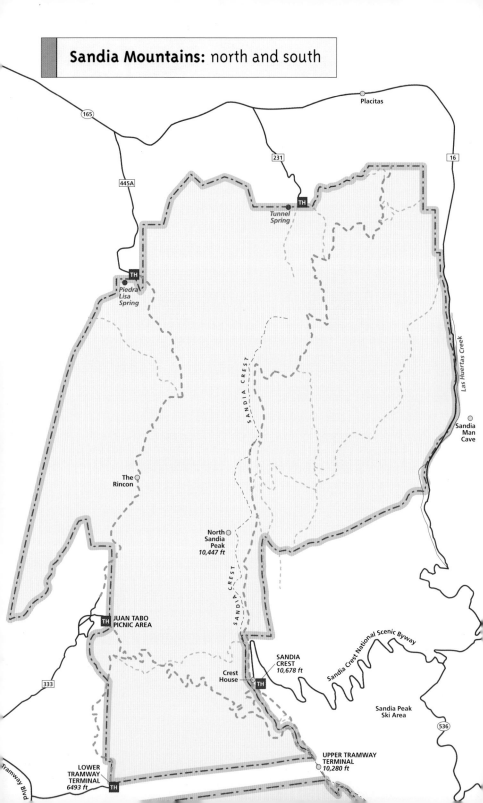

Sandia Mountains: north and south

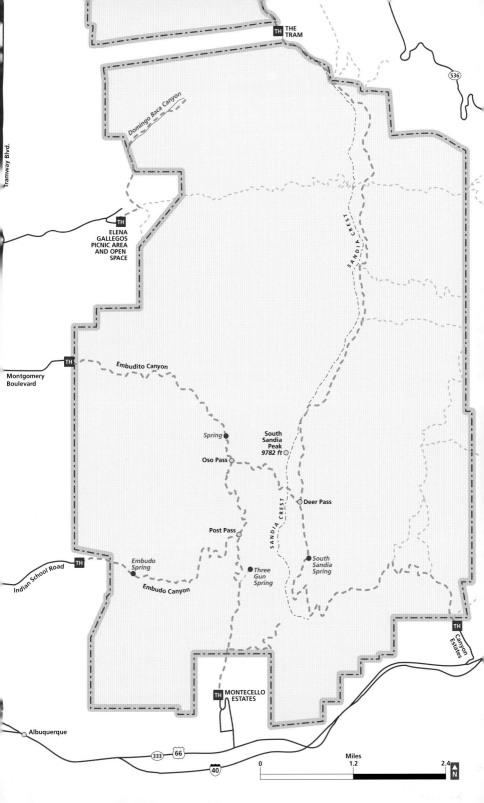

THE
TRAM

536

Domingo Baca Canyon

SANDIA CREST

ELENA
GALLEGOS
PICNIC AREA
AND OPEN
SPACE

Tramway Blvd.

Montgomery
Boulevard

Embudito Canyon

Spring

South
Sandia
Peak
9782 ft

Oso Pass

Deer Pass

SANDIA CREST

Post Pass

Embudo
Spring

Three
Gun
Spring

South
Sandia
Spring

Indian School Road

Embudo Canyon

Canyon
Estates

MONTECELLO
ESTATES

Albuquerque

333   66

40

Miles

0   1.2   2.4

N

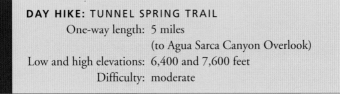

DAY HIKE: NORTH PEAK
One-way length: 2.0 miles
Low and high elevations: 10,000 and 10,678 feet
Difficulty: easy

This popular hike begins at the Sandia Crest, which you can reach by driving east from Albuquerque on I-40, taking the Tijeras exit to Highway 14, driving north six miles to Highway 536, and then following the signs for 12 miles. From the parking lot's north end, the Crest Trail, No. 130, heads north and follows or parallels the Sandia Crest. At 1.25 miles, as the main trail again begins descending into the forest, a faint branch trail leads uphill to the west, coming out after a few hundred yards atop a cliff whose level, open top runs north. North Sandia Peak, 10,447 feet, is just 0.3 mile farther north along the Crest Trail and slightly west, although the route isn't well marked. The peak's summit is forested, but if you hike west just about 50 feet down some rock ledges you come to an overlook offering spectacular views into Del Agua Canyon and the west face of the northern Sandias. If you miss the route to North Peak, don't fret; just a little ways farther on the Crest Trail is the Del Agua Canyon Overlook (and the junction with the North 10K Trail, No. 200), with views comparable to those from North Peak. The hike back to the Crest House is all uphill, but the gradients are gentle.

DAY HIKE: TUNNEL SPRING TRAIL
One-way length: 5 miles
(to Agua Sarca Canyon Overlook)
Low and high elevations: 6,400 and 7,600 feet
Difficulty: moderate

This modest hike, especially scenic in the fall, appears on most maps simply as the northern terminus of the Crest Trail, No. 130. The mine tunnel at the trailhead that gave this site its name has collapsed, but the spring is still there. You reach it by driving 5.4 miles east on Highway 44 from I-25 to a dirt road and sign indicating Tunnel Spring and the Crest Trail, No. 130. Drive about 1.5 miles south on this to the spring and the trailhead. The trail ascends gradually as it slabs around to the north, giving great views of the village of Placitas and the Rio Grande Valley. It climbs through piñon-juniper forest before coming to a west-facing overlook. From here, the trail returns to the woods before reaching the overlook into Agua Sarca Canyon after five miles. Continuing on for eight miles, you'll come to yet another overlook into Del Agua Canyon. As you return, you might look for a shortcut trail down into Del Orno Canyon; it's rough, very steep, and certainly not recommended for going up.

DESTINATION HIKE: LA LUZ TRAIL – SANDIA TRAM
One-way length: 7 miles to the Crest House,
7.8 miles to tram
Low and high elevations: 6,200 to 10,678 feet
Difficulty: strenuous

This is the most popular hike in the Sandias and deservedly so. Its difficulty comes primarily from length and elevation gain, rather than steepness. Spectacular scenery, a variety of ecosystems, and facilities at the Crest House allow for some intriguing combinations. My favorite scenario is to begin the hike at the base of the tram (reached from Tramway Boulevard), follow a connecting trail to the La Luz Trail, then hike to the top of the tram, have some cocoa, coffee, or whatever at the restaurant, and ride the tram back down. (Of course, you also can ride the tram up and hike down.)

The more standard hiking route begins at the trailhead near the Juan Tabo Picnic Area, reached by driving on Tramway Boulevard north until it begins to curve west. Here take paved Forest Road 333 east toward the mountains. After two miles, drive between two stone pillars to the trailhead. The trail ascends gradually via broad switchbacks with the scenery becoming more impressive as you climb. After five miles you'll reach the bottom of a large talus slope. At its top, after seemingly endless switchbacks, you'll come to a saddle where the trail splits. The northern trail takes you to the Crest House; the other trail, slightly longer, takes you to the tram.

DESTINATION HIKE: HAWK WATCH TRAIL (RAPTOR ROUTE)
One-way length: 2 miles
Low and high elevations: 6,325 and 7,500 feet
Difficulty: moderate

From late February through early May, literally thousands of hawks, kites, falcons, eagles, and other raptors, migrating northward, soar over this southern Sandia knob, which you can reach by the appropriately named Hawk Watch Trail. The trail branches from the Three Gun Spring Trail. To reach Three Gun Spring Trail, drive east from Albuquerque on I-40 to the Carnuel exit. Then take Highway 333 east into Tijeras Canyon for 2 miles to Montecello Estates, where you'll turn left and follow USFS signs to the Three Gun Spring Trail, No. 194. Hike the Three Gun Spring Trail approximately 0.5 mile to the sign indicating the Sandia Wilderness boundary. At this sign the Hawk Watch Trail, marked by a sign, branches right to head downhill and east. The trail crosses a dry wash and winds persistently up the canyon's east flank to arrive, after approximately 1.5 miles, at a level spot high on the mountain.

During the raptor migration, a raptor conservation group called HawkWatch International has observers at the site who welcome visitors and share information about the birds. The eagles tend to arrive first, in late February. Then come the hawks, falcons, and other raptors, as many as 20 species in all, including such rarities as the zone-tailed hawk and the black-shouldered kite.

SHUTTLE HIKE: EMBUDO CANYON – EMBUDITO VIA OSO PASS
One-way length: 7.2 miles
Low and high elevations: 6,200 and 8,540 feet at Oso Pass
Difficulty: moderate to strenuous

This route combines two popular trails of the western Sandias. Beginning at the south end at Embudo Canyon (trailhead at the end of Indian School Road), the Embudo Trail, No. 193, climbs three miles to the junction with the Three Gun Spring Trail, No. 194, at Post Pass. From there, Trail 194 continues another 1.25 miles to Oso Pass, a major trail junction. Heading due west is the Whitewash Trail, which returns you to the Embudo Trailhead, but this route can be very steep and difficult to follow. A more obvious choice is the Embudito Trail, No. 192. From Oso Pass this climbs steeply one mile to the Sandia Crest, with access to South Peak and the Crest Trail, No. 130, This is a challenging but worthwhile side trip. To descend from Oso Pass, hike the Embudito Trail northward, passing a fairly reliable spring less than a half-mile from the pass. The trail continues its descent through spruce-fir, then ponderosa pine, and finally piñon-juniper until, three miles from Oso Pass, you reach the trailhead near the eastern end of Montgomery Boulevard.

BOB JULYAN'S FAVORITE HIKE
CREST HOUSE – SOUTH PEAK – THREE GUN SPRING
One-way length: 16 miles (Crest House to Canyon Estates)
Low and high elevations: 6,280 and 10,678 feet
Difficulty: strenuous

Because of their proximity to Albuquerque, the Sandia Mountains rarely are regarded as a backpacking setting, yet this route is as scenic, wild, and challenging as many in better-known backpacking wilderness areas. It begins at one of several points: the Crest House, reached by a paved road, the tram, or one of the trails connecting with the Crest Trail, No. 130. The hike consists of taking the Crest Trail south to the meadows near 9,782-foot South Peak—its summit is a worth-while sidetrip—with excellent undeveloped campsites. Unlike many other features in the Sandias, there is no short, easy route to South Peak, and while you might meet a few hardy day hikers, you'll likely camp in blissful solitude. Regrettably, you've passed no water sources on your hike so far. The next morning you face two choices. Either you continue on the Crest Trail to its terminus at Canyon Estates and pass by reliable South Sandia Spring about two miles from the peak, or you can take the slightly longer but more scenic route down from Deer Pass to Oso Pass and then follow Trail 194 to Three Gun Spring Canyon. The reliable spring is only 1.5 miles from the trailhead, so this route is essentially dry.

OTHER RECREATIONAL OPPORTUNITIES

Although the wilderness is off-limits to mountain bikes, Albuquerque Open Space in the western foothills has an extensive network of excellent mountain biking trails, especially around the Elena Gallegos Picnic Area. These trails, along with several hiking trails, are also popular with trail runners. The Sandia Ski Area on the mountain range's east side has downhill lifts and runs. A limited but expanding number of cross-country ski trails are also on the upper eastern slopes, as well as snowshoeing routes. And the western escarpment's solid granite cliffs and crags offer outstanding technical rock climbing.

FOR MORE INFORMATION

CIBOLA NATIONAL FOREST, Sandia Ranger District, Highway 337, Tijeras, NM 87059; (505) 281-3304.

25 Sierra Ladrones Wilderness Study Area

The small, isolated, and very rugged desert mountains of Sierra Ladrones lack trails and are perennially challenging and fascinating to hikers.

Sierra Ladrones at dawn

LOCATION	West of I-25, 60 air miles southwest of Albuquerque
SIZE	45,308 acres Size recommended by the NM Wilderness Alliance: 36,244 acres
ELEVATION RANGE	5,200 to 9,210 feet at Ladron Peak
MILES OF TRAILS	No marked or maintained trails
ECOSYSTEMS	Desert scrub and grassland, piñon-juniper, ponderosa and Douglas fir
ADMINISTRATION	BLM
TOPOGRAPHIC MAPS	Ladron Peak, Riley, Carbon Springs, and Silver Creek USGS 7.5-minute quadrangles
BEST SEASONS	Spring, fall
GETTING THERE	Almost all approaches to the mountains begin at the Bernardo exit from I-25, where a paved road heads west across the Rio Puerco, soon becoming dirt County Road B12. This loops north around the mountains and eventually arrives at the ghost town of Riley, far to the southwest of the Ladrones on the Rio Salado. From this county road several dirt tracks head toward the mountains, but none is marked as an access; a topographic map is perhaps the best guide.
HIKING	Hiking in the Sierra Ladrones is limited by the lack of trails and ruggedness of the terrain; a topographic map and good route-finding skills are essential for hiking here. Lack of water severely limits overnight trips.

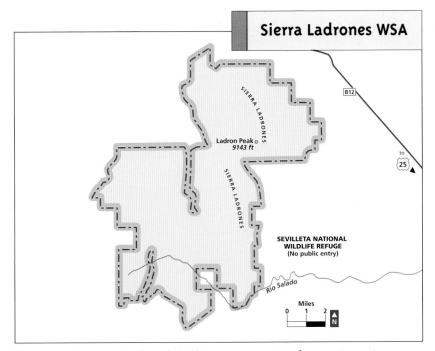

THIS MOUNTAIN RANGE has a forbidding reputation out of proportion to its modest size. The Spanish name means "thieves' mountains," and during Spanish colonial times Indian raiding parties would retreat here with livestock stolen from villages along the Rio Grande. Later, Hispanic and Anglo rustlers and thieves used the numerous steep-sided canyons—excellent ambush sites— as a refuge from pursuit. Even today, tales persist of stolen treasure concealed in remote caves and of gold veins discovered by prospectors who never returned to claim them.

Perhaps hikers will find them one day as they bushwhack routes over the rough terrain: trails are conspicuously absent in the Sierra Ladrones. On the east, the mountains break wavelike into a series of rocky canyons, giving the appearance of an enormous pile of boulders. The southern and western sections are characterized by rocky cliffs, mesa rimrock, badlands, and steep slopes cut by numerous canyons and ravines.

There is little water. Springs and seeps are occasionally nestled in a few of the many canyons, but they're easy to miss. Look for slight vegetational differences as clues. The high saddle that separates the twin summits can be reached from the southwest or via a long fin extending to the northwest. But neither route is marked, and both are extremely rough, especially near the top. At the saddle, it's easy to imagine no one has been there before.

While some acreage in the Sierra Ladrones is still in private hands, most is administered by the BLM, whose lands adjoin the Sevilleta National Wildlife Refuge, which is closed to the public. The core of the Sierra Ladrones is the wilderness study area, and because of its conspicuous wilderness character, the range was chosen as a reintroduction site for desert bighorn sheep. Other wildlife includes black bear, mountain lion, mule deer, and pronghorn.

Western New Mexico

The Western New Mexico region includes some of the state's oldest landscapes—and some of its youngest. This region encompasses the New Mexico portion of the Colorado Plateau, a sprawling upland of sedimentary rocks, eroded into striking mesas and canyons. A region where fossils protrude from ancient sea deposits, where the petrified trunks of giant trees litter a landscape that can no longer support trees, where crevices in canyons and cliffs hide the remains of prehistoric people long departed. The overall impression is of an ancient land where time has depth beyond human imagining. This is a place where, as Anne Zwinger said of the Grand Canyon and the Colorado Plateau, the second hand moves once a century. This is the landscape people see with their mind's eye if they've never been to the Southwest—Navajos herding sheep among tawny mesas and over arid plains beneath an endless turquoise sky.

Yet also within this region are landscapes that better fit the stereotypes of Hawaii: volcanic landscapes formed just yesterday in geologic time; Indian peoples who tell of their ancestors beholding rivers of fire. Valleys bordered by ancient sandstone contain frozen rivers of lava whose black swirls would seem more appropriate on a Pacific island. This, above all, is a region of contradictions.

The most prominent characteristic of this region is that it is conspicuously arid. The only major rivers are in the northwest where the San Juan, Animas, and La Plata Rivers—all rising in Colorado—converge briefly. Persons driving on I-40 near Grants see signs indicating the Rio San Jose, then look in bewilderment into a narrow, muddy slough that would be shamed by a large irrigation ditch. Most drainages appear on maps as washes— broad sand and gravel channels. Water occasionally flows on the surface, particularly after thunderstorms (resulting in flash floods), but most water is underground. You can dig for it in an emergency, but it will typically taste unpleasantly alkaline.

The vegetation in this region reflects its aridity. Widely spaced junipers and pines are the most common trees, with an occasional stand of ponderosa pine. The uplands here once supported rich grasslands, but overgrazing, especially by sheep, has allowed sagebrush, rabbitbrush, and other shrubs to invade and dominate.

In this region, the designated wildlands are defined by landscape features other than mountains. Not that mountains are absent: the Zuni Mountains

Pueblo Bonito in snow
Chaco Culture National Historical Park

are here, as well as the Chuska Mountains. But compared to the Sangre de Cristo Mountains or even the Sandia and Manzano Mountains, these ranges are small and tame. The exception is Mount Taylor, at 11,301 feet a hulking volcanic giant that dominates this part of the state. But even though Mount Taylor encompasses considerable wild Forest Service land and offers some magnificent hiking, roads and other human works have precluded formal wilderness designation here.

The Continental Divide runs through this region, and so does the Continental Divide Trail, although not always in the same place. The Divide and the trail coincide fairly closely in the stretch of BLM land from Pie Town to El Malpais National Monument. The trail crosses the lava flow on the ancient Zuni–Acoma Trail, following cairns erected by Zuni and Acoma

Indians. The actual divide runs farther west, but because it crosses private and Navajo lands, the trail has been routed through Grants, then over Mount Taylor and on to the BLM lands in the Rio Puerco Valley. Local Indian tribes have expressed concern about the trail obtruding upon sacred sites in the Mount Taylor area, so the trail's actual route is still evolving. The largest wilderness complex in Western New Mexico is the array of public lands centered on El Malpais National Monument. This array includes not only the monument itself but also the adjacent Cebolla and West Malpais Wildernesses, the Chain of Craters Wilderness Study Area, and National Conservation Area lands—a complex whose combined acreage of 376,000 makes it New Mexico's second largest wild area (after the Gila Wilderness). Yet curiously, it doesn't seem that large or that wild. Its various units are balkanized by paved and dirt roads, so you don't feel far removed from civilization like in other wildernesses such as the Gila. Hiking trails are sparse and mostly short; few backpackers ever spend the night here. With its lava flows and cinder cones flanked by high sandstone bluffs, this area is a photographer's delight, but seldom attracts hikers. In fact, it seldom attracts anyone, despite the fact that it's just off I-40, near the nation's busiest interstate highways and the route by which millions of vacationing Americans travel to places like the Grand Canyon, the Petrified Forest, and other attractions farther west.

Also overlooked by most out-of-state travelers is the nationally significant Chaco Culture National Historical Park. Again, few people come here to hike and none to backpack, although not because the park lacks backcountry appeal. Rather, people come here, over a long, out-of-the-way route, to see North America's greatest prehistoric ruins north of Mexico. The canyon here—remote, arid, and exposed—improbably became the center of a Puebloan civilization that, about a thousand years ago, extended throughout northwestern New Mexico and into Arizona, Utah, and Colorado. Today, the once-bustling canyon is a place of silence, beauty, and mystery. But the designated hiking trails here are short and few, and off-trail hiking and backcountry camping are not allowed, to safeguard the fragile prehistoric remains found throughout the park.

Farther west, in the badland complex that includes the Bisti—De-na-zin Wildernesses and the BLM Ah-shi-sle-pah Wilderness Study Area, the opposite situation exists: backcountry camping is allowed, and hikers have no choice but to go cross-country—because there are no trails. In fact, there are no facilities of any kind except what the wilderness itself provides. This is geology "in the nude" like photographer Edward Weston would have appreciated. There is little or no vegetation, and the land is eroded into strange shapes and formations descriptively termed hoodoos, toadstools, and the misleading term, badlands. Petrified wood is abundant; fossils of national paleontological significance have been found here. This is, indeed, wilderness, although not in the popular sense of vast forests and pristine wildlife habitat. Here, the forests and animals lived millions of years ago.

Regrettably for lovers of wilderness, however, the accumulation of these plants and animals produced extensive and economically valuable coal, oil, and gas deposits throughout the Colorado Plateau. These pose the greatest threat to the region's wilderness. The Bisti area was designated as wilderness in part to preempt strip-mining for coal (the wilderness is bordered on the west by dormant coal-mining operations). In early 1998, a public outcry arose when an oil-gas company sought to develop leases it had purchased from the BLM in the corridor connecting the Bisti and De-na-zin Wildernesses. Such threats to the region's wildlands are likely to continue as demand for fossil fuels increases and Indian groups seek revenue from tribal land with little other economic value.

Western New Mexico also includes several wilderness study areas aside from those mentioned above. Petaca Pinta is a rugged, remote area of mesas and canyons, west of Albuquerque and south of I-40. The contiguous areas of Mesita Blanca and Eagle Peak west of Quemado are also characterized by mesas and canyons, as well as volcanic cinder cones and lava flows. The Techado proposed wilderness southeast of El Malpais National Monument is centered upon a high mesa.

Western New Mexico is Indian country. Almost all the wildlands in this book are contiguous with or near Indian lands. The El Malpais complex abuts Acoma Pueblo and Ramah Navajo tribal lands, while Zuni lands are just to the southwest and Laguna lands are to the northwest. Chaco Culture National Historical Park and the Bisti—De-na-zin—Ah-shi-sle-pah complex are surrounded by the Navajo Nation. The region's three largest towns—Farmington, Gallup, and Grants—have sizable Indian populations and base much of their economies on being within Indian country. Also, because Navajos tend to live in widely dispersed family units, the land is far less empty of people than it often appears, and a very extensive and complex network of dirt roads links these dwellings. For most visitors, this Indian presence adds an interesting dimension to the region, but it also imposes a responsibility to understand and respect lifestyles and values.

26 Ah-shi-sle-pah Wilderness Study Area

This area features scenic, multicolored badlands, as well as low, sparsely vegetated hills and mesas that contain highly significant fossil remains.

Erosion forms

AH-SHI-SLE-PAH IS ONE PART of New Mexico's Colorado Plateau badlands wilderness complex that also includes the Bisti and De-na-zin Wilderness areas and the 10,000-acre corridor linking them. All are located around broad washes flanked by hills and mesas eroded into unusual formations containing highly significant fossils. The nearly complete skeleton of a dinosaur was found in the Ah-shi-sle-pah WSA, and fossils of other dinosaurs and early mammals have been found here, as well.

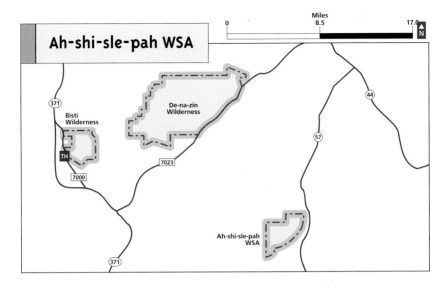

Regrettably, the WSA overlies substantial coal deposits, and the possibility also exists of at least some lands being transferred to the Navajo Nation. For these reasons, its status as wilderness is in jeopardy.

Like the other wild areas, this lends itself to cross-country exploration (especially as there are no trails). The country is open, and the only other people you're likely to encounter are Navajos tending livestock. Water is scarce, and the country is exposed to wind and sun. Also, the topography can be very complex and confusing, so a compass is very helpful. For more information about the history and hiking in this area, see Bisti and De-na-zin Wildernesses.

LOCATION	Southeast of Farmington, just north of Chaco Culture National Historical Park
SIZE	6,563 acres Size recommended by the NM Wilderness Alliance: 6,563 acres
ELEVATION RANGE	6,200 to 6,500 feet
MILES OF TRAILS	No marked or maintained trails
ECOSYSTEMS	Sagebrush, piñon-juniper, Great Basin scrubland and grassland
ADMINISTRATION	BLM
TOPOGRAPHIC MAPS	Pretty Rock and Pueblo Bonito NW USGS 7.5-minute quadrangles
BEST SEASONS	Spring, fall
GETTING THERE	From Highway 44, maintained gravel Highway 57 runs southwest to Chaco Canyon and forms the WSA's eastern and southern boundaries.
HIKING	Though the Ah-shi-sle-pah WSA lacks marked or maintained trails, the terrain readily allows for cross-country travel. Old roads and livestock trails, ridges, and drainages offer routes for exploration of the terrain as well.

27 Bisti—De-na-zin Wilderness Areas

This wilderness area showcases a diverse environment of rolling grasslands and broken rugged badlands cut by broad washes and gently sloping mesas.

Evening clouds over badlands

LOCATION	About halfway between Farmington and Crownpoint, just east of Highway 371
SIZE	37,100 acres (combined plus corridor)
ELEVATION RANGE	5,770 to 6,800 feet
MILES OF TRAILS	No designated trails
ECOSYSTEMS	Piñon-juniper, sagebrush, Great Basin scrubland and grassland
ADMINISTRATION	BLM
TOPOGRAPHIC MAPS	Alamo Mesa East, Alamo Mesa West, Tanner Lake, Bisti Trading Post, and Huerfano Trading Post SW USGS 7.5-minute quadrangles
BEST SEASONS	Spring, fall
GETTING THERE	These two wildernesses are reached from Highway 371, south of Farmington and north of Crownpoint. Navajo Road 7000 passes by the western edge of the Bisti Wilderness, while Navajo Road 7023 goes along the southern edge of the De-na-zin Wilderness.
HIKING	Though the Bisti—De-na-zin Wilderness lacks marked or maintained trails, the terrain readily allows for cross-country travel. Hikers can follow ridges and drainages in their explorations. Lack of water limits overnight trips.

THE WIND WAS RAGING and the air was dense and dark with dust the first time I camped at the Bisti—De-na-zin Wildernesses. My youngest daughter was three, and—undaunted by the storm—we explored the strange, barren hills. The swirling tempest reminded her of a scene from a movie we'd recently seen, *The Neverending Story*, in which the universe was about to be devoured by a formless chaos called The Nothingness. "We're in the Nothingness," she repeated.

Not a bad image, actually, for the wilderness known as the Bisti (pronounced BIS-tie), a name derived from a Navajo word meaning "badlands." A strange, otherworldly sort of place. Stone trunks of ancient trees protrude from the lifeless soil, calcite crystals glitter in the intense sun, and the land is contorted like an amoeba with weathered formations known as hoodoos and toadstools. It's an easy place for a three-year-old to enter the realm of fantasy.

To geologists, however, the Bisti—De-na-zin Wildernesses exhibit a different richness. Here chapters of the Earth's history are laid bare, open and easy to read. And very interesting chapters they are, too, for they include the period that began about 70 million years ago and ended about 54 million years ago, the period spanning the controversial transition during which the dinosaurs declined, and died out, and mammals began their era. During this period, this area was covered alternately by seas and vast swamps. In this fluctuating environment, successive mineral and organic deposits were laid down that, when buried, compacted, and then later, exposed by erosion, appeared as interbedded layers of shale, sandstone, and coal.

It's the coal and associated oil and gas deposits that have worried wilderness advocates most. Literally billions of tons of coal underlie the wildernesses. When the two wildernesses were designated in 1984, it was at least in part to preempt strip-mining. The two areas remained separate (Bisti, 3,946 acres, and De-na-zin, 22,454 acres) until 1996 when the BLM completed a land exchange with the Navajo Nation that created a 10,700-acre wilderness corridor linking the two. A fourth component of this Colorado Plateau wilderness complex is the 6,563-acre Ah-shi-sle-pah Wilderness Study Area, which is similar in character to the Bisti—De-na-zin Wilderness areas and located southeast of them. Regrettably, in 1991 the BLM a granted a private oil and gas company lease rights to 1,500 acres of the corridor, and early in 1998 the company applied for permits to exercise those rights. This has resulted in a campaign, with broad public support, to compensate the company and protect the wilderness. This campaign is underway as of this writing.

Hikers who want to explore the Bisti—De-na-zin Wildernesses face special challenges. First, while there is a trailhead of sorts at the Bisti Wilderness, there aren't really any marked trails. You can use maps to formulate a route, although even with a map the topography is extremely confusing. But following a preset route is contrary to the entire spirit of this area, which invites random venturing, following your nose, and trusting to serendipity. If ever there was a poking-around wilderness, this is it.

This is also an extremely fragile wilderness. The landforms here have little vegetation to stabilize them, and the soil is highly subject to erosion. Footprints on the patterned soil last a long time. This area definitely deserves a "Leave No Trace" ethic. Furthermore, the area's geologic treasures and curiosities are like items in an unlocked case in an unattended jewelry store. Calcite crystals and petrified wood fragments are

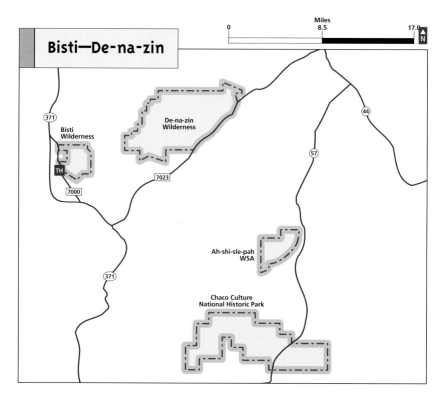

everywhere, and there are no park rangers looking over your shoulder. The temptation is great to grab a chunk as a souvenir, but please resist. In Arizona's Petrified Forest National Park, literally tons of petrified wood are removed from the park each year, one chunk at a time, in the pockets of people who couldn't resist the temptation and who think one piece won't be missed.

The wilderness badlands here, as their name implies, are without water. They're highly exposed to sun and wind, and shade trees are rare. Hikers should not only bring plenty of water but, also, wear protective clothing and sunscreen. Summer is not a good season to explore these areas, except in the early morning or late evening. In winter, the temperatures are reasonable, but the soils here, with their high clay content, have a statewide reputation for being horrendous when wet. Thus fall or late spring are probably the best seasons for hiking.

I'm glad I visited this area when my children were small because they made it easy to enter the fantasies that this strange landscape inspires. But even without kids, the Bisti—De-na-zin Wildernesses give proof to the dictum that it's never too late to have a happy childhood. Bring your imagination and your sense of wonder and let yourself wander.

BOB JULYAN'S FAVORITE HIKE
One-way length: 2.0 miles or more
Low and high elevations: 5,700 and 5,800 feet
Difficulty: easy

As mentioned, trails don't really exist in the Bisti—De-na-zin Wildernesses, so this is more of a route than a defined trail. It begins at the BLM Bisti parking area where a dirt road that parallels Highway 371 crosses a broad wash. From the parking area, an old road heads east along the wash's north side, but the more interesting formations are on the wash's south side, so cross over and then head east. Little ravines branch chaotically from the wash, so use your compass to determine where you are relative to the wash.

OTHER RECREATIONAL OPPORTUNITIES

Although mountain biking may be marginally appropriate on the dirt roads in the general vicinity of the wilderness areas, it is definitely out of place in the wilderness because of damage to sensitive soils and landforms.

The recreation for which the area is most suited, aside from hiking, is photography. This is one of the most photogenic areas in the Southwest.

FOR MORE INFORMATION

BUREAU OF LAND MANAGEMENT, Farmington Field Office, 1235 La Plata Highway, Farmington, NM 87401; (505) 599-8900.

28 Cebolla Wilderness

The broad, grassy valleys in this wilderness area are flanked by sandstone cliffs rising to extensive forested mesas. Interesting remains of the area's human history are found throughout.

La Ventana Natural Arch

LOCATION	On the southeast side of El Malpais National Monument
SIZE	62,800 acres
ELEVATION RANGE	7,300 to 8,340 feet
MILES OF TRAILS	Approximately 10 miles
ECOSYSTEMS	Piñon-juniper, ponderosa pine, grassland
ADMINISTRATION	BLM
TOPOGRAPHIC MAPS	Bonine Canyon, Sand Canyon, North Pasture, Laguna Honda, and Los Pilares 7.5-minute USGS quadrangles
BEST SEASONS	Spring, fall
GETTING THERE	Most public access to the Cebolla Wilderness is from Highway 117, which runs south of I-40 east of Grants. County Road 41 branching south from Highway 117 also parallels the wilderness's western side.
HIKING	Hiking here is limited by a general paucity of trails, though cross-country hiking is not difficult. Water is scarce throughout.

THE PATTERN IS REPEATED throughout west-central New Mexico—tawny sandstone cliffs rising to tiered, forested mesas, all separated by broad grassy valleys veined with a network of deep arroyos—but only here, abutting El Malpais National Monument, has this subtly beautiful landscape been preserved as wilderness.

Few New Mexicans know that the Cebolla Wilderness exists; even fewer have ever explored it. Not designated until 1987, with the establishment of El Malpais National Monument, Cebolla is one of those puzzle-piece wilderness areas that needs to be put into the larger context of the surrounding lands. Here the larger puzzle includes El Malpais National Conservation Area, abutting the Cebolla Wilderness; El Malpais National Monument, just to the west; the West Malpais Wilderness, to the west; and still farther west, more lands of the El Malpais National Conservation Area—376,000 acres in all.

The youngest lava in El Malpais National Monument is only 1,000 years old; the residents of Acoma Pueblo, whose lands are just to the east, have oral traditions in which their ancestors witnessed fiery rivers in the valleys. Today, hikers on the Zuni-Acoma Trail can see lava that looks like it solidified only yesterday—black and jagged, with congealed swirls and burst bubbles. But the sandstone bluffs and mesas of the Cebolla Wilderness have an older tale to tell. No humans were here 138 to 63 million years ago to behold seas advancing and retreating. When the granite core of the Zuni Mountains was uplifted, these sandstone layers, called the Zuni sandstone, were shoved to the surface. Then they eroded into today's landscape.

This was the landscape that became home to the Puebloan culture group known as the Anasazi, and from their great cultural center in Chaco Canyon 80 miles north, they created the greatest pre-Columbian civilization in the United States. At the far southern edge of the Chacoan world were small villages, some of whose ruins are within the Cebolla Wilderness. Probably the best-known of these is the Dittert Site, where the remains of walls form a haunting presence at the mouth of Armijo Canyon at the southwest edge of the wilderness. But throughout the wilderness, hikers are likely to find potsherds, flint flakes, and rubble mounds that once were dwellings. On rock faces you'll find petroglyphs, symbols, and designs pecked into the rock by ancient artists for purposes unknown.

What became of the Anasazis? Well, if you're hiking in the Cebolla Wilderness, you might meet some of them. They might be hunting small game, harvesting piñon nuts, or gathering medicinal herbs or edible plants (the Spanish name *cebolla*, "onion," refers to the wild onions growing here). They won't identify themselves as Anasazis, a somewhat pejorative Navajo-applied name in any case; rather, they'll say they're from Zuni Pueblo, or more likely, Acoma Pueblo. But there's no doubt either among themselves or among anthropologists that they are indeed the descendants of the Anasazis. That's one reason, among many, to protect and respect the artifacts and sites you might find: the people to whom they have cultural and spiritual meaning are still here.

While hiking the Cebolla Wilderness—especially the valleys—you might come across decaying log cabins. From 1918 to 1940, a group of English-speaking pioneers arrived by pickup and jalopy to find new homes. They had the same courage and tenacity of the pioneers who came west in covered wagons. They were homesteaders; many came from Texas and Oklahoma. Most filed claims to the allowed 640 acres with the State Land Office and paid the $34 filing fee—some simply squatted. To "prove up," they had to live on the land seven months a year for three years, make at least $800 in improvements, and pay another $34 for title.

They built one- and two-room cabins from ponderosa logs, or constructed picket houses from smaller piñon poles. Their Hispanic neighbors showed them how to make adobe. Life was hard. Most sites lacked water; it had to be hauled (hikers, take note!). Many struggled, gave up, and moved on. Necessity, lack of alternatives, and sometimes sheer stubbornness forced the survivors to stay. When World War II caused the economy to boom, most homesteaders left for better jobs and an easier life elsewhere. Today their abandoned cabins, their descendants, and the stories passed on by old-timers are all that remain. One cannot but wonder how the people whose cabins we see today in Armijo Canyon, Homesteader Canyon, and Lobo Canyon would react to knowing their former homesteads have been designated wilderness.

After the war, the area was ignored. After all, it was *el malpais*, a Spanish term that means literally "the bad land." The BLM, however, viewed this area differently and in 1969 began an 18-year process of studying how the land should be designated. Finally, in 1987, with support from New Mexico's congressional delegation and local businesses who saw tourism as a replacement for the failed uranium-mining industry, El Malpais National Monument and associated conservation and wilderness areas were established.

Today, the Cebolla Wilderness still awaits the expected visitors. The scenery can be spectacular, especially in a wet year, but trails are few. This is poking-around country—a place to leave one's vehicle on one of the dirt roads heading into the wilderness and then hike cross-country through the valleys and onto the mesas, trusting serendipity to lead to whatever you were meant to discover. Archaeological sites are scattered throughout the wilderness, including impressive rock art panels. The area is also rich in wildlife, including elk, deer, coyotes, black bear, pronghorn antelope, wild turkey, and many more. The rimrock country and vertical sandstone cliffs are prime nesting areas for raptors, including golden eagles, red-tailed hawks, prairie falcons, and great horned owls.

All road access to the wilderness begins on Highway 117, a very scenic road that heads south from I-25 east of Grants. Spring and fall are the best hiking seasons, although summer mornings, evenings, and nights can be delightful. Chances of encountering other hikers are remote, and you'll have to improvise a campsite if you spend the night (established campsites are rare). You'll also have to carry water because water sources are infrequent.

Few New Mexico wilderness experiences equal a place like the Cebolla Wilderness. Here at night atop a sandstone bluff overlooking a valley frequented by wildlife—the soft, dry, air scented with pines—you might imagine yourself an Indian centuries ago, when the world was wide and wild. Or, you might ponder the meaning of the strange symbols you found earlier that day etched on the ancient rocks.

DAY HIKE: NARROWS RIM
One-way length: 3.0 miles
Low and high elevations: 7,084 and 7,500 feet
Difficulty: moderate

Probably the most popular hike in the Cebolla Wilderness, this easy-to-follow but rocky trail parallels the rim of the sandstone bluffs overlooking the lava flow in the section known as the Narrows. After a short but steep initial ascent, the trail climbs gradually through piñon-juniper forest to end at an overlook of La Ventana, New Mexico's second largest natural arch (a good side trip on your drive down on Highway 117). The trail begins at a turnoff from Highway 117, 19 miles south of the intersection with I-25, where it is marked with a sign.

DAY HIKE: LOBO CANYON
One-way length: 3.0 miles
Low and high elevations: 7,200 and 7,550 feet
Difficulty: moderate

No trail leads into Lobo Canyon—no signs even indicate its existence—so you'll have to use a map and compass to find your way. But the broad valley and adjoining mesas provide a pleasant day of hiking and exploration. At Mile Marker 31 on Highway 117, south of I-25, an unlocked gate opens onto a dirt road heading east. In dry weather the road poses no problems for most cars, but it can be slippery during and after rains. After about three miles, the road forks; take the left fork, which continues heading east. After more than four miles, the broad valley you've been following will make a T. The road follows the south branch into Cebolla Canyon; the canyon running north is Lobo Canyon. Although the hiking generally is easy, you'll probably be confronted by some very deep arroyos that may prove a challenge to cross. And be sure to carry plenty of water.

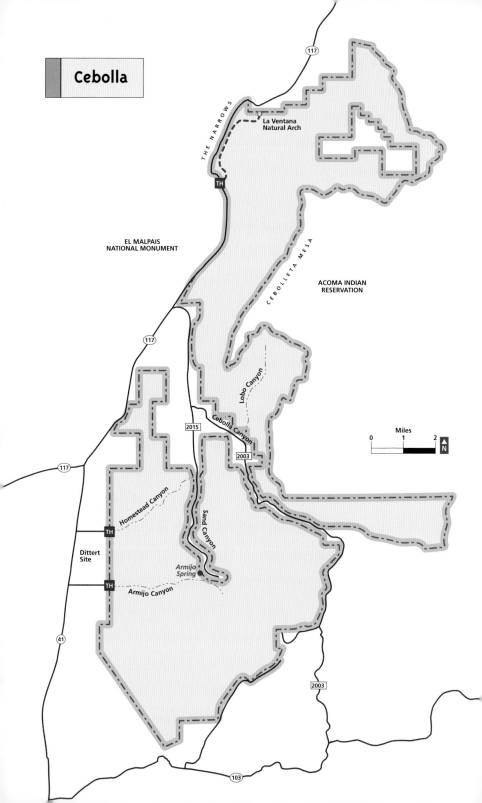

Cebolla

La Ventana
Natural Arch

THE NARROWS

TH

EL MALPAIS
NATIONAL MONUMENT

CEBOLLETA MESA

ACOMA INDIAN
RESERVATION

117

Lobo Canyon

2015

Cebolla Canyon

2003

Miles
0   1   2

N

117

Homestead Canyon

Sand Canyon

TH

Dittert
Site

Armijo
Spring

TH

Armijo Canyon

41

2003

103

DESTINATION HIKE: DITTERT SITE
One-way length: 0.5 mile
Low and high elevations: approximately 7,200 feet
Difficulty: easy

Few people would come here solely to hike to this site, but if you're already in the area, it makes an interesting side trip. The hike begins at the same place as the Armijo Homestead hike (see directions below). No sign or clear trail shows the way to the Dittert Site, but if you head northeast across a broad arroyo you'll have no trouble finding it. Archaeologists once suspected the site to have been a remote outlier of the far-flung Ancestral Puebloan civilization centered on Chaco Canyon, but construction occurred at the Dittert Site around A.D. 1200, long after the Chacoan civilization dissolved. So the site's real history remains a mystery. A pamphlet available at the El Malpais National Monument Visitor Center (north on Highway 117) provides more information.

DESTINATION HIKE: ARMIJO HOMESTEAD SITE
One-way length: 2.0 miles
Low and high elevations: 7,260 and 7,700 feet
Difficulty: easy to moderate

Ancient and recent history are juxtaposed in this hike, beginning with the thirteenth century Chacoan ruins known as Dittert Site and ending with ruined homesteader cabins abandoned early in the twentieth century. To reach the trailhead, drive about 33 miles on Highway 117 south from I-25 to the unpaved Pie Town road. Drive on this 3.3 miles to a still smaller dirt road heading east and ending after 1.3 miles at the wilderness boundary. The Dittert Site will be about half a mile to the northeast. The mouth of Armijo Canyon is not obvious, but if you head southeast from the Dittert Site, you'll enter it. Follow what remains of a ranch road until you reach the ruins. Here, look for what remains of a very rough road leading up the mesa immediately opposite the buildings (behind an earthen dam). Follow this uphill to Armijo Spring. Inside the recent protective structure is the niche where once the Hispanic ranchers placed a *santo* to bless and protect the place.

LOOP HIKE: ARMIJO CANYON – HOMESTEAD CANYON
Round-trip length: approximately 10 miles
Low and high elevations: 7,260 and 7,800 feet
Difficulty: strenuous

This hike is a longer version of the Armijo Canyon hike. From Armijo Spring, climb onto the unnamed mesa separating the two canyons. Then go north cross-country until you are able to drop into the head of Homestead Canyon. Here you'll encounter old roads that lead downhill in a southwest direction, but eventually you'll have to go cross-country again to return to your vehicle, most likely passing the Dittert Site (described above) en route.

OTHER RECREATIONAL OPPORTUNITIES

While mountain biking is prohibited in the wilderness itself, the entire El Malpais complex, including the Cebolla Wilderness, is interlaced with dirt roads of varying stages of maintenance that offer truly outstanding mountain biking. Examples in the Cebolla Wilderness include the roads in Sand and Cebolla Canyons.

FOR MORE INFORMATION

NATIONAL PARK SERVICE, P.O. Box 939, Grants, NM 87020; (505) 285-4641.

BUREAU OF LAND MANAGEMENT, P.O. Box 846, Grants, NM 87020; (505) 285-5406.

Chaco Culture
National Historical Park

*Set in a remote canyon in northwestern New Mexico,
Chaco is the nation's largest group of prehistoric ruins.
We are still faced with many questions about the
culture that created this memorable site.*

Morning clouds, Pueblo Bonito

LOCATION	Southeast of Farmington, south of Highway 44, on the Navajo Indian Reservation
SIZE	36,864 acres
ELEVATION RANGE	6,010 to 6,658 feet at Tsin Kletzin Ruins
MILES OF TRAILS	Approximately 10
ECOSYSTEMS	Piñon-juniper, sage, Colorado Plateau scrub, grassland
ADMINISTRATION	National Park Service
TOPOGRAPHIC MAPS	Kin Klizhin Ruins, Sargent Ranch, and Pueblo Bonito USGS 7.5-minute USGS quadrangles
BEST SEASONS	Spring, summer, fall
GETTING THERE	Chaco Culture National Historical Park is reached from Highway 44 via Navajo Reservation roads leading southwest from Nageezi or Blanco Trading Post or via Navajo roads heading northeast from Crownpoint.
HIKING	Hiking here is strictly limited to the few short trails designated and maintained by the Park. No backcountry camping is permitted.

You'll find North America's most impressive pre-columbian ruins north of Mexico in Chaco Canyon on the Navajo Reservation in northwestern New Mexico. This broad canyon would otherwise go unnoticed in this vast, seemingly empty land of many canyons. Why this canyon became the center of the culture known as the Anasazi is but one of many mysteries surrounding this hauntingly beautiful place.

"Anasazi" is derived from a Navajo word meaning "ancient enemies," but modern Pueblo Indians, who include the Indians at Chaco Canyon among their ancestors, regard the term Anasazi as pejorative. (No consensus has emerged as to what term should replace Anasazi, which is why I've continued using it in this book, but one suggested alternative is "Ancestral Puebloan.") By the time Navajos arrived in the Southwest, they found only ruins in Chaco Canyon; the inhabitants of the masonry towns left centuries earlier. By A.D. 1200 the hundreds of dwellings, complex irrigation works, and mysterious roads had been abandoned. This preceded the eventual migration out of the entire Four Corners area. What became of these people is not a mystery: they traveled south to where their descendants live today as modern Pueblo Indians, in villages at Hopi, Zuni, Acoma, Laguna, and the pueblos along the Rio Grande. The oral histories of these peoples allude to migrations from the north.

But why they left—that has long been hotly debated. Drought, famine, raids by nomadic peoples, and warfare have been advanced as theories. More recently, some archaeologists have noted that the abandonment coincided with the global cooling known as the Little Ice Age, which would have caused a shorter growing season in a region where the agriculture was marginal even in the best of times. The food shortages resulting from this would have been accompanied by severe social stress. Perhaps all of these factors led to the move.

Today, thousands of archaeological sites are poignant reminders of these people's presence in the Four Corners area, and of these sites none testify more eloquently about the level of culture they achieved than the ruins at Chaco Canyon. Early Spanish and American explorers noted them, but the first of many excavations did not begin until 1896 with the Hyde Exploring Expedition. In 1907 Chaco Canyon National Monument was established to preserve the ruins. In 1980 the monument was enlarged and redesignated Chaco Culture National Historical Park. It was designated a World Heritage Site in 1987.

Visitors to the park approach via all-weather dirt Highway 57, 29 miles south from Highway 44 at Nageezi or 26 miles northeast from Crownpoint. You'll find a small, seasonal campground near the visitor center at the park's south end; there are no other accommodations near the park. Most visitors understandably go first to the major ruins, such as Pueblo Bonito and Casa Rinconada, which you can reach via a paved park road. But trails also extend to other ruins, such as Peñasco Blanco and Tsin Kletzin (described below). To forestall vandalism, no overnight camping is allowed in the backcountry.

The trails leading to the backcountry ruins are usually relatively short and of moderate difficulty. But while the backcountry ruins typically are less impressive than those in the canyon, it is in the backcountry away from roads, cars, often-numerous visitors, and Park Service facilities and personnel that you get a sense of the place's isolation and subtle beauty. The effect can be haunting. Why here? you'll ask, and the canyon walls echo your question.

What shaped the civilization here? The outlying ruins were carefully placed to be within sight of each other—why? At Fajada Butte at the canyon's south end, a dagger of sunlight pierces a spiral petroglyph on the morning of the summer solstice—why? Radiating out from Chaco Canyon are wide arrow-straight roads that ignore terrain irregularities, built with enormous effort by people who had neither wheeled conveyances nor pack animals—why? And the ultimate question: Why did they leave?

Chaco Culture National Historical Park isn't wilderness in the traditional sense; nor is it a likely destination for backpacking. But after you've driven here and hiked to the ruins, you'll not question why Chaco Canyon belongs in a book about New Mexico's wildlands.

> ### DESTINATION HIKE: PEÑASCO BLANCO
> One-way length: 2.2 miles
> Low and high elevations: 6,115 to 6,175 feet
> Difficulty: easy

Peñasco Blanco ("white rocky outcrop") is an isolated ruined pueblo; along the way you'll pass several very interesting petroglyph panels. The hike begins at Casa Chiquita ("pretty little house") at the canyon's north end. The trail runs north, paralleling Chaco Wash. Crossing it after thunderstorms, can be dangerous as the normally modest drainage becomes rapid moving water. Just before the wash lies a cairn-marked trail to the right that leads across the wash 0.5 mile to another petroglyph site. A star-shaped figure here has been thought to depict the super-nova visible in A.D. 1054. This trail loops back to the main trail.

Peñasco Blanco is a so-called great house village, with an unusual oval shape. When it was inhabited from circa A.D. 913 until the general abandonment of Chaco Canyon in the 1100s, it was three stories high and had at least 160 rooms. The site is unexcavated, and the fragile walls are easily damaged by people crawling over them.

> ### DESTINATION HIKE: TSIN KLETZIN
> One-way length: 1.5 miles
> Low and high elevations: 6,150 and 6,658 feet
> Difficulty: easy

Tsin Kletzin ("charcoal house") is a modest D-shaped Chacoan site on South Mesa with expansive vistas of Chaco Canyon. Tree-ring analysis of timbers in the ruins indicate construction around A.D. 1112—not long before the area's abandonment. The site also intersects several lines-of-sight connecting other Chacoan villages— Kin Klizhin, Bas'sa'ani, Peñasco Blanco, Kin Kletso, Casa Chiquita, and Pueblo

Chaco Culture National Historical Park

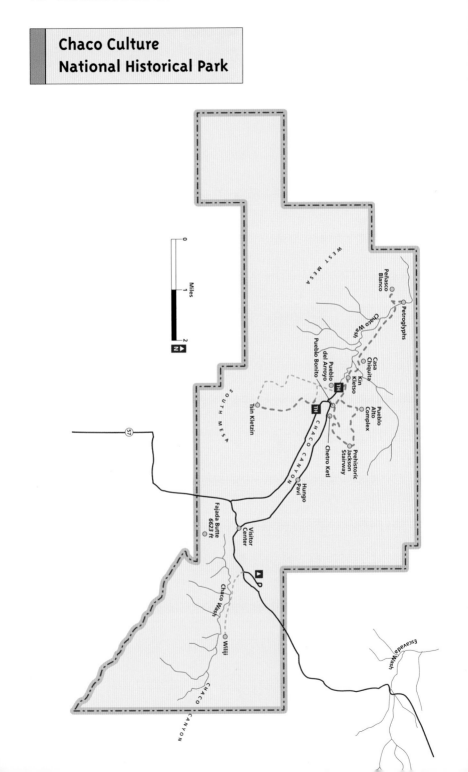

Alto. Had Tsin Kletzin been shifted 30 feet in any direction, not all of these great houses could have been seen from each other. Why was this so important to these peoples?

The Tsin Kletzin Trail begins at Marker 9, just south of the great kiva of Casa Rinconada on Chaco Wash's south side. The trail immediately ascends the steep, rocky slope to the mesa top. Then it climbs more gradually through soft sand until reaching the ruin.

LOOP HIKE: ALTO MESA LOOP
Round-trip length: 4.8 miles
Low and high elevations: 6,090 and 6,440 feet
Difficulty: moderate

Allocate more time than you would expect to complete this route so you can see most of its many interesting archaeological sites and vistas. Pueblo Alto, meaning "high town" in Spanish, is aptly named because it sits atop a mesa. The trail begins directly behind the ruin of Kin Kletso and ascends to a bench (look for some stone basins here). From the bench, the trail runs east to the loop's beginning. Near this junction is an overlook of Pueblo Bonito, the park's largest ruin. From here the trail ascends again, to the mesa top, or continues along the bench to ascend farther east. Once on top, this route passes the stairs ancient Indians carved in the sandstone for their route to the mesa top. Don't use the stairs: they're unsafe and subject to erosion by hard-soled shoes. From the stairs, Pueblo Alto is 0.75 mile.

Actually, six ruins comprise the Pueblo Alto Complex, four of which are visible. And by the time you reach the main ruin, you will have crossed some of the prehistoric roads that converge at Pueblo Alto. You likely won't know it; they were discovered only by aerial photography and evidence of them on the ground is very subtle. The Great North Road, aligned within one degree of true north, runs about 40 miles for reasons that are still a mystery.

OTHER RECREATIONAL OPPORTUNITIES

The loop road connecting the various sites in Chaco Canyon is paved, and bicycling is an easy, fun, and environmentally friendly way to visit the sites. The ruins of Chaco Canyon, as well as the canyon itself, lend themselves well to photography.

FOR MORE INFORMATION

SUPERINTENDENT'S OFFICE, Chaco Culture National Historical Park, P.O. Box 220, Nageezi, NM 87037; (505) 786-7014.

Chain of Craters
30 # Wilderness Study Area

This area of open conifer forest on old lava soil features a group of volcanic cinder cones.

New Mexico Wilderness Alliance

Chain of Craters

LOCATION	Southwest of Grants, adjoining the West Malpais Wilderness to the east, southwest of El Malpais National Monument
SIZE	15,200 acres Size recommended by the NM Wilderness Alliance: 17,440 acres
ELEVATION RANGE	7,400 to 8,345 feet at Cerro Lobo
MILES OF TRAILS	No marked or maintained trails
ECOSYSTEMS	Piñon-juniper, ponderosa pine, open grassland
ADMINISTRATION	BLM
TOPOGRAPHIC MAPS	Cerro Brillante and Cerro Hueco USGS 7.5-minute quadrangles
BEST SEASONS	Spring and fall
GETTING THERE	The best access is from the north, which you can reach from I-40 by taking Exit 81 at the west end of Grants, which puts you on Highway 53 leading to San Rafael, El Morro National Monument, and Zuni Pueblo. Take County Road 42 after the Ice Caves turnoff. This passes briefly through El Malpais National Monument before entering BLM land. Later, it skirts more of the monument and the West Malpais Wilderness as it goes south before eventually turning east and exiting at Highway 117. Under dry conditions, the county road is passable by most passenger cars, but you should avoid it in wet weather. Numerous dirt tracks branch off C42.
HIKING	Though no designated trails are here, interesting day hikes among the craters are possible over numerous seldom-traveled dirt roads.

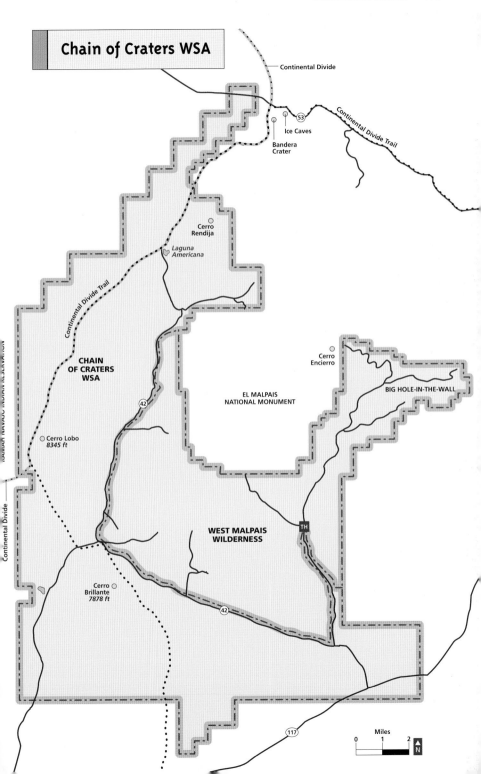

Chain of Craters WSA

Continental Divide

53

Continental Divide Trail

Ice Caves

Bandera Crater

Cerro Rendija

Laguna Americana

Continental Divide Trail

CHAIN OF CRATERS WSA

Cerro Encierro

EL MALPAIS NATIONAL MONUMENT

BIG HOLE-IN-THE-WALL

Cerro Lobo 8345 ft

42

WEST MALPAIS WILDERNESS

TH

Continental Divide

Cerro Brillante 7878 ft

42

NAVAJO INDIAN RESERVATION

117

Miles
0   1   2

N

AS ITS NAME IMPLIES, this wilderness study area on the west side of El Malpais National Monument features a series of volcanic cinder cones, part of the larger volcanic complex here and intended to be part of the overall land-management mosaic. The craters were created during eruptions 110,000 to 200,000 years ago. Some are only a few feet high, yet others tower hundreds of feet above the ground, the tallest in the study area being 8,345-foot Cerro Lobo ("wolf hill"). Among nearby cinder cones, Cerro Alto ("high hill") is higher at 8,512 feet, but it's on the Ramah Navajo Indian Reservation. Other craters in the WSA chain include 8,062-foot Cerro Brillante ("bright hill"), 7,878-foot Cerro Colorado ("red hill"), 8,164-foot Cerro Piedrita ("little rock hill"), and 8,247-foot Cerro Chato ("blunt hill").

The cones sit perched upon the generally flat landscape where a thin soil overlays the old lava flow and where ubiquitous lava chunks make for ankle-twisting footing. The soil also readily absorbs moisture, so the area is devoid of surface water. The area is interesting for day hikes but less so for backpacking. There are no trails leading to the cones' summits, although none really are needed. A few old roads exist, currently used mostly by hunters and piñon-nut gatherers, although they would be excellent for mountain biking exploration. Indeed, the area is used little by hikers because, truthfully, far more interesting volcanic sites are more readily accessible in the nearby monument and wilderness areas.

El Malpais
National Monument **31**

*This large, complex national monument contains
geologically recent volcanic features, including lava flows,
lava tubes, and cinder cones as well as sandstone bluffs.
This area also includes numerous archaeological sites.*

*Sandstone Bluffs at sunset
El Malpais National Monument*

LOCATION	Approximately 60 miles west of Albuquerque, south of Grants
SIZE	Size: 115,000 acres (monument); 263,000 (conservation area)
ELEVATION RANGE	Range: 6,000 to 8,372 feet
MILES OF TRAILS	26
ECOSYSTEMS	Open grassland, occasional piñon-juniper and ponderosa pine
ADMINISTRATION	National Park Service, BLM
TOPOGRAPHIC MAPS	El Malpais Recreation Guide Map, El Malpais National Monument
BEST SEASONS	Spring, fall
GETTING THERE	Vehicular access to El Malpais National Monument is via two paved roads heading southwest from I-40: Highway 117 east of Grants and Highway 53 at the west end of Grants. Dirt County Road 42 goes around the monument's southern and southwestern borders.
HIKING	The forbidding nature of the volcanic terrain limits hiking here to just a few trails designated and maintained by the monument.

IT'S CURIOUS HOW A LANDSCAPE AS BEAUTIFUL and interesting as this can have a name meaning "the bad land," which is one way to translate *el malpais*. To be sure, few people would argue that for commercial and agricultural purposes, the lava-filled valley south of Grants is indeed "bad." But for geologists, naturalists, archaeologists, and hikers, El Malpais is a place of discovery and delight—lava formations reminiscent of those in Hawaii, cinder cones, sinuous lava tubes, caves with perennial ice, natural arches, prehistoric rock art, homesteader cabins, and much more.

This area's story began about 290 million years ago when a sea advanced and retreated here, laying down deep deposits of sandstone and shale. This process continued intermittently until 70 million years ago when the sea withdrew not to return (at least not in foreseeable human history). Today, these sedimentary layers are spectacularly visible in the bluffs and formations along the monument's eastern side. I personally find the sandstone formations at least as fascinating as the better-known lava. Ten miles south of I-40 on Highway 117, just south of the visitor center, a dirt road branches right to lead to Sandstone Bluffs Overlook and a truly spectacular panorama of the monument. But the sandstone bluffs themselves are interesting to explore, and when my children were small we spent hours here, scrambling over the convoluted formations, looking into puddles for spadefoot toads and aquatic insects, and playing fantasy games. South of here, the Sandstone has weathered into isolated formations with evocative names like La Vieja, "the old woman." Still farther south, 17 miles south of I-40 on Highway 117, near a marked parking area, you'll find 165-foot-long La Ventana, "the window"—New Mexico's second largest natural arch. (Snake Bridge in western New Mexico on the Navajo Indian Reservation is the largest at 204 feet long, but it is generally inaccessible to the public.) Just south of La Ventana are the scenic cliffs known as the Narrows (Spanish, La Angostura). With the final departure of the seas, the sandstone and shale were eventually eroded into a broad valley, likely resembling so many others in the Four Corners area.

But volcanism has never been absent for long in New Mexico's geologic history—indeed, the present, with no active volcanoes, is an anomaly. Beginning about a million years ago, the placid sandstone valley was changed dramatically when the earth split and fiery molten rock spewed forth, eventually filling the valley with a river of lava 40 miles long and five miles wide. Many people seeing the lava flows near Grants assume they came from Mount Taylor, the 11,301-foot volcano looming conspicuously to the north, but in fact Mount Taylor had long been extinct by the time the lava flowed. Rather, most of the lava came from basalt and cinder cones to the west and south of the flows. Geologists have identified several flows—five major ones—ranging in age from about 700,000 years old to only 1,000 years. Indeed, oral traditions at nearby Acoma Pueblo tell of ancestors witnessing rivers of fire. Even non-geologists quickly develop a sense of the relative age of lava, especially as the young lava looks as if it flowed just last week.

One local geologist called El Malpais "poor man's Hawaii," and the resemblance to the lava formations there is striking. The New Mexican volcanic fields have even borrowed Hawaiian terminology; *pahoehoe* (pa-HOY-hoy) refers to "ropy" lava, while *aa* (AH-ah) is broken, crumbly lava. Exploring the lava flows is a uniquely interesting and challenging hiking experience. The youngest lava flows are by far the most

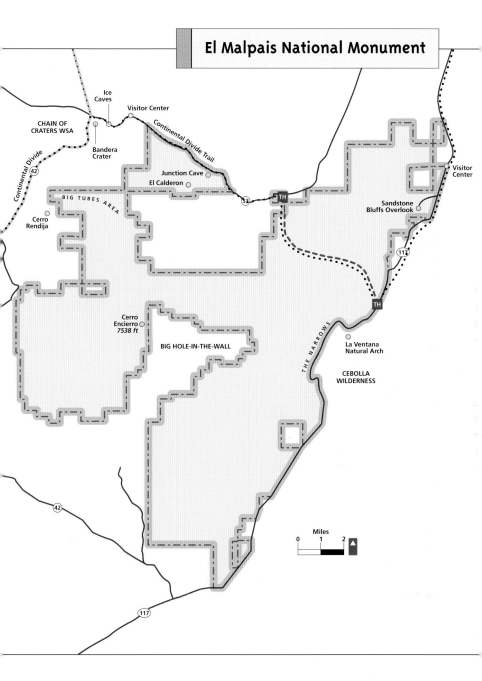

El Malpais National Monument

Ice Caves

Visitor Center

Continental Divide Trail

CHAIN OF CRATERS WSA

Continental Divide

(42)

Bandera Crater

Junction Cave

El Calderon

BIG TUBES AREA

(53)

TH

Cerro Rendija

Visitor Center

Sandstone Bluffs Overlook

(117)

TH

Cerro Encierro
7538 ft

BIG HOLE-IN-THE-WALL

THE NARROWS

La Ventana Natural Arch

CEBOLLA WILDERNESS

(42)

Miles
0   1   2

(117)

interesting; my favorite lava hike is on the Zuni-Acoma Trail from Highway 117 (see hike description p. 179). Here you hike past a few old-lava outliers and over sandy trails until you climb onto the McCarty's Flow, the monument's youngest. Here are collapsed lava bubbles, formations like frozen black caramel, and deep fissures.

But hiking on lava can be daunting. The surface is extremely uneven, and even old lava has wickedly sharp edges; most hikers welcome walking sticks here. Also, retracing your route can be very difficult because everything starts to look the same and the lava is impervious to worn trails. The few hiking routes you'll find here are marked with cairns. Precipitation vanishes in the porous lava, so you'll need to take water. And lava is heat-absorbing black, so hiking here in the summer can be like walking across a griddle. Except for the Zuni-Acoma Trail (see p. 179) and a few routes leading to lava tubes and other volcanic features, no hiking trails exist in the lava flows.

The lava flows are best explored from the east, from Highway 117, while the cinder cones, ice caves, and lava tubes are best accessed from the west, from Highway 53. A drive from Grants over Highway 53 to El Morro National Monument provides a spectacular overview of many volcanic features. Also, County Road 42 branches from here, giving access to the West Malpais Wilderness and the Chain of Craters Wilderness Study Area.

For centuries, most travelers simply avoided El Malpais. The desolate, difficult land became the realm of folklore with tales of hidden treasure and supernatural occurrences. By 1969, however, the BLM began acting to preserve and call attention to what increasingly was recognized as an area of national scenic and scientific significance. Studies of management alternatives culminated on December 31, 1987, when the area was declared a national monument and national conservation area. Management of the 114,000-acre monument was given to the National Park Service, while responsibility for the 263,600-acre conservation area went to the BLM.

Yet despite the area's size—with more than 376,000 acres, the combined monument and conservation area constitute the second largest section of wildland in New Mexico—and despite being easily accessible not only from Albuquerque but also from I-40, the monument conservation area remains relatively unknown and seldom visited.

DAY HIKE: EL CALDERON AREA
One-way length: 1.5 miles
Low and high elevations: 7,277 and 7,612 feet
Difficulty: easy

This hike takes you to one of the more accessible lava tubes at El Malpais National Monument. To reach the trailhead, drive south 20 miles on Highway 53 from I-40 at Grants. On the highway's left side, a sign reading "El Calderon Area" marks a rutted dirt road leading south 0.25 mile to a parking area. Just south of the parking area is a collapsed lava tube; don't descend here but follow a well-worn trail from the parking area about 100 yards east to Junction Cave.

You don't need to be a spelunker to explore the cave, but you do need protective clothing—the sharp-edged lava makes this no place for shorts and tennies. And you'll need several reliable sources of light because the cave quickly becomes very dark. Something to help you maintain sure footing, such as a walking stick, would be a good idea. Don't panic if you encounter a sleeping bat clinging to the walls; both you and the bat will be happier if you leave it alone.

*Sandstone outlier along Continental Divide Trail
El Malpais National Monument*

After exploring Junction Cave, return to the parking area and the trail leading to Bat Cave. After 0.25 mile you'll pass between dramatic double sinkholes. Another 0.5 mile over pleasant open country brings you to Bat Cave, with two entrances: the west is for exploring and is similar to Junction Cave; the east entrance leads to a cave inhabited by a colony of Mexican freetail bats. In the summer, their exits from the cave can be observed at dusk from the knoll above the cave's entrance. Note that the cave's east entrance is closed to hikers, not only to protect the bats but, also, because they can carry diseases dangerous to humans. Please respect the bats' sanctuary. This colony has declined in recent years, devastated by pesticides used years ago but still lingering in the soil, and human disturbance further threatens the colony.

After exploring Bat Cave, hike uphill 0.75 mile west to El Calderon Crater. There's no obvious trail; stay to the right of the fence and watch for a large lava trench on your right. The modest crater, nestled among ponderosa pines, is among the oldest in the monument.

DAY HIKE: ICE CAVES AND BANDERA CRATER
One-way length: 0.2 mile to the Ice Cave;
0.6 mile to Bandera Crater
Low and high elevations: 7,855 and 8,000 feet
Difficulty: easy

As of this writing, negotiations still were underway to see if this property would become part of El Malpais National Monument, rather than operated privately as a fee-charging attraction. I find the ice cave, touted as the main attraction, somewhat underwhelming, but it's interesting nonetheless. And Bandera Crater is well worth the fee and the hike. You can reach Ice Cave and Bandera Crater by driving 24.7 miles south of I-40 on Highway 53 to a turnoff marked by a sign. From the parking area, the routes to both are clearly marked. El Malpais has six ice caves, but this is the largest, and one cannot help but appreciate the irony of a perennial layer of ice nestled beneath once-fiery lava. And while El Malpais has numerous cinder cones, Bandera Crater—1,000 feet high, 200 feet across, and 640 feet deep—is the largest and most spectacular. The trail is an old road of moderate grade that takes you about halfway up the crater until suddenly you turn a corner and are confronted with the crater's huge gaping maw.

DAY HIKE: SANDSTONE BLUFFS OVERLOOK
One-way length: 1 to 2 miles
Low and high elevations: 6,700 and 7,000 feet
Difficulty: easy
(except for scrambling up and down)

Although rarely advertised as such, Sandstone Bluffs Overlook makes an excellent short hike. You reach the bluffs by driving south from I-25 on Highway 117 10 miles. A sign on the right indicates the short drive to the bluffs. You won't find a trailhead at the bluffs, but I've always simply headed north, keeping fairly close to the rim. The eroded formations are fun to explore, especially with children. Eventually there's a break in the rim, allowing a descent to the valley below where a dirt track leads you along the lava's edge back to the base of the bluffs. From here you simply scramble back up the cliffs to the top; it's easier than it looks.

SHUTTLE HIKE: ZUNI – ACOMA TRAIL
One-way length: 7.5 miles
Low and high elevations: 6,850 and 6,865 feet
Difficulty: moderate to strenuous

This hike traverses the lava flow, following a route used since pre-Columbian times by Puebloan Indians in their travels. Cairns dot the trackless lava. The recommended crossover is from east to west because this brings you sooner to the youngest and most interesting lava flows. Footing can be very treacherous on the sharp lava, and it's easy to get lost. So don't leave one cairn without having spotted the next. You won't find any water, and a black lava field is no place to be during hot weather.

To reach the eastern trailhead from I-40 take the Highway 117 exit east of Grants and drive 15 miles south. The trailhead is on the right. To hike from the west, exit from I-40 at the west end of Grants onto Highway 53. Then drive 18 miles south. You'll find the trailhead to the left.

OTHER RECREATIONAL OPPORTUNITIES

While the lava itself allows no activities but hiking, in the public lands surrounding the lava are numerous old roads that would be excellent for mountain biking; be sure to check with the visitor centers as to where bike access is allowed.

FOR MORE INFORMATION

EL MALPAIS NATIONAL MONUMENT, P.O. Box 939, Grants, NM 87020; (505) 285-4641.

Visitor centers are located on the monument's east side, along Highway 117, and on its west side, along Highway 53.

32 Mesita Blanca and Eagle Peak Wilderness Study Areas

Characterized by broken mesas, canyons, cinder cones, and associated lava flows, these two contiguous areas include significant archaeological and historical sites.

LOCATION	West of Quemado, north of Highway 60
SIZE	Mesita Blanca, 16,429 acres; Eagle Peak, 49,960 acres Size recommended by the NM Wilderness Alliance: 33,167 acres (combined)
ELEVATION RANGE	6,400 to 7,679 feet
MILES OF TRAILS	No marked or maintained trails
ECOSYSTEMS	Piñon-juniper, ponderosa pine, grassland
ADMINISTRATION	BLM
TOPOGRAPHIC MAPS	Zuni Salt Lake, Lake Armijo, Tejana Mesa Southwest, and Blaines Lake USGS 7.5-minute quadrangles
BEST SEASONS	Spring, summer, fall
GETTING THERE	From Highway 60 west of Quemado, County Road A007 separates the two WSAs and provides vehicular access.
HIKING	Limited. While no designated trails exist here, remnants of primitive roads facilitate foot travel.

Petaca Pinta Wilderness Study Area

Petaca Pinta ("painted box") is a small, very isolated area characterized by colorful eroded mesas, rolling piñon-juniper woodlands, desert scrublands, and the deep gorge of Blue Water Canyon.

New Mexico Wilderness Alliance

Mouth of Blue Water Canyon

LOCATION	50 miles southwest of Albuquerque, 20 miles south of Laguna Pueblo
SIZE	11,668 acres Size recommended by the NM Wilderness Alliance: 14,680 acres
ELEVATION RANGE	6,100 to 7,300 feet
MILES OF TRAILS	No marked or maintained trails
ECOSYSTEMS	Piñon-juniper, desert scrub, canyon riparian
ADMINISTRATION	BLM
TOPOGRAPHIC MAPS	Broom Mountain, Cerro del Oro, East Mesa, and Marmon Ranch USGS 7.5-minute quadrangles; Acoma Pueblo 1:100K map
BEST SEASONS	Spring, fall
GETTING THERE	From I-40 west of Albuquerque, take Highway 6 southeast for almost 2 miles. From here you will need to follow a current map, such as the USGS 1:100K.
HIKING	Limited. Although you won't find delineated routes here, cross-country hiking is relatively easy.

Techado Mesa
Wilderness Inventory Unit

34

The basalt-capped Techado Mesa dominates the heavily wooded mesas, slopes, and small, cliff-edged valleys of this wild place.

LOCATION	Southeast of the Cebolla Wilderness and southeast of Grants
SIZE	19,000 acres Size recommended by the NM Wilderness Alliance: 19,480 acres
ELEVATION RANGE	7,540 to 8,430 feet at Techado Mesa
MILES OF TRAILS	No marked or maintained trails
ECOSYSTEMS	Ponderosa pine, piñon-juniper, scrub oak, as well as meadow grassland and playa wetlands
ADMINISTRATION	BLM
TOPOGRAPHIC MAPS	Wiley Mesa and Wild Horse Canyon USGS 7.5-minute quadrangles
BEST SEASONS	Spring, summer, fall
GETTING THERE	Access via seldom-used dirt roads separating the unit from the Cebolla Wilderness.
HIKING	The complex system of mesas, cliffs, and canyons begs exploration by experienced cross-country hikers and campers.

West Malpais Wilderness

*This wilderness area features rolling grassland
and a ponderosa forest atop a bed of lava flows.*

Pahoehoe lava

LOCATION	South of Grants, south and west of El Malpais National Monument
SIZE	39,700 acres
ELEVATION RANGE	7,100 to 7,808 feet
MILES OF TRAILS	Open ponderosa forest, grassland
ECOSYSTEMS	No designated trails
ADMINISTRATION	BLM
TOPOGRAPHIC MAPS	Ice Caves, Cerro Hueco, Ice Caves Southeast, and Cerro Brillante USGS 7.5-minute quadrangles
BEST SEASONS	Spring, fall
GETTING THERE	Access to the West Malpais Wilderness is via dirt County Road 42, which parallels the wilderness on the south and southwest to connect paved Highways 117 and 53.
HIKING	Hiking here is severely limited by the forbidding nature of the volcanic terrain and the lack of trails.

TO PEOPLE FOR WHOM WILDERNESS is synonymous with natural grandeur—Yellowstone, the Colorado Rockies, Canyonlands—the West Malpais Wilderness will probably be a disappointment. Sure, the nearby El Malpais National Monument is spectacularly scenic. But the wilderness here is south of the great lava flows, the dramatic cinder cones, and the towering sandstone cliffs. When hiking here, you stumble over chunks of lava, a reminder that beneath these rolling grasslands and ponderosa-capped hummocks is a volcanic soul. But when you leave you'll remember more than volcanism. You'll appreciate the subtle natural forces of the inexorable weathering of even the hardest rocks, of wind filling swales and hollows with dust and sand, of grass colonizing and becoming dominant, and of ponderosa pines establishing outposts.

From a management perspective, the West Malpais Wilderness is perhaps more fragile than the better-known *malpais*; after all, the *malpais* almost by definition is "bad land," good for nothing but interesting photographs. The West Malpais grasslands, however, are good for something—grazing. You'll see ranch roads, stock tanks, man-made water impoundments, windmills, and cattle. As with other New Mexico wilderness areas, grazing continues within the West Malpais Wilderness. Indeed, it's not uncommon for a rancher to ride up to a hiker simply to check him or her out: "No hard feelings, just checking. By the way, if you get caught in a storm up in the Hole, there's an old house you can use for shelter. Be careful of lightning. The *malpais* seems to draw it, and it really gets to popping in there."

The wilderness was established in 1987 with the legislation that established the monument and associated National Conservation Area. The areas combined make a large complex of land management. Consider the non-wilderness area of El Malpais National Conservation Area lands to the west and east, the Cebolla Wilderness to the east, and El Malpais National Monument to the north—376,000 acres in all. The West Malpais Wilderness encompasses 39,700 acres, a fraction of this total area. Like the other units, the West Malpais Wilderness has volcanism as its dominant theme, although here the volcanic presence is understated. The majority of the wilderness area is covered with some of the area's oldest basalt flows. The area includes, however, a 6,000-acre ponderosa parkland island (or *kipuka*, to use the Hawaiian term) known as Big Hole-in-the-Wall. Beneath the *kipuka* are old flows and more recent lava encircles the island, including portions of the McCarty's flow (at 500 to 1,000 years old, it's the area's youngest). You don't have to be a geologist to tell the difference: the old lava is encrusted with lichens, often in a matrix of soil and weathered a dusty brown, whereas the very young lava looks like it hardened only yesterday.

You can access the wilderness from County Road 42, which connects Highway 117 on the south and Highway 53 on the north and forms the wilderness's south and west boundaries. Under good conditions this dirt road is passable by passenger cars, although a high-clearance vehicle is desirable. The road can be impassable to almost all vehicles when it's wet and muddy.

The West Malpais Wilderness is not a hiker's wilderness. It's not that you can't hike here, but there are no trails, no hiking guides, and few obvious routes or destinations. Backpackers will find no established backcountry campsites. And you won't find water, except for what humans have captured with earthen impoundments or windmills or the rare and ephemeral puddle following a rainstorm. (Summer is not the best hiking season.) You'll take home no backpack patches as souvenirs, no "I hiked the West Malpais Wilderness" bumper stickers. No, as stated before, the appeal of the West Malpais Wilderness is more subtle. A Zen wilderness, if you will.

Wildlife is abundant here. The combination of eco-types supports deer, pronghorn antelope, Abert's squirrel, turkey, and band-tail pigeon. If you're attentive, you'll also see coyotes, foxes, bobcats, rabbits, and bats. And the area includes a rich assembly of birds, especially raptors. Yet as you hike the grasslands and ponderosa parks, you have a sense of something missing—large animal species like bear, bison, and elk—whose presence would give the cachet of wilderness to this area. Something besides cows.

If you do hike here, heed the following caveats. First, what might appear from a distance to be smooth, easy ground is actually peppered with chunks of lava, making for very unstable footing. In other areas, the lava is more obvious, but you'll still need to wear sturdy leather boots, and preferably ones you won't mind cut and scuffed; nothing is harder on boots than lava. So leave your dog at home, unless you can improvise boots for your pet's paws. Wearing shorts is not a good idea either; the lava and ubiquitous cacti can be brutal. Take plenty of water and sunscreen. And find some means to record your positions, especially if you're going cross-country. The lava formations and ponderosa stands may seem distinctive, but after a mile or two they'll all look the same. And give yourself a broad time margin. Trying to hike out of the *malpais* at night would be a nightmare.

Despite all the caveats and reservations, the West Malpais Wilderness remains . . . wilderness. I recall driving near the wilderness on a dirt road one evening, watching a thunderstorm approach from the west. Dark rain streamers hung down like the chaps of ghostly buffalo, and the light from the declining sun filtered through the clouds. The grasslands became a surreal, iridescent green and highlighted the strange stone cairns heaped atop a couple of ridges. I realized that seldom had I beheld a scene more beautiful, or more elusive.

DAY HIKE: BIG HOLE-IN-THE-WALL
One-way length: 4.0 miles
Low and high elevations: 7,120 and 7,260 feet
Difficulty: moderate

With 6,000 acres of rolling grassland and old lava hummocks topped by ponderosa pines, Big Hole-in-the-Wall is the largest *kipuka* (island surrounded by a lava sea)

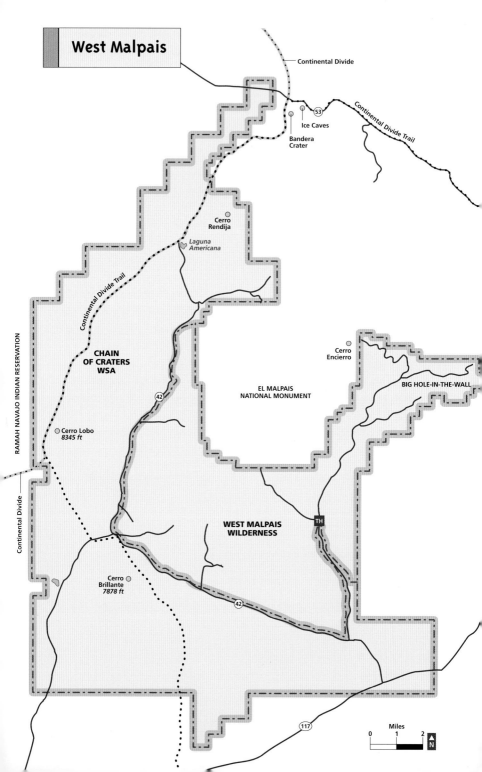

West Malpais

Continental Divide

Ice Caves

53

Continental Divide Trail

Bandera
Crater

Cerro
Rendija

Laguna
Americana

Continental Divide Trail

CHAIN
OF CRATERS
WSA

RAMAH NAVAJO INDIAN RESERVATION

Cerro
Encierro

EL MALPAIS
NATIONAL MONUMENT

BIG HOLE-IN-THE-WALL

42

Cerro Lobo
8345 ft

Continental Divide

WEST MALPAIS
WILDERNESS

TH

Cerro
Brillante
7878 ft

42

117

Miles
0   1   2

N

in El Malpais complex. To reach the trailhead from I-40, drive 34.5 miles south on Highway 117 to where dirt County Road 42 branches right. Follow this two miles to a wilderness sign, where you take another right-branching dirt road. After four miles you arrive at the trailhead. (Note: avoid these roads during and after heavy rains.) No trails are marked, but an old road heads north across open country for about a mile and then into the lava area that hosts an open, grass-carpeted ponderosa forest. It's easy hiking, but stick to the road; the ubiquitous lava makes hiking cross-country here harder than it might appear, and the topography is very confusing. After about two miles, you enter the Hole.

FOR MORE INFORMATION

EL MALPAIS NATIONAL MONUMENT, P.O. Box 939, Grants, NM 87020; (505) 285-4641.

BUREAU OF LAND MANAGEMENT, P.O. Box 846, Grants, NM 87020; (505) 285-5406.

The Datil-Mogollon Volcanic Plateau

This region has New Mexico's greatest wilderness array, containing not only the state's first and third largest wildernesses but also its greatest ecological diversity. The concept of setting aside land solely to protect its wildness was born here with the creation of the Gila Wilderness in 1924. In 1998, this was the setting where Mexican wolves were returned to the wild. Here was the last redoubt of grizzlies in New Mexico, and streams here contain the endangered Gila cutthroat trout. Within this region, in the Gila Wilderness, is the farthest you can get from a road in New Mexico. The human history of this area is long and fascinating, albeit often tragic, and includes prehistoric and vanished cliff dwellers, Spanish explorers, mountain men, and miners. Army troops and Chiricahua Apaches who fought many of their final battles here. Today, bitter conflicts between the opposing views of land ownership and land use, and the clash between the New West and the Old West, continue some of these age-old battles. Nevertheless, the region is rich in beautiful hot springs—nature's way of saying, "Welcome, and be healed."

The Datil-Mogollon Volcanic Plateau is bounded on the south by I-10, on the west by Arizona, on the east by the Rio Grande, and on the north by Highway 60. The landforms within this vast region are united by their origin—the widespread, cataclysmic volcanism that occurred throughout southwestern New Mexico during the early Cenozoic Era (40 to 25 million years ago). These were perhaps the greatest volcanic events ever to happen in New Mexico—and that's saying a lot, given the state's volcanic history. The lava flows, breccias, pumice, and compressed ash, as well as subsurface igneous rocks, created the Datil-Mogollon Volcanic Plateau.

While the region is generally arid, it nonetheless includes several large drainages, and the Gila Wilderness has numerous streams and springs. (Hikers still need to consider water availability in their planning.) The largest and most significant of these is the Gila River, whose watershed includes much of the vast Gila and Aldo Leopold Wildernesses. Within the Gila Wilderness, the river has three named forks: East, Middle, and West. These were traditional travel routes, and much of today's wilderness hiking follows these rivers. Because these rivers run within narrow, vertical-sided canyons, hiking these routes usually requires many river crossings. The lower Gila River is particularly popular with river rafters.

View of peaks and buttes, Apache Kid Wilderness

The San Francisco River also drains the region. With headwaters in Arizona, it enters New Mexico west of Luna and, paralleling Highway 180, runs south through a broad, fertile valley. South of Glenwood the river heads west to re-enter Arizona but not before passing through the Gila National Forest's Lower San Francisco Box Wilderness Study Area, an 8,800-acre wild and scenic canyon visited by boaters and rafters more than hikers.

The region's third major drainage is the Mimbres River, which heads on the western Black Range, southwest of Reeds Peak, and runs south through a wide, pleasant valley. It eventually travels past Deming on its way toward the Mexican border, but long before it reaches Mexico it has ceased flowing, at least on the surface.

The region's other major physiographic feature aside from the mountains, is the vast, treeless, enclosed basin south of Highway 60 and southeast of Highway 12 known as the Plains of San Agustin. Once the bed of a long-gone lake, 45 miles long and 12 miles wide, the plains are now mostly grazing land except in their northeast part. Here you'll find the Very Large Array, the world's largest radio telescope—an assemblage of twenty-seven 2.5-ton antennas mounted on rails.

The topography in this region is extremely complex and often extremely rugged, but the presence of numerous large wildernesses here has less to do with geology than with ethnology, or in a word: Apaches. Early maps drawn by Spanish explorers show Apaches living here, and for centuries these fierce, resourceful, implacable people discouraged settlement; even as late as the 1880s, prospectors entered the Gila Country at their peril. The man who discovered the fabulously rich silver lode at Lake Valley was killed by Apaches on the day of his discovery. The renegade Apache Kid was killed in the San Mateo Mountains in 1894. Although popularly depicted as a desert tribe, the Apaches in fact were a mountain people, and in their mountain strongholds they were all but invincible. This fact became real for me during a trip into the Black Range, when I found the 30 graves of soldiers ambushed by Victorio's Apaches. As I looked upon the silent mounds, and then at the craggy outcrops above me, I sensed just how vulnerable non-Apaches would be in these mountains.

So while Europeans had explored and settled New Mexico for centuries, especially along the Rio Grande, they had made few inroads into the numerous mountains of the Datil-Mogollon region. Indeed, when young Aldo Leopold arrived here in 1909 to become a forest ranger, he found one of America's last great wildernesses.

Today, the Gila Wilderness he fought to create in 1924 is New Mexico's largest wilderness. At 558,065 acres, it is more than twice as large as the next largest wilderness, the Pecos. It was even larger before 202,016 acres were cut out of it to create the Aldo Leopold Wilderness. And while the Gila Wilderness is almost as well-known as the Pecos Wilderness, it receives significantly less use simply because it is far from large population centers. From Albuquerque I can be at a Pecos trailhead in just a couple of hours, but I have to endure a minimum of five hours driving to hike the Gila. Day trips are practical only if you're based in Silver City or another nearby community. For most New Mexico hikers, exploring the Gila requires commitment.

It's worth it, of course. The wilderness has an extensive and well-developed trail network. Finding water is not as problematic as elsewhere in New Mexico. The scenery is interesting and beautiful, and the terrain is diverse, from piñon-juniper-ponderosa pine uplands to river bottoms lined with deciduous trees—cottonwoods, sycamores, willows, and walnuts—to 10,000-foot summits cloaked in spruce and fir. The area is rich in unexpected delights, from hot springs to cliff dwellings. Wildlife is abundant. When groups, whether the Boy Scouts or the Sierra Club, want their members to have a wilderness experience, they often come to the Gila Wilderness—and are rarely disappointed.

By contrast, the region's second largest wilderness, the Aldo Leopold, is little-known even in New Mexico. Centered on the Black Range—steep, rugged, and remote—the Aldo Leopold Wilderness has not had the same publicity, and its access and logistical problems are even greater. Mention the Black Range to most New Mexicans, and they'll say they think they've heard of it—but don't really know where it is. The Forest Service is considering abandoning some hiking trails simply because not enough people use them.

That wasn't true 100 years ago, however. This densely forested region of a million steep, dry canyons and ridges was scoured by prospectors, and small, ephemeral mining camps sprang up, particularly on the range's east side. When the minerals played out or proved disappointing, the miners left, and today the mountains primarily attract hunters. In the absence of humans, game is abundant—mule deer, elk, and wild turkeys. (On one trip into the Black Range I saw more wild turkeys than during the rest of my life combined; I actually yelled at them to stop gobbling around my campsite in the morning because I wanted to sleep!)

The Continental Divide and the Continental Divide Trail go over the northern Black Range in the Aldo Leopold Wilderness. Although the Black Range Ranger District of the Gila National Forest is enthusiastically committed to putting the route on the ground, much work remains.

Northeast of the Black Range are the Magdalena and San Mateo Mountains, two mid-size ranges whose gray and pinkish volcanic rocks reveal roots in the Datil-Mogollon Volcanic Plateau. The Magdalena Mountains, located west of Socorro and just south of Magdalena, resemble the Black Range with piñon-juniper-ponderosa forests rising to spruce-fir forests and grassy meadows above 9,000 feet. The Magdalenas, however, include no designated or proposed wilderness, although the BLM Devils Backbone Wilderness Study Area is at the range's southern extremity—without any legal access. This lack of wilderness designation is not because the mountains aren't wild, but rather because of longstanding mining claims (dream on!) and the presence of roads and other human artifacts. In reality, the Magdalenas include large tracts of wildland and deserve more hiking attention than they've received.

That can also be said of the Magdalenas' slightly larger sister range to the southwest, the San Mateo Mountains. Geologically and ecologically similar to the Magdalenas (and to the Black Range as well), the San Mateos are not close to any population centers (even counting the village of Magdalena as a population center!), and can only be reached by long drives over dirt roads of varying roughness.

The San Mateos include the Withington and Apache Kid Wildernesses. (Actually, these should be one wilderness.) Like their sibling ranges, the Magdalenas and the Black Range, the San Mateos are characterized by arid lower slopes vegetated with piñon-juniper (including some impressive alligator junipers), yucca, Apache plume, and Gambel oak, changing to ponderosa pine and eventually spruce-fir as the steep slopes culminate at summits and plateaus over 9,000 feet.

Wildlife is abundant in the San Mateos; Aldo Leopold, when he was with the Forest Service in the Southwest, considered the San Mateos one of the richest wildlife habitats he'd ever seen. And water, while scarce, is not absent. The San Mateos have a well-developed trail system that receives very little use. (On one hike in the San Mateos I realized that bears used the trail more than humans—talk about mixed emotions!) People who complain about "humans loving the wilderness to death" are not talking about the San Mateo wilderness.

Nor are they talking about the Blue Range Wilderness, along the Arizona border. Geologically and ecologically, this wilderness is more akin to the nearby Gila Wilderness than to the wildlands of the Black Range, the San Mateos, or the Magdalenas. Indeed, the Blue Range Wilderness is separated from the Gila Wilderness only by the San Francisco River valley. The Blue Range Wilderness is much smaller and much less known than the Gila Wilderness, but is similarly characterized by uplands and mountains to 8,000 feet, forested with piñon-juniper, oak, and ponderosa pines,

Along the Gila River

and cleft by meandering steep-walled canyons. The Blue Range Wilderness, managed by the Gila National Forest—Glenwood Ranger District, is adjacent to the Blue Range Primitive Area in Arizona, managed by the Apache National Forest. It was here that in January 1998, a family of Mexican gray wolves was released into the wild, finally restoring this species to the Southwest.

In addition to the designated wildernesses, the region also includes several BLM and Forest Service Wilderness Study Areas. The BLM Continental Divide WSA is in the mountainous uplands south of the Plains of San Agustin and at 68,761 acres is the among the state's largest WSAs. Its two salient features are 9,212-foot Pelona Peak and the Continental Divide.

West of the Plains of San Agustin is the small BLM Horse Mountain WSA—5,032 acres centered on the volcanic cinder cone of 9,450-foot Horse Mountain.

The remaining WSAs are along the region's western margin near the Arizona border; most are centered on streams. South of the Lower San Francisco Box WSA (already described) is the 18,680-acre Gila National Forest Hell Hole WSA, on Blue and Sawmill Creeks. Adjacent and complementary to the Hell Hole WSA is the 932-acre BLM Apache Box WSA on Apache Creek.

Further south, like a sleeve around the Gila River as it prepares to leave New Mexico, are the 21,656-acre BLM Blue Creek WSA and the adjacent 8,555-acre BLM Gila Lower Box WSA. To the east, along the Gila River, is the 41,645-acre Gila Middle Box Wilderness unit.

In recent times, some of New Mexico's fiercest environmental battles have occurred in the Datil-Mogollon Volcanic Plateau region, with traditional economies and lifestyles pitted against changing concerns and priorities. When the Gila Wilderness was created in 1924, it was with the enthusiastic support of local ranchers, who felt wilderness designation would protect their grazing lands. Now, environmental groups have sued—successfully—to have cattle grazing reduced or prohibited in the wilderness, charging overgrazing and habitat destruction, especially along riparian areas. Similarly, concern for protecting old-growth forest, vital habitat for species such as the Mexican spotted owl, has clashed with local logging economies.

The region has become one of heated emotions and highly polarized opinions. Sparsely populated (modest Silver City and Socorro, on the region's periphery, are the two largest population centers), the area has few economic alternatives. Primary industries have traditionally been resource-based—mining, logging, and ranching. Furthermore, deep family roots in the area have instilled in many people a sense of ownership that sometimes borders on xenophobia. Dislike and distrust of government, especially the federal government, are deep and intense here, in part because the overwhelming majority of the land is federally owned.

At the same time, environmentalists see the area as too precious to lose to short-term financial gain. The region has a history of environmental disasters, including the extermination of large predators, strip-mining, wilderness-dissecting road construction, and more. If ever there was a situation where human resolve could lead to lasting and significant benefit—and actually restore wilderness to its full potential—it will be here. Much of what was lost, including exterminated species like Mexican wolves, river otters, and even jaguars, grizzlies, and bison, can be restored. But first it is imperative to protect what exists now against further degradation.

As I hiked along the West Fork of the Gila River, I reflected on the irony of this serenely beautiful place staging such a tumultuous history. Apaches, prospectors, and feuding homesteaders filled my mind. But very real conflicts over the Gila Country continue to the present day.

36 Aldo Leopold Wilderness

One of New Mexico's three wilderness giants,
Aldo Leopold is a seldom-visited, relatively little-
known wilderness centered on the extremely
rugged Black Range.

Broad view of the Aldo Leopold Wilderness

LOCATION	West of Truth or Consequences, north of Highway 152
SIZE	202,016 acres
ELEVATION RANGE	6,000 to 10,165 feet at McKnight Mountain
MILES OF TRAILS	Approximately 200
ECOSYSTEMS	Chihuahuan Desert scrub and grassland, piñon-juniper, ponderosa pine, spruce-fir
ADMINISTRATION	Gila National Forest–Black Range and Wilderness Ranger Districts
TOPOGRAPHIC MAPS	Gila National Forest–Aldo Leopold Wilderness
BEST SEASONS	Spring, summer, fall
GETTING THERE	Access to the Aldo Leopold Wilderness from the east is greatly limited by private land. From the south, access is by hiking along the Black Range crest from Emory Pass and Highway 152. From the west, access is from forest roads heading east from Forest Road 150. Access from the north is from forest roads heading south of Highway 59.
HIKING	Hiking in this vast and interesting wilderness is limited only by poor access sometimes to trailheads. For this reason, this wilderness is best explored by persons prepared for multi-day trips.

IN 1976, AN ARTICLE in the *Denver Post Empire Magazine* called the Black Range "the Wildest Wilderness in the West." One would hate to get into wilderness one-upmanship, but the Black Range, which includes much of the Aldo Leopold Wilderness, is indeed wild and nothing has happened since 1976 to diminish this. Mention to most New Mexicans, even hikers, that you're going backpacking in the Black Range of the Aldo Leopold Wilderness, and you're likely to hear, after a brief pause, "Where is that?" Curious, as the Aldo Leopold is the state's third largest wilderness, only slightly smaller than the Pecos Wilderness and more than three times larger than number four. Curious, as the Black Range, stretching 100 miles north to south, is the state's largest mountain range.

Well, maybe not so curious when you consider that the wilderness is in such a sparsely populated part of the state. It must compete with the far-better-known Gila Wilderness, adjacent to the west; and access from the east, from whence most hikers would arrive, is extremely poor. The mountains are dauntingly difficult and lack the charismatic attractions of other wildernesses. Yet people who, despite all this, have visited the Aldo Leopold Wilderness will say it has everything one would want in a wilderness and more; it's just more difficult to get to and lacks publicity.

What publicity the mountains have received historically has been negative. Spanish-speaking New Mexicans living along the Rio Grande called the range *Sierra Diablo*, "devil range." They looked upon these mountains with fear and aversion with good reason. In the deep canyons and along the high ridges of the Black Range, fierce and well-armed Apaches led by Mangas Coloradas, Cochise, Nana, Victorio, and Geronimo lived and controlled all entry to their territory. It was perfect country for them: remote and mountainous, containing plants and animals they needed for sustenance, eminently suited for ambush and defense. I once hiked into Animas Canyon, on the range's east side, and encountered an unexpected reminder of this fact. I was seeking a place called Victorio Park, where Victorio and his people camped near a spring. Nearby was a tributary canyon named Massacre Canyon. On a flat near the canyon's mouth, I came upon rows of oblong, low earthen mounds—the mute graves of U.S. Army soldiers killed in an ambush on September 18, 1879. The fear that people had for these mountains was based on more than superstition. Even today, the mountains, when viewed from the east, have a dark, somber, forbidding appearance; the name Black Range is easy to understand.

In 1846, the year New Mexico became part of the U.S., Lt. William H. Emory, guided by Kit Carson, led an expedition over the mountains, crossing at a pass now bearing his name, Emory Pass—a major access point for the mountains.

In 1877, prospectors found gold in the range's eastern foothills north of Hillsboro, and soon several ephemeral mining camps sprang up, but they had little impact on the wilderness. The Apache threat was always formidable: George Daly, the man who discovered the fabulously wealthy silver deposit called the Bridal Chamber, at Lake Valley, was killed by Apaches the same day he made his discovery. By 1900 the Apaches were gone, but then so were most of the minerals. A few of the towns survive: Winston, Kingston, Chloride—all the haunts of ghosts and hidden relics.

Now even the prospectors are gone, and fewer people travel in these mountains than in previous centuries. As wilderness advocate Corry McDonald observed:

"If Lt. Emory, Victorio, Geronimo, or any other of those of the shadowed past could visit the area today, they would find it much as they last saw it."

So when the vast Gila Wilderness was designated in 1924, it was only natural that the lands that now constitute the Aldo Leopold Wilderness be included. The two became separate after 1932, when the Forest Service created an "administrative road" up North Star Canyon to North Star Mesa. Because this affected the area's wilderness status, in 1933 the lands east of the road became the Black Range Primitive Area. In 1970, the Forest Service proposed a 150,731-acre wilderness; the New Mexico Wilderness Study Committee countered with 231,737 acres. The area took the name of the conservationist responsible for the original Gila Wilderness.

Ironically, Aldo Leopold surely would have disapproved of splitting the wilderness, even if what was created does bear his name. It's tantalizing to dream about the two reunited into a super-wilderness that could support all kinds of exciting possibilities, including the reintroduction of vanished species (the grizzly, for example).

In the words of a retired forest ranger I once met, the Black Range is "damned rough country," and for that we should be grateful, because that is what has kept these mountains wild and untamed. Unlike the Gila Wilderness, with its sinuous, flat canyon bottoms, rolling uplands, and grassy parks, the Aldo Leopold Wilderness guards its mountains with steep slopes, narrow canyons, and difficult access.

Furthermore, the Black Range has undergone several forest fires in the last ten years, wreaking havoc upon an already decrepit trail system. On the other hand, these fires have effectively jump-started the ecosystem, with extensive aspen stands now adding diversity to the conifer forest. A forest ranger has predicted that as the aspen stands become established, their brilliant yellow fall foliage will make the Black Range Crest, Trails 74 and 79, among the premier fall hikes in the Southwest.

But for now, many trails in the Aldo Leopold Wilderness are more evident on the map than on the land. Some trails may be abandoned simply because so few people travel them. Once a friend and I were trying to find a tributary to the trail we were hiking. The map indicated it was right where we were, but nothing on the ground looked like a trail. Then suddenly my friend said, "Here, I found it." He pointed to a single, weathered blaze on a ponderosa pine. That was it, only a distant memory of a tread on the ground. Corry McDonald put it well: "The Black Range is an archetype of a wilderness, defending itself."

Poor access has indeed retarded hiking in the Aldo Leopold Wilderness. On the east are private ranch lands, including the sprawling Ladder Ranch now owned by media mogul Ted Turner, who has removed cattle and introduced bison. From the south, the best access is along the Black Range Crest north of Emory Pass, although trailheads such as Railroad Canyon (farther west on Highway 152) also lead into the wilderness. From the west, the most popular trail is probably that along the headwaters of the Mimbres River leading to the crest and 10,011-foot Reeds Peak and 10,165-foot McKnight Peak, the range's two highest summits. From the north, access is over many miles of Gila National Forest trails and roads heading south from Highway 59. The Continental Divide and the Continental Divide Trail both run through the Aldo Leopold Wilderness, which may with time result in more hikers through the area. For now, most people who use the area are hunters. All the species one associates with New Mexico mountain wilderness are here and in abundance: deer, elk, black bears, mountain lions, wild turkeys, and more. On my Animas Canyon trip, I saw more wild turkeys than in my entire hiking career. In fact, their enthusiastic gobbling woke me up in the morning. I never thought I'd be yelling at wildlife to shut up!

Spring in the Black Range is utterly magnificent. Summers are hot, but the elevation mitigates this somewhat. Fall is a pleasant and beautiful time of year; winter can bring savage storms and deep snow. Water is infrequent and unreliable on mountain slopes, but springs do exist, and the canyons often have perennial streams. (Cattle graze in the wilderness, especially along streams, so treat your water.) A few drainages even have isolated populations of rare native cutthroat trout. Still, you should plan carefully for extended trips here and check with the Forest Service regarding current conditions.

An excellent way to become acquainted with this vast and challenging wilderness is by volunteering to work in it. The Forest Service has an active and well-coordinated effort to use volunteers for such things as trail maintenance, trail construction, and other projects. In return the volunteers receive an educational program and an up-close-and-personal encounter with the wilderness. To volunteer, contact one of the ranger districts below: the Black Range Ranger District has responsibility for most of the Black Range area.

I confess I'm like most New Mexico hikers in having limited personal knowledge of the Black Range and the Aldo Leopold Wilderness, although my boots have left their tread on some of its trails. But this landscape calls to me, promising to deliver an experience of what the great American wilderness was like many generations ago.

DESTINATION HIKE: HILLSBORO PEAK
One-way length: 4.7 miles
Low and high elevations: 8,166 and 10,011 feet
Difficulty: moderate

This is probably the most popular hike in the Aldo Leopold Wilderness (although it's only barely in the wilderness), at least in part because it has the easiest access. The trailhead is at Emory Pass, named for Lt. William H. Emory who led an 1846 exploring expedition through here. It can be reached either from Silver City on the west or Hillsboro on the east by Highway 152.

From the parking area at the pass, follow a paved side road north to Trail 79, which continues heading north, passing radio towers and other facilities. Beyond a gate the trail briefly follows an old road before becoming a footpath. Two miles of hiking through Douglas fir, ponderosa pine, and occasional scrub oak, with some spectacular views, bring you to the wilderness boundary. At three miles is the junction with Trail 412, the Hillsboro Peak Bypass, which goes around the peak's southwest side to return to Trail 79 to the west. Following this makes a good loop trip around the peak. The peak itself has a fire tower and associated cabin, located in a pleasant meadow. Several good campsites are along the trail, as well as at the meadow, and water is generally available at Hillsboro Spring, north-west of the peak. Snow can linger into May on north slopes; afternoon thunder-storms are a hazard in late summer.

LOOP HIKE: UPPER GALLINAS CANYON – RAILROAD CANYON
Round-trip length: 12.0 miles
Low and high elevations: 7,000 and 9,200 feet
Difficulty: moderate to strenuous

West of Emory Pass on Highway 152 and west of Iron Creek Campground, the Upper Gallinas Canyon Trail, No. 129, begins at the undeveloped Railroad Canyon Campground. From here it heads north to meet the Black Range Crest and Trail 79 at Sids Prong Saddle. Water is available intermittently in Upper Gallinas Canyon, or more reliably in Sids Prong or Holden Prong on the crest's east side. At the crest, hike east on Trail 79 along the crest to Holden Prong Saddle, where Trail 128 follows Railroad Canyon down to its junction with Gallinas Canyon, near where you started.

LOOP HIKE: SIDS PRONG CANYON – PRETTY CANYON
Round-trip length: 11.0 miles
Low and high elevations: 8,000 and 9,600 feet
Difficulty: moderate to strenuous

From Highway 35 north of Mimbres, take Forest Road 152 (the McKnight Road) northeast. This high-clearance-vehicle road is rough and little-used. Forest Road 152 junctions with Trail 79 at the Black Range Crest. From here go south on Trail 79 to Sids Prong Saddle, where Trail 121 goes north, dropping into Sids Prong Canyon. The lower section is a good place to camp, with grassy meadows and a perennial stream. Trail 121 leaves Sids Prong, goes over a ridge, and descends just a short distance into Pretty Canyon, which also has grassy meadows and intermittent water. From here Trail 812 goes uphill and west to Forest Road 152 which takes you south, completing the loop.

SHUTTLE HIKE: BLACK RANGE CREST –
CONTINENTAL DIVIDE TRAIL
One-way length: 40.0 miles
Low and high elevations: 7,424 and 10,165 feet at McKnight Mountain
Difficulty: strenuous

Beginning at 8,194-foot Emory Pass, hike north on the Crest Trail, No. 79, following the directions for the Hillsboro Peak hike. From the peak, Trail 79 con-tinues north, joining Forest Road 152 for about three miles, and going over

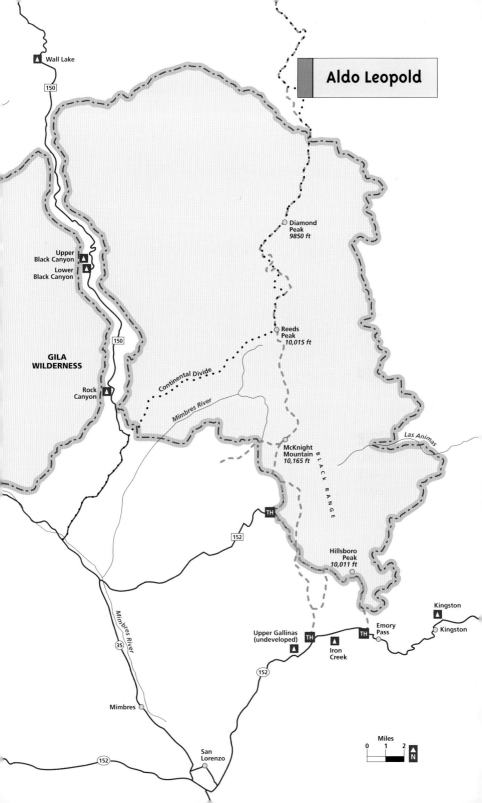

Aldo Leopold

Wall Lake

150

Upper
Black Canyon
Lower
Black Canyon

GILA
WILDERNESS

Rock
Canyon

150

Diamond
Peak
9850 ft

Reeds
Peak
10,015 ft

Continental Divide

Mimbres River

McKnight
Mountain
10,165 ft

Las Animas

B L A C K   R A N G E

TH

152

Hillsboro
Peak
10,011 ft

Kingston

Kingston

Mimbres River

35

Upper Gallinas
(undeveloped)   TH

Iron
Creek

TH   Emory
Pass

152

Mimbres

San
Lorenzo

152

Miles
0   1   2

N

McKnight Mountain. Then shortly before 10,015-foot Reeds Peak, the Continental Divide Trail enters from the southwest, which you would follow down to your vehicle parked along Forest Road 150.

A much longer shuttle hike would be to continue north on the Continental Divide Trail, exiting the wilderness north of Diamond Peak to meet a high-clearance vehicle at Forest Road 226. You also could continue along the Continental Divide (without a trail as of early 1998), north for another 16 miles to end at paved Highway 59, a total distance of about 70 miles.

FOR MORE INFORMATION

GILA NATIONAL FOREST – BLACK RANGE RANGER DISTRICT,
1804 North Date Street, Truth or Consequences, NM 87901; (505) 894-6677.

GILA NATIONAL FOREST – WILDERNESS RANGER DISTRICT,
Mimbres Station, HC 68, Box 50, Mimbres, NM 88049; (505) 536-2250.

GILA NATIONAL FOREST, 3005 E. Camino del Bosque, Silver City, NM 88061;
(505) 388-8201.

ALDO LEOPOLD

Aldo Leopold is regarded as the father of wildlife ecology, but his influence was much more far-reaching than just that discipline. Leopold articulated the concept of a land ethic, and also spearheaded the drive to create the world's first formally protected wilderness area—the Gila Wilderness of New Mexico.

Leopold was born in 1887 in Burlington, Iowa, where the family home sat on a bluff overlooking the Mississippi River. A flyway hosted hordes of migrating birds. At that time a hunter was limited only by how many birds he could kill and carry, and market hunters sent literally wagonloads of game back east. Leopold and his father hunted along the flyway, but they saw wildlife populations dwindling and voluntarily imposed conservation measures upon themselves.

At 16 young Leopold was sent east for schooling, first to Lawrenceville Academy in New Jersey, and then to Yale University, where he studied forestry. In letters home he expressed nostalgia for hunts along the river, but in 1904 he also wrote: "I am very sorry that the ducks are being slaughtered as usual. . . . When my turn comes to have something to say

New Mexico State Records Center and Archives, Bergere Collection, No. 21358

and do against it and other related matters I am sure that nothing in my power will be lacking to the good cause."

Upon graduation in 1909, he joined the Forest Service and was assigned to the Apache National Forest, which then straddled the New Mexico–Arizona border and included some of the Gila Country and the Blue Range. He was quickly immersed in the issues of the time. Among these was predator control, which as an avid hunter he took to readily. Grizzlies, wolves, mountain lions, coyotes—if only they could be curtailed, then wildlife such as deer and elk would flourish. In 1916, writing about the prospects of restoring Arizona's wildlife, he said: "Nature is with us—only man and predatory animals are against us." Years later, in *A Sand County Almanac,* he wrote: "I was young then, and full of trigger-itch; I thought that because fewer wolves meant more deer, that no wolves would mean hunter's paradise."

But even then changes were stirring in the sensitive young conservationist. In 1909 he and some companions came upon a family of wolves, and almost by reflex they began pumping lead into them. They killed a pup and wounded the mother. "We reached the old wolf in time to watch the fierce green fire dying in her eyes. I realized then, and have known ever since, that there was something new to me in those eyes, something known only to her and to the mountain."

Leopold moved up rapidly in the Forest Service. In 1911 he became deputy supervisor of the Carson National Forest. He became supervisor in 1912, the same year he married pioneer New Mexico family member Estella Bergere. Among his employees at the Carson was a young man, about the same age, who was to have a similar evolution as a wildlife conservationist and wilderness advocate: Elliott Barker (see Pecos Wilderness). The two became lifelong friends. Leopold then moved to the regional office in Albuquerque. During this time he witnessed the wilderness dwindling as had the waterfowl along the Mississippi. He also met others who shared his concern about preserving wild nature for future generations. These people included William T. Hornaday, Chief Forester Henry Graves, and Arthur Carhart, another young Forest Service planner, who most echoed his own evolving philosophy about preserving wilderness and the value of the wilderness experience. Leopold soon became a passionate and articulate spokesman, and with his friend Fred Winn, supervisor of the Gila National Forest, he mapped the boundaries of the world's first area to be set aside solely to preserve its wild character.

In 1924, the same year the Gila Wilderness was created, Leopold left the Southwest to join the U.S. Forest Products Laboratory in Madison, Wisconsin. In 1928 he began teaching at the University of Wisconsin. There he wrote his seminal *Game Management* (1933), and soon after became first chair of the newly created Department of Game Management.

Then in 1935, Leopold and his family purchased a worn-out farm in what was known as Wisconsin's "sand counties." Here he put into practice many of his land stewardship ideas. And here he crafted many of the essays that articulated a philosophy that had been evolving ever since his youth along the Mississippi.

The most famous collection of essays he titled *A Sand County Almanac.* He prefaced the work by saying: "There are some who can live without wild things and some who cannot. These essays are the delights and dilemmas of one who cannot." In this work he wrote: "That land is a community is a basic concept of ecology, but that land is to be loved and respected is an extension of ethics. That land yields a cultural harvest is a fact long known but latterly often forgotten."

But for many people, the most moving passage Leopold ever wrote was about watching the "fierce, green fire" die in the eyes of the old wolf he'd shot. On January 26, 1998, the fiftieth anniversary of Leopold's death, a family of three wolves was brought in pens to Hannagan Meadow in the Blue Range Primitive Area of Arizona, prior to eventual release into the wild. Wolves were finally back in the Gila Country. Aldo Leopold would have approved.

Apache Box
Wilderness Study Area

Sheer cliffs rise 600 feet to form this deep, narrow canyon on Apache Creek, with riparian habitat below and table lands above. This area is contiguous on the north with the Forest Service's Hell Hole WSA.

LOCATION	45 miles west of Silver City, 35 miles east of Safford, Arizona
SIZE	932 acres Size recommended by the NM Wilderness Alliance: 6,229 acres
ELEVATION RANGE	4,150 to 6,540 feet
MILES OF TRAILS	No marked or maintained trails
ECOSYSTEMS	Desert shrubs and grasses, piñon-juniper, riparian
ADMINISTRATION	BLM
TOPOGRAPHIC MAPS	Crookson Peak USGS 7.5-minute quadrangle
BEST SEASONS	Fall, winter, spring
GETTING THERE	Several county roads head south from Highway 78 to end near the Hell Hole WSA. From there, you can reach Apache Box by going cross-country.
HIKING	The area's small size and difficult access limit recreational use.

38 Apache Kid Wilderness

This remote wilderness features deep canyons, steep slopes, jagged ridges, and vegetation ranging from desert scrub to montane conifer forest. It is a place where savage and gentle beauty coexist.

Ramparts of Vicks Peak

LOCATION	In the southern San Mateo Mountains, southwest of Socorro, northwest of Truth or Consequences
SIZE	44,650 acres
ELEVATION RANGE	7,000 to 10,336 feet at West Blue Mountain
MILES OF TRAILS	62
ECOSYSTEMS	Semidesert grassland and scrub, piñon-juniper, ponderosa pine, Douglas fir, aspen, spruce
ADMINISTRATION	Cibola National Forest Magdalena Ranger District
TOPOGRAPHIC MAPS	Cibola National Forest—Apache Kid, Withington Wildernesses
BEST SEASONS	Spring, fall
GETTING THERE	Access to the Apache Kid Wilderness is on long, often rough dirt forest roads, the main one being Forest Road 225, which heads west toward the wilderness from Highway 1 near I-25 north of Truth or Consequences.
HIKING	Difficult access is the main impediment to hiking in the Apache Kid Wilderness, which has an extensive system of marked backcountry trails.

IMAGINE YOU'RE AN APACHE RENEGADE pursued by white soldiers and civilians alike. You choose the mountains for refuge, for after all, your people traditionally prefer mountain environments. Your refuge is rugged and remote, far from white settlements, and not easily accessible by soldiers on horseback. You know where springs are, which drainages might have water, and where game might be found. Several ranges in southern New Mexico would have met these criteria, but the renegade known as the Apache Kid chose the San Mateo Mountains.

The Apache Kid, a White Mountain Apache, was born near Globe, Arizona, around 1860. He spent his youth first as a captive of Yuma Indians, then as a street orphan in U.S. Army camps. The name Apache Kid was given to him by Army scout Albert Sieber, who befriended the youth and employed him as a scout in the Geronimo campaigns. But whiskey and an Apache feud led the young Apache into trouble with the Army, and in 1889 he was convicted of wounding Sieber in a shootout: the Apache Kid denied the charge. While being taken to prison, he escaped. Outlawed by the whites, and with his Apache friends and relatives in prison, the Apache Kid became a renegade and for four years conducted a campaign of terror in the region. Finally, in September, 1894, New Mexico cattleman Charles Anderson and some cowboys ambushed rustlers in the San Mateo Mountains, killing one—the Apache Kid. He was buried near what later was known as Apache Kid Peak, a 10,048-foot mountain in the heart of the wilderness between Blue Mountain and San Mateo Peak. Appropriately, another major peak in the wilderness, Vicks Peak, bears the name of another Apache also dreaded and pursued by whites throughout the Southwest—Victorio.

Today, the Apache Kid Wilderness vies for being New Mexico's least known, least visited wilderness, and for the same reasons the Apache Kid chose it for a refuge. It's far from population centers, and road access is difficult. The dirt roads are usually long, dusty, and rough. The terrain is forbidding, the trails typically steep, rocky, and scorching hot in the summer. Finally, the wilderness has no obvious attractions, no ghost towns to visit, no major summits to bag, no extraordinary natural or geologic features, no outstanding historical significance (the Apache Kid will never upstage Billy the Kid as New Mexico's premier outlaw)—nothing, except some of the state's wildest wilderness.

The Apache Kid Wilderness was established by the New Mexico Wilderness Act of 1980. During the RARE II process, the Forest Service identified 132,700 acres here as suitable for wilderness, a rare instance in which the Forest Service advocated more wilderness than the New Mexico Wilderness Study Committee, a wilderness advocacy group. The Forest Service proposed protection for the entire area, including what became the Withington Wilderness to the north, but opposition from a local rancher resulted in a drastic acreage reduction. Prospectors, who dug infrequent prospect holes, never found any minerals to make mining a threat to the wilderness. In the 1970s a telephone microwave tower was proposed for the top of Vicks Peak, but the Forest Service concurred with the Wilderness Study Committee that less expensive alternatives existed.

Most hikers enter the wilderness from the Forest Service Springtime Campground because the campground, one of only two near the wilderness, is easy to get to from

Forest Road 225 connecting with I-25 Exit 115 via Highway 1. From here, the most popular trip is the 4.2-mile route to the fire tower atop San Mateo Peak. This trail, the Apache Kid Trail, No. 43, connects with other wilderness trails that receive less traffic. Spring and fall are the best hiking seasons in the Apache Kid Wilderness; the highcountry can be pleasant in summer. In winter, snowstorms rake the range and seal off the high mountains. Several summits here exceed 10,000 feet, including West Blue Mountain, 10,336 feet; East Blue Mountain, 10,319 feet; Vicks Peak, 10,252 feet; San Mateo Peak, 10,139 feet; San Mateo Mountain, 10,145 feet; and Apache Kid Peak, 10,048 feet.

Ridges and valleys in the wilderness are steep, craggy, rock outcrops. Rock glaciers of rhyolite boulders slump down from the peaks. In the foothills and lower slopes, yucca, prickly-pear cactus, tough grasses, piñon-juniper trees, and other plants of the Upper Sonoran life zone thrive. As elevation rises, ponderosa pines appear and, still higher, aspen, Douglas fir, and spruce. Despite numerous springs in the backcountry, water is always problematic. Because of their isolation, the San Mateo Mountains are rich wildlife habitat. Many trails have more black bear traffic than human visitors. In 1919 the conservationist Aldo Leopold described a hunting trip he'd taken in the San Mateos, then within the Datil National Forest (now Cibola National Forest):

The Datil Forest, from the sportsman's standpoint, is the cream of the Southwest, and there is no part of the Datil country as interesting to hunt in as the San Mateos. It is a very rough region with a fair amount of water, and endless miles of yellow [ponderosa] pine forest interspersed with oak and piñon. Any year that the oak fails to produce acorns it is pretty certain that the piñons will produce nuts, so that the game is nearly always hog-rolling fat.

On this particular trip, Leopold found the game sparse, which he attributed to hungry cowboys, sheepherders, and Indians who jerked meat at hidden camps. Today, while poaching occasionally still occurs, the presence of hunters has declined. Wildlife populations have consequently expanded.

Were Aldo Leopold to return to the San Mateo Mountains of the Apache Kid Wilderness today, he'd find them just as wild as he did 80 years ago—perhaps wilder.

DESTINATION HIKE: SAN MATEO PEAK
One-way length: 4.2 miles
Low and high elevations: 7,360 and 10,139 feet at San Mateo Peak
Difficulty: moderate to strenuous

People driving south on I-25 should take Exit 115 onto Highway 107, then quickly take Highway 1 south to the junction with Forest Road 225. This good dirt road leads after 13 miles to Springtime Campground (no potable water) and the head of the Apache Kid Trail, No. 43. This route provides access to the heart of the wilderness. The trail climbs drainages and ridges, passing San Mateo Spring, until after 3.4 miles from the campground it intersects the Cowboy Trail, No. 44, which takes you on a relatively easy finish to the San Mateo Peak summit. There a fire tower affords expansive views.

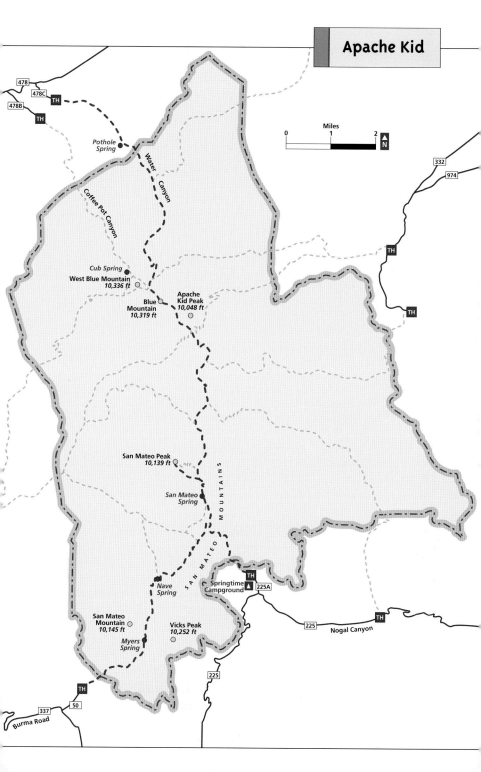

Apache Kid

478
478C TH
478B TH

Pothole Spring

Water Canyon

Coffee Pot Canyon

332
974

TH

TH

Cub Spring

West Blue Mountain
10,336 ft

Blue Mountain
10,319 ft

Apache Kid Peak
10,048 ft

Miles
0   1   2
N

San Mateo Peak
10,139 ft

San Mateo Spring

SAN MATEO MOUNTAINS

Nave Spring

Springtime Campground
TH
225A

225
Nogal Canyon

TH

San Mateo Mountain
10,145 ft

Vicks Peak
10,252 ft

Myers Spring

225

337 50 TH
Burma Road

LOOP HIKE: BLUE MOUNTAIN VIA COFFEE POT CANYON AND APACHE KID TRAILS
Round-trip length: 15.0 miles
Low and high elevations: 7,270 and 10,336 feet at West Blue Mountain
Difficulty: strenuous

This long hike takes you to the highest point in the San Mateo Mountains. To reach the trailhead at the range's northwest side, drive on Highway 60 west of Magdalena until Highway 52 heads south. Follow this 37 miles to where Forest Road 478 heads east toward the mountains.

Follow this approximately 13 miles into Red Canyon to a good campsite; you may be able to drive father, but the walking is easy. The two trailheads are a short distance up Coffee Pot and Water Canyons, a half mile apart, which you can reach by Forest Roads 478B and 478C (both difficult under adverse conditions). Starting from the Water Canyon Trailhead for Trail 43, the Apache Kid Trail, hike along the stream for 3.1 miles to the wilderness boundary and reliable water at Pot Hole Spring. From here the trail swings south and climbs more steeply until at 3.6 miles from the wilderness boundary you pass Trail 81. Continue 0.5 mile farther to pass Trail 90 at the saddle between Blue and West Blue Mountains. By following the ridge northwest you reach the summit of West Blue with its decrepit Forest Service cabin. To return, pick up Trail 90 on the north side of West Blue. Less than half a mile downhill, on Trail 69, you reach reliable Cub Spring. The trail follows ridges downhill until, about 0.5 mile outside the wilderness boundary, the trail switchbacks down a steep slope to join Coffee Pot Canyon, which it follows back to Forest Road 478.

BOB JULYAN'S FAVORITE HIKE: SHIPMAN CANYON
One-way length: 3 miles (to Myers Cabin)
Low and high elevations: 7,440 and 9,394 feet
Difficulty: moderate to strenuous

Despite a long and often difficult approach, this beautiful trail is worth it. The easiest access is to drive south on I-25, take the Red Canyon exit, and then travel about one mile south on the frontage road until packed dirt Forest Road 139 heads west. After approximately 10 miles, Forest Road 377 heads northwest. The road is rough, and while a four-wheel-drive isn't necessary, you'll appreciate high clearance if you have it. After approximately 10 miles, a two-track branches right and goes about 0.5 mile to the start of the Shipman Trail, No. 50. The trail soon enters the narrow canyon marked by a small, intermittent stream. It follows this uphill to Myers Spring. Here the trail becomes steeper as it climbs past dramatic rock glaciers. To the west are the cliffs of San Mateo Mountain. To the east, the ramparts of Vicks Peak rise. After about three miles the trail reaches the saddle between the two peaks. Here are the remains of the large log cabin known as Myers Cabin. It's a pleasant, beautiful spot—level grassland shaded by tall ponderosas and slender aspens. From here the trail continues north, following another drainage downhill to Nave Spring and, nearby, the Nave Trail, No. 86, junction. The Shipman Trail, No. 50, continues on into the wilderness, crossing dry, rough country eventually to end at the Apache Kid Trail, No. 43.

FOR MORE INFORMATION

CIBOLA NATIONAL FOREST – MAGDALENA RANGER DISTRICT, P.O. Box 45, Magdalena, NM 87825; (505) 854-2281.

CIBOLA NATIONAL FOREST, 2113 Osuna Road NE, Suite A, Albuquerque, NM 87113-1001; (505) 346-2650.

39 Blue Creek Wilderness Study Area

Dominated by Black Mountain in the south, this terrain features rolling and sometimes rugged desert hills and drainages. The area complements the Gila Lower Box WSA to the south and the proposed Gila Middle Box Wilderness to the east.

LOCATION
North of the Gila River, northwest of Redrock, northeast of Virden

SIZE
14,896 acres
Size recommended by the NM Wilderness Alliance: 21,656 acres

ELEVATION RANGE
4,000 to 5,600 feet on Black Mountain

MILES OF TRAILS
No marked or maintained trails

ECOSYSTEMS
Desert scrub and grassland, riparian woodland, scattered piñon-juniper

ADMINISTRATION
BLM

TOPOGRAPHIC MAPS
Nichols Canyon, Canador Peak, Walker Canyon, and Steeple Rock USGS 7.5-minute quadrangles

BEST SEASONS
Fall, winter, spring

GETTING THERE
From Highway 82, 1 mile east of Virden, County Road A039 leads to the WSA's northern boundary. On the south, County Road A030 runs east from Highway 82, 0.5 mile east of the Gila River Bridge.

HIKING
This area is seldom used for hiking. However, this could change as this area and others nearby become better known as an integrated wilderness unit.

Blue Range Wilderness 40

*This wilderness area features forested uplands and
deep canyons with few trails and even fewer hikers.
The Blue Range encompasses portions of the Brushy
Mountains and the Mogollon Rim.*

Cholla buds in the Blue Range

LOCATION	West of Highway 180, southwest of Reserve, along the Arizona border
SIZE	29,304 acres
ELEVATION RANGE	5,000 to 8,765 feet at Whiterocks Mountain
MILES OF TRAILS	30
ECOSYSTEMS	Ponderosa pine, piñon-juniper, oak, willow, and other riparian vegetation
ADMINISTRATION	Gila National Forest
TOPOGRAPHIC MAPS	Gila National Forest—Saliz Pass, Blue, Alma, and Alma Mesa 7.5-minute USGS quadrangles
BEST SEASONS	Spring, fall
GETTING THERE	The primary vehicular access to the Blue Range Wilderness is the smooth dirt Forest Road 232, which heads west from Highway 180 southwest of Reserve.
HIKING	While trails are relatively few in the Blue Range Wilderness, extended wilderness trips are possible by linking this area with the adjacent Blue Range Primitive Area in Arizona.

THE APPARENTLY SMALL SIZE OF THE BLUE RANGE WILDERNESS is deceptive. It may appear dwarfed in comparison to the 558,065-acre Gila Wilderness nearby, but at 29,000 acres it still is larger than seven other New Mexico wildernesses. More importantly, it's an integral appendage of the 173,762-acre Blue Range Primitive Area across the border in Arizona's Apache National Forest. Indeed, the New Mexico portion of the Blue Range wasn't formally designated wilderness until 1980 with the New Mexico Wilderness Act. Taken together, the primitive area and the wilderness constitute a wild area of 203,066 acres, slightly larger than the vast Aldo Leopold Wilderness.

This "appendage" quality also helps explain why the Blue Range wilderness complex is far less well known in New Mexico than in Arizona, even among New Mexico hikers. Here, the Blue Range Wilderness is usually overshadowed by the nearby Gila Wilderness, despite the two being similar in character: forested mountains and hills etched by numerous drainages and deep canyons. But the Blue Range Wilderness has the distinction of including, in its southwest section, the Mogollon (pronounced muggy-YONE) Rim, the important escarpment made famous as the Tonto Rim in the western novels of Zane Grey. The Blue Range Wilderness, like the Gila Wilderness, is good habitat for deer, elk, black bear, and mountain lions. Prehistoric humans found it appealing country as well and likely drew few distinctions between the two areas. In both areas they left reminders of their presence in the form of abandoned pit houses and pueblos. The Blue Range, however, has fewer trails and is more primitive than the Gila Wilderness.

The primary access to the Blue Range Wilderness is Forest Road 232, a graded dirt road heading west from Highway 180 southwest of Reserve and south of Luna. The road skirts the northern boundary of the wilderness. Most visitor activity in the Blue Range Wilderness begins at Pueblo Park Campground, 5.6 miles from Highway 180. Situated beneath tall ponderosa pines, the campground is open free of charge April 1 through November 30. Although Pueblo Creek is nearby, it's often dry, and there's no potable water at the campground. The campground does have privies, however, built in the 1930s by the Civilian Conservation Corps. The campground attracts rockhounds because of nearby deposits of bytownite, a semi-precious stone used in jewelry.

Also at the campground you'll find a 1.5-mile interpretive trail whose loop includes historic and prehistoric settlement sites. While the Blue Range certainly was visited by hunter-gatherers thousands of years ago, more permanent settlements occurred 1,500 years ago when people of the Mogollon Culture began building pit houses. Later, they used stone and mortar to build their dwellings above ground. If you're planning to hike in the Blue Range Wilderness, take time to walk the interpretive trail because it will sensitize you to the kind of artifacts you're likely to encounter in the backcountry.

The Pueblo Park Campground is the trailhead for the WS Mountain Trail, which bisects the wilderness and is the main trunk for other wilderness trails. Dependable, potable water is lacking along the route; your chance of encountering other hikers is small.

But while the Blue Range Wilderness has largely been ignored or overlooked by hikers and campers, that could change dramatically in the next few years. The reason?

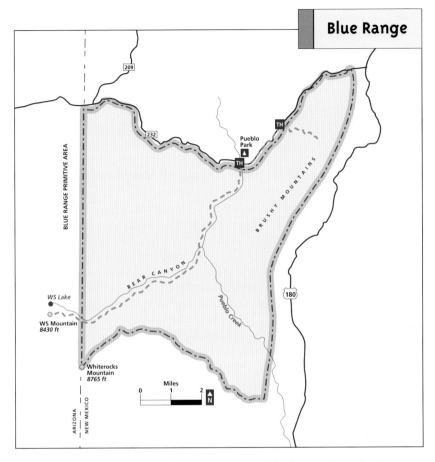

One word: wolves. On January 26, 1998, Secretary of the Interior Bruce Babbitt accompanied wildlife biologists to Hannagan Meadow in the Blue Range Primitive Area just over the border in Arizona. They carried cages holding a family of three Mexican wolves to pens where they were kept before release into the wild. Other wolves will follow. If all goes well, in a few years campers in the Blue Range might hear the howl of wolves, the ultimate cachet of wilderness.

When that happens, the Blue Range Wilderness will emerge from its obscurity and be recognized for the significant wild area it truly is.

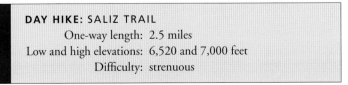

DAY HIKE: SALIZ TRAIL
One-way length: 2.5 miles
Low and high elevations: 6,520 and 7,000 feet
Difficulty: strenuous

This trail, No. 22, follows an old wagon road into the wilderness. The trailhead is on the southeast side of Forest Road 232, 3.7 miles from its junction with Highway 180. The trail heads east initially and begins rather gently but then becomes steeper before turning south, where it continues climbing along a ridge. At its terminus are good vistas of the wilderness and the aptly named Brushy Mountains.

BACKPACK HIKE: WS MOUNTAIN TRAIL
One-way length: 8.8 miles
Low and high elevations: 5,700 and 8,430 feet
Difficulty: moderate to strenuous

Trail No. 43 is the main route for exploring the Blue Range Wilderness, as it traverses the wilderness's western half from northeast to southwest. A canyon bottom trail, it follows the Pueblo Creek and Bear Canyon drainages and consequently provides access to numerous tributary canyons. Gradients along the trail are gentle—the first half is even downhill—but rugged nonetheless. And although you'll be hiking along stream beds, don't count on finding water. The trail begins just south of the entrance to the Pueblo Park Campground. It heads south along Pueblo Creek, passing the junction with Chimney Rock Canyon, which it follows south to its junction with Bear Creek at about four miles. It then begins following Bear Creek upstream until just over the Arizona border. There you reach WS Mountain, 8,430 feet, where you'll find good camping.

OTHER RECREATIONAL OPPORTUNITIES

Forest roads north of the wilderness, as well as Forest Road 232, are suitable for mountain biking. Forest Road 232 goes into Arizona, and Forest Road 281 offers excellent mountain biking with two Forest Service campgrounds north of the junction. Farther north in New Mexico, Forest Road 33 heads southwest from Highway 180, past its junction with Highway 12.

FOR MORE INFORMATION

GILA NATIONAL FOREST – GLENWOOD RANGER DISTRICT, P.O. Box 8, Glenwood, NM 88039; (505) 539-2481.

GILA NATIONAL FOREST, 3005 E. Camino del Bosque, Silver City, NM 88061; (505) 388-8201.

Continental Divide Wilderness Study Area

Capped by 9,212-foot Pelona Mountain and bisected by the Continental Divide, the Continental Divide Wilderness Study Area is one of New Mexico's largest, characterized by high, rolling grasslands to the south and east, and canyon country with ponderosa pines to the west. This area is outstanding wildlife habitat.

New Mexico Wilderness Alliance

Scenic view of Continental Divide Wliderness Study Area

LOCATION	30 miles south of Datil, at the southwest end of the Plains of San Agustin, south of Highway 12
SIZE	68,761 acres Size recommended by the NM Wilderness Alliance: 105,704 acres
ELEVATION RANGE	6,785 to 9,212 feet at Pelona Mountain
MILES OF TRAILS	No marked or maintained trails
ECOSYSTEMS	Grassland, piñon-juniper, ponderosa pine
ADMINISTRATION	BLM
TOPOGRAPHIC MAPS	Pelona Mountain USGS 7.5-minute quadrangle
BEST SEASONS	Spring, summer, fall
GETTING THERE	While Highway 12 passes near the northern and western boundaries, the roads leading to the WSA all cross private land. The only public access is via Highway 163 on the east, an all-weather dirt road.
HIKING	Limited by access. You'll find few trails here, although the Continental Divide is a natural route. Spacious, wild, and scenic, the area doesn't have much water.

42 Devils Backbone Wilderness Study Area

Remote, rugged, and rocky, the "Backbone" refers to a knife-edged hogback within this domain currently surrounded by private land.

LOCATION	East of the Rio Grande, southwest of Socorro, at the south end of the Magdalena Mountains
SIZE	8,904 acres Size recommended by the NM Wilderness Alliance: 15,184 acres
ELEVATION RANGE	5,400 to 8,100 feet
MILES OF TRAILS	No marked or maintained trails
ECOSYSTEMS	Piñon-juniper forest in the north, rocky grassland in the south
ADMINISTRATION	BLM
TOPOGRAPHIC MAPS	Puertecito Gap USGS 7.5-minute quadrangle
BEST SEASONS	Fall, winter, spring
GETTING THERE	You can't, at least not legally.
HIKING	Very limited; no delineated routes; no public access.

Gila Lower Box
Wilderness Study Area

43

The Gila River flows through here with tributary canyons flanked by rolling upland hills.

New Mexico Wilderness Alliance

The serene Gila River

LOCATION	5 miles down the Gila River from Redrock
SIZE	8,555 acres Size recommended by the NM Wilderness Alliance: 19,595 acres
ELEVATION RANGE	3,775 to 4,300 feet
MILES OF TRAILS	No marked or maintained trails
ECOSYSTEMS	Riparian, including cottonwood, sycamore, hackberry, and mesquite; arid species include creosote bush, yucca, cacti; Chihuahuan Desert grassland and scrub.
ADMINISTRATION	BLM
TOPOGRAPHIC MAPS	Nichols Canyon and Canador Peak USGS 7.5-minute quadrangles
BEST SEASONS	Fall, winter, spring
GETTING THERE	From Redrock county roads lead to Fishermans Point and traverse along the eastern and southern boundaries.
HIKING	The constricted nature of the "box" section of this WSA limits hiking along the river, but ranch and mine roads offer hiking routes through the rolling uplands of the WSA's southern section.

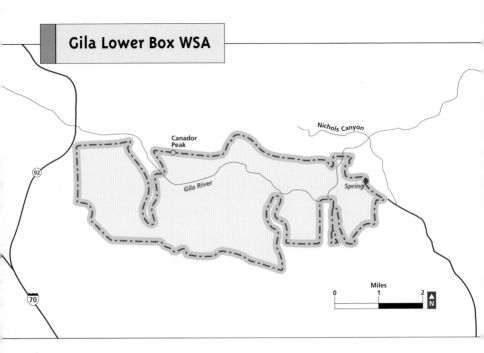

Gila Lower Box WSA

EXPLORING GILA LOWER BOX WSA   Three potential wilderness areas—the
Gila Lower Box, the Blue Creek to the north, and the Middle Gila Box to the east—
form a wilderness complex of exceptional ecological value. Among the ecosystems are
the riparian areas along the Gila River and tributary creeks, as well as nearby canyons
and adjoining uplands. The combination defines a naturalist's paradise. Soaring on
thermal air currents above the river and ridges are several species of raptors, including
endangered bald eagles and peregrine falcons. Gila monsters have been seen in the
area. Mammals include black bears, mountain lions, javelina, coatimundi, ringtails,
beavers, mule and Coues deer—indeed, this ecologically rich area is estimated to
include almost half of all the vertebrate species found in New Mexico. Furthermore,
the area has been mentioned for possible reintroduction of desert bighorn sheep and
river otters. And if the reintroduction of Mexican wolves in the Blue Range to the
north succeeds, visitors here might one day be thrilled by the howl of wild wolves.

The area also has great archaeological significance, with numerous prehistoric
dwellings and large petroglyph panels.

This rich natural and cultural diversity also makes the three-area complex
rich in outdoor recreation opportunities—backpacking, day hiking, rockhounding,
photography, bird watching, and—during the spring runoff—rafting and kayaking
on the Gila River (at other seasons pools invite swimming). Recreational use of the
area is relatively light, but this could change because the entire Gila River drainage
is a focus for recreation and exploration, not only for New Mexico recreationists but
also for those in Arizona. For this reason alone, the area deserves wilderness protection.

Gila Middle Box
Wilderness Inventory Unit   44

*This area features 10 miles of the rugged and scenic
Gila River Middle Box Gorge, as well as tributaries and
surrounding mountains.*

New Mexico Wilderness Alliance

The winding Gila River

LOCATION	In the Big Burro Mountains along the Gila River, 25 miles southwest of Silver City
SIZE	19,660 acres Size recommended by the NM Wilderness Alliance: 41,645 acres
ELEVATION RANGE	4,000 to 5,300 feet
MILES OF TRAILS	No marked or maintained trails
ECOSYSTEMS	Pines, evergreen oak, Chihuahuan Desert grassland and scrub, riparian cottonwoods, sycamores, and walnuts
ADMINISTRATION	BLM, Gila National Forest
TOPOGRAPHIC MAPS	Mangas Springs, Brushy Mountain, Bullard Peak, and Redrock USGS 7.5-minute quadrangles
BEST SEASONS	Fall, winter, spring
GETTING THERE	From Highway 180, 1.5 miles southeast of Riverside, take Bill Evans Road toward Bill Evans Lake.
HIKING	This unit was dropped by the BLM and Forest Service during their inventories because of the size of the two administrative units (as well as a now-defunct dam proposal). It has the same high ecological values and recreational potential as the nearby Gila Lower Box WSA and Blue Creek WSA. (See Gila Lower Box WSA for more information.)

45 Gila Wilderness

The Gila Wilderness is New Mexico's largest formally designated wilderness and the world's first—a vast, wild tract of high mountains, arid uplands, and rivers flowing through steep canyons. The area is rich in natural and human history.

Ruin along Gila River

LOCATION	North of Silver City, east of Highway 180
SIZE	558,065 acres
ELEVATION RANGE	4,700 feet on the Gila River to 10,895 feet at Whitewater Baldy
MILES OF TRAILS	Approximately 700
ECOSYSTEMS	Spruce-fir at high elevations, ponderosa pine, piñon-juniper, riparian deciduous
ADMINISTRATION	Gila National Forest Wilderness Ranger District and Glenwood Ranger District
TOPOGRAPHIC MAPS	Gila National Forest shaded relief map; Forest Service Gila Wilderness topographic map
BEST SEASONS	Spring, summer, fall
GETTING THERE	The vast Gila Wilderness is accessible from several areas. The main population center, Silver City, is to the south. Access from the north and east is limited to dirt forest roads. The high peaks of the wilderness's western section are reached from Highway 180. From Silver City, Highway 15 leads into the heart of the wilderness, as well as campgrounds and a Forest Service visitor center.
HIKING	The Gila Wilderness offers the greatest extent and diversity of hiking opportunities of any wilderness in New Mexico.

THE GILA WILDERNESS is one of America's great wildernesses. But its significance lies not only in its size—more than twice as vast as the next largest wilderness in New Mexico, the Pecos—but also in its creation, for it was the first area anywhere in the world set aside solely to protect its character as wilderness. It's a story worth telling.

The mountain and rolling grassland complex known as the Gila Country was first born with volcanic activity beginning 65 million years ago and later with cataclysmic volcanic eruptions that produced a huge caldera (a geologic formation created when empty magma chambers collapsed). The vague outline of this caldera, huge in its dimensions, is visible on satellite images of the area. Portions of the caldera's rim are preserved in the Mogollon, Diablo, and Jerky Mountains within the wilderness. On the ground, evidence of this fiery birth remains in the compacted volcanic ash, known as tuff, that makes up the tawny cliffs along drainages and in the area's numerous hot springs.

Certainly these hot springs, warm springs, and lukewarm springs would have attracted early Indians, just as they attract hikers today. Of the very earliest Indians here little evidence remains, but by about 300 B.C. a culture began to emerge from the earlier Cochise Culture that would leave enduring remains. They have been labeled the Mogollon (pronounced muggy-YONE) people, and at least part of their subsistence included domesticated plants such as maize, beans, and squash, requiring at least semi-permanent dwellings. Thus, these people constructed pithouses. But around A.D. 1000 a cultural shift occurred, for reasons still open to speculation; the pottery style changed dramatically, and the people emerged from their pit houses and began living above ground, often in masonry structures wedged into alcoves high on cliffs. Remains of these dwellings are found throughout the wilderness, but they are best represented at Gila Cliff Dwellings National Monument near the wilderness center.

Then they left. Around A.D. 1300 the people who had lived here for centuries, perhaps millennia, abandoned the area completely. Where they went and what became of them is still hotly debated. Even more controversial is why they left—especially as their leaving roughly coincided with the abandonment by the distinct but related Anasazi Culture to the north, whose vast territory centered on the Four Corners area. As you come upon cliff dwellings in the Gila Wilderness, spend a moment imagining people living their routine day-to-day lives here. Then imagine these people walking away from their homes with their belongings, never to return.

For whatever reason they left, they'd been long gone by the time a new people arrived in the area from the north: they spoke an Athabaskan language and called themselves N'de, "the people." We know them as Apaches. Organized into several bands, they ranged throughout southern New Mexico, Arizona, and northern Mexico. The Gila Country was the territory of the Chiricahua and Mimbres Apaches. Geronimo said he was born near the Gila River headwaters around 1829.

The Apaches were a raiding culture, and they were fierce, formidable defenders of their territory. Not until the surrender of Geronimo in 1886 did the Apache threat to outsiders begin to subside. Until then, non-Apaches entered the Gila Country only at great peril, something that helped preserve the area's wild character. Today, the only reminders of the Apaches' presence here are place names: Apache Creek, Lookout Mountain, Indian Creek, and others.

With the Apaches gone, new settlers moved in with a vengeance. They clear-cut forests to feed a huge demand for timber; they prospected for minerals (rarely finding any in the wilderness); they grazed and overgrazed cattle; and they slaughtered wildlife. So sudden and devastating was their impact that in 1899, just 13 years after Geronimo's surrender, President McKinley withdrew the land from settlement by designating the Gila River Forest Preserve. The reserve was transferred to the newly created Forest Service in 1909, the same year young Aldo Leopold arrived in the Gila Country on his first assignment.

The story of how the Gila Country affected the thinking of Leopold, who went on to become America's foremost wilderness philosopher, is told elsewhere in this book. The Gila Country first taught Leopold to "think like a mountain," a key phrase of his, and it was here that his burgeoning philosophy first bore fruit: in 1924, stimulated by Leopold's leadership, the U.S. Secretary of Agriculture created the Gila Wilderness by executive order.

The wilderness originally encompassed 775,000 acres and included all the lands to the north and east now within the Aldo Leopold Wilderness, including much of the Black Range. The two wilderness areas became separated in 1933 after an "administrative" road was built up North Star Canyon. Since then, other acreage and boundary adjustments have occurred to create the present configuration.

Environmentalists and wilderness advocates dream of the Gila Wilderness forming the core of a vast "Sky Island" wilderness, encompassing not only much of southwestern New Mexico but also southeastern Arizona. Such a super-wilderness, they say, would be truly sustainable as a self-perpetuating wild area, a place to which long-vanished indigenous species such as the river otter, the grizzly, the Mexican wolf, and the jaguar could return with viable populations. It's not an implausible dream, especially as the concept of biodiversity gains acceptance and the public recognizes the enormous economic potential of eco-tourism and outdoor recreation. By the time you read this, wolves will again be running free in the Blue Range Wilderness just to the north.

For now, however, hikers will have to imagine the lupine howling at night, an otter splashing as it frolics in a stream, a jaguar's scream, and a grizzly's ruckus as it scavenges wild plants in a meadow.

Even now, hikers in the Gila Wilderness aren't exactly wildlife-deprived. The area teems with wildlife: mountain lions, black bears, elk, Rocky Mountain bighorn sheep, mule and white-tailed deer, javelina, coatimundi, pronghorn, Arizona coral snake, Gila monsters, turkeys, blue grouse, common black hawks, zone-tailed hawks, northern goshawks, Mexican spotted owls, and bald eagles, among many others.

The Gila Wilderness is an exceptionally rich and diverse habitat. It has more species of deciduous trees—more than 20—than anywhere else in the West. The Chihuahua pine reaches its northern limit here, and the world's largest remaining virgin ponderosa forest is here. This biological diversity results, in part, from topographic diversity. Within the half-million acres are 10,000-foot summits with steep snow-catching slopes, broad rolling uplands and mesas, and deep stream-cut canyons. A hiker's dream.

Hikers can enter this vast wilderness from several points. Probably the most popular, and deservedly so, is from the south following Highway 15 north from Silver City. Don't underestimate the time it will take to drive the interminable serpentine curves of this road. And don't be impatient. Relax, enjoy the scenery. Eventually you arrive at the tiny private enclave of Gila Hot Springs, a pleasant and welcome source of gas, supplies, commercial camping, and hot springs. Nearby you'll find the Forest Service Forks and Grapevine Campgrounds. A little farther is the Gila Center and visitor center. From here it's a short drive to Gila Cliff Dwellings National Monument and the Forest Service's Scorpion Campground. (I've never seen a scorpion here, so the chances of a sting are not high. But an overly bold skunk once terrorized my oldest daughter.)

Where you hike in the Gila Wilderness will depend somewhat on time of year. The area can be divided into three physiographic regions: the Mogollon Mountains, the uplands, and the canyon bottoms. The mountains attract hikers during the summer when lower-elevation trails are baking hot. The uplands, with their open ponderosa and piñon-juniper forests, are a delight in the spring when everything is green and wildflowers are blooming. The canyon bottoms are used at all times of the year except winter and during the spring runoff. These are especially enchanting in the fall when the deciduous trees and shrubs turn color—cottonwoods, willows, box elders, maples, iridescent sycamores, and scarlet Virginia creepers.

The canyon bottom trails are unquestionably the most popular, but they do demand some concessions. Foremost of these are stream crossings. Prepare for interminable stream crossings—some routes average three per mile. They'll drive you crazy if you're not physically and mentally prepared for them. Also, they limit when you can hike the route, because the crossings can be difficult and dangerous during high water. By summer the rivers generally are low enough not to pose serious problems. You'll find a walking stick very helpful, and you should also wear old sneakers and keep them on until you stop or leave the streams behind.

At the bottoms of these canyons you won't have to worry about water. Nor will you have to look far for good campsites, as people for generations have camped along the rivers. But you are more likely to encounter other hikers here, and you're under greater responsibility to practice "Leave No Trace" ethics.

I've probably spent more time reading about the history of this wild and wonderful area than I have actually hiking it; it's an imbalance I intend to correct. And when I do hike here, I always wonder at the irony of such a beautiful, serene place having such a tragic and violent history. The answer that comes to me is that the history is not so much of the place as of the humans here, and that we as humans can always write another history, one more in keeping with the essence of the wilderness. At least that's what I tell myself as I'm reclining beneath a sycamore or soaking in a hot spring, watching clouds float overhead.

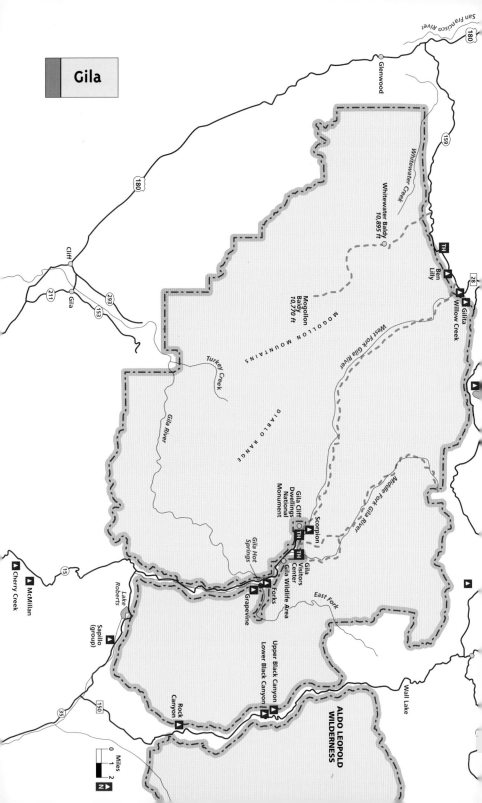

DESTINATION HIKE: MOGOLLON BALDY VIA THE CREST TRAIL
One-way length: 6.0 miles
Low and high elevations: 9,132 and 10,895 feet
Difficulty: strenuous

The drive to this popular high-mountain hike is almost as interesting as the hike itself, for the drive along Highway 159 takes you from the pleasant little town of Glenwood northeast along Whitewater Creek through the all-but-ghost mining town of Mogollon. Highway 159 continues east eight miles to the well-marked trailhead at Sandy Point. The trail ascends steeply to a ridge, which it follows through dense spruce-fir forest and aspen groves south-southwest, crossing very scenic Hummingbird Saddle just before passing over 10,895-foot Whitewater Baldy (check out the observation tower). From here the trail rollercoasters past 10,535-foot Center Baldy to end at 10,770-foot Mogollon Baldy.

LOOP HIKE: WEST FORK – MIDDLE FORK LOOP
Round-trip length: 10.5 miles
Low and high elevations: 5,700 and 6,300 feet
Difficulty: moderate

This hike allows you to experience the Gila Wilderness uplands as well as the popular canyon bottoms. It begins just before the Scorpion Campground near Gila Cliff Dwellings National Monument. Trail 729 climbs not too steeply through grassy meadows onto the upland separating the West Fork and Middle Fork drainages. Here you meander through open ponderosa forest before an interesting descent through a tributary canyon of the Middle Fork. At about 3.5 miles you reach the Middle Fork. To make the loop, take the Middle Fork Trail, No. 157, downstream (lots of stream crossings) about 5.5 miles to the ranger station and visitor center. Just before the ranger station is a small hot spring near the river. From the visitor center it's about a 1.5-mile hike back to the campground.

SHUTTLE HIKE: MIDDLE FORK OF THE GILA RIVER
One-way length: 41.0 miles
Low and high elevations: 5,680 and 8,300 feet
Difficulty: strenuous
(due to length of hike and pack weight)

This trail runs through the heart of the Gila Wilderness and doggedly follows the Middle Fork along its tortuous course. It is likely the longest continuous trail in the wilderness. And if the sheer miles don't make this trek seem long, the river crossings will: they total more than 100. But there are compensations: because the trail stays in the canyon bottom, you won't do much climbing; you'll see cliff dwellings in the buff-colored canyon walls; you can enjoy excellent trout fishing amid beautiful scenery; and here and there you'll soak in hot (or warm) springs at day's end.

The Middle Fork Trail, No. 157, starts in the south at the Wilderness Ranger Station Visitor Center, directions described above. The trail then follows the Middle Fork to end either at the Snow Lake Campground or, for the full 41 miles, at the Gilita Campground a few miles farther along Gilita Creek.

BOB JULYAN'S FAVORITE HIKE
WEST FORK OF THE GILA RIVER
One-way length: 3 miles (or more, possibly much more)
Low and high elevations: 5,700 and 6,200 feet
Difficulty: easy to moderate

The entire West Fork of the Gila River Trail, No. 151, is more than 34 miles long, the second longest in the wilderness. It eventually runs all the way through the heart of the wilderness to the Willow Creek Campground on the northwest. This is my favorite simply because it's such a great day hike for adults and an easy overnighter for people with children. A somewhat truncated description follows. The trail begins at Gila Cliff Dwellings National Monument and wanders through wetlands and open forest for about a mile before arriving at the first of many river crossings. Just after you emerge from the water here, take a short sidetrip south to the remains of a small cabin in a clearing. Look for a grave nearby, with a weathered headstone that reads: "William Grudging waylaid and murdered by Tom Wood Oct. 8 1893 age 37 years 8 mos." Local people still debate the tragic outcome of that old feud.

From here the trail continues to follow the river, crossing it several times as it winds between the canyon's steep walls. After about two miles, you'll begin noticing obvious campsites. Three-mile Ruin—three miles from the trailhead—is the most popular West Fork destination for hikers. It's a tiny, very fragile cliff dwelling in a shallow cave on the river's west side.

OTHER RECREATIONAL OPPORTUNITIES

Little mountain biking occurs in the area immediately around the Gila Wilderness, primarily because of the region's remoteness and mountainous terrain. People interested in mountain biking should contact outdoor stores in Silver City. The area offers several outstanding mountain biking areas, such as the nearby Burro Mountains.

Similarly, little cross-country skiing or snowshoeing occurs in the wilderness, again because of remoteness but also due to the fact that the best snow tends to be in the wilderness's center, which requires trudging through miles of mud. An exception is the Crest Trail, No. 182. It runs from the Sandy Point Trailhead to the high peaks of the Mogollon Mountains. You can reach the trailhead by Highway 159 east of the village of Mogollon, although this road isn't always open in the winter.

Many people explore the remote wilderness with pack animals, specifically horses and mules, available at stables and outfitters. Llamas, despite their initial popularity, are used less because of the animals' sensitivity to heat.

Next to hiking and horseback riding, the most popular way to experience the Gila Wilderness is by floating on the Gila River from a put-in at the Highway 15 bridge to a take-out at the junction with Turkey Creek, which you can reach by Forest Roads 153 and then 155. You can float an additional nine miles down the river outside the wilderness to the village of Gila. (Actually, you can float farther, but the river becomes rougher.) The total distance through the wilderness is 32 miles. Most parties allocate five days for the trip. Flow levels vary widely, even during spring runoff, with the highest water being mid-March through mid-April.

FOR MORE INFORMATION

GLENWOOD RANGER DISTRICT, P.O. Box 8, Glenwood, NM 88039; (505) 539-2481.

GILA NATIONAL FOREST, 3005 E. Camino del Bosque, Silver City, NM 88061; (505) 388-8201.

GILA CENTER, Route 11, Box 100, Silver City, NM 88061; (505) 536-9461.

GILA NATIONAL FOREST—WILDERNESS RANGER DISTRICT, Mimbres Station, HC 68, Box 50, Mimbres NM 88049; (505) 536-2250.

46 Hell Hole Wilderness Study Area

Varied, rolling mountainous terrain features cliffs along drainages. The Hell Hole WSA adjoins the BLM's Apache Box WSA to the south.

LOCATION	South of Highway 78, southwest of Mule Creek, abutting the Arizona border
SIZE	18,680 acres
ELEVATION RANGE	5,400 to 7,470 feet at McMullen Peak
MILES OF TRAILS	No marked or maintained trails
ECOSYSTEMS	Ponderosa pine, piñon-juniper, scrub oak, semi-desert shrub and grassland
ADMINISTRATION	Gila National Forest
TOPOGRAPHIC MAPS	Tillie Hall Peak, Crookson Peak, Big Lue Mountains, and Mule Creek USGS 7.5-minute quadrangles
BEST SEASONS	Spring, summer, fall
GETTING THERE	Access from the north is via Highway 78 west of Mule Creek. Also, a county road heads south from Mule Creek to form the WSA's eastern border.
HIKING	Little hiking occurs in this area, and there are no trails or trailheads, although old roads could provide hiking routes. Dense stands of scrub oak could make cross-country travel difficult on the west.

47 Horse Mountain Wilderness Study Area

This rugged, remote area of canyons and ridges is named for 9,450-foot Horse Mountain—an extinct volcano rising 2,000 feet above the nearby Plains of San Agustin.

LOCATION	25 air miles southwest of Datil, near New Horse Springs, just north of Highway 12
SIZE	5,032 acres Size recommended by the NM Wilderness Alliance: 8,272 acres
ELEVATION RANGE	7,500 to 9,490 feet at Horse Mountain
MILES OF TRAILS	No marked or maintained trails
ECOSYSTEMS	Ponderosa pine and piñon-juniper woodlands, grassland
ADMINISTRATION	BLM
TOPOGRAPHIC MAPS	Horse Mountain West USGS 7.5-minute quadrangle
BEST SEASONS	Spring, summer, fall
GETTING THERE	From Highway 12, two county roads, B040 and B034, head north. These and the ancillary dirt roads branching from them provide access to the WSA's western and northern sections.
HIKING	Limited. This area has no designated trails, although several jeep trails approach the mountain. The area's dramatic scenery would reward people seeking solitude and self-contained camping.

Lower San Francisco Wilderness Study Area

48

Along the San Francisco River as it enters Arizona, this WSA is part of a river corridor of mesas that feature steep box canyons.

LOCATION	Southwest of Glenwood, west of Highway 180
SIZE	8,800 acres
ELEVATION RANGE	4,200 to 6,900 feet
MILES OF TRAILS	No marked or maintained trails
ECOSYSTEMS	Piñon-juniper, ponderosa pine
ADMINISTRATION	Gila National Forest
TOPOGRAPHIC MAPS	Wilson Mountain, Glenwood, Harden Cienega, and Maple Peak USGS 7.5-minute quadrangles
BEST SEASONS	Spring, summer, fall
GETTING THERE	From Highway 180 south of the community of Pleasanton, a dirt road heads southwest to drop down to the San Francisco River, ultimately ending at the San Francisco Hot Springs.
HIKING	The main recreational activity in this WSA is running the river because the boxes downriver from San Francisco Hot Springs limit foot travel along the river. Most boaters put in at the hot springs and float down to take out at Martinez in Arizona. Boaters need to be aware that sheer cliffs can make some sections extremely isolated.

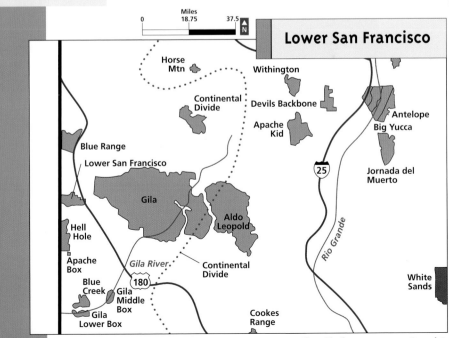

Detail of map on pages 8 and 9.

49 Withington Wilderness

This wilderness of arid, steep volcanic mountains is accessible only by two trails, both in narrow canyons through which tiny streams sometimes flow.

Bob Julyan

*Waterfall in
Withington Wilderness*

LOCATION	Southwest of Magdalena, in the northern San Mateo Mountains
SIZE	18,869 acres
ELEVATION RANGE	6,675 to 10,116 feet
MILES OF TRAILS	18
ECOSYSTEMS	Semidesert grassland, piñon-juniper, ponderosa pine, Douglas fir, aspen, and spruce
ADMINISTRATION	Cibola National Forest – Magdalena Ranger District
TOPOGRAPHIC MAPS	Apache Kid and Withington Wildernesses; Cibola National Forest; Mount Withington and Grassy Lookout 7.5-minute USGS quadrangles
BEST SEASONS	Spring, fall
GETTING THERE	Forest Road 549 heads south from Highway 60 west of Magdalena to connect with Forest Roads 138 and 330 as they go along the Withington Wilderness's western and southern boundaries. From Magdalena, all-weather dirt Highway 107 heads south, where the smaller and rougher Forest Road 52 provides access to the wilderness's eastern and northern sections.
HIKING	The relatively small size of the Withington Wilderness and the paucity of marked and maintained trails limit hiking here to day hikes and short backpack trips. Cross-country travel is difficult over the rough terrain.

GEOGRAPHIC ISOLATION, a paucity of trails, and arid, forbidding mountains make this wilderness among New Mexico's least visited. Yet for many hikers, therein lies the appeal of the Withington Wilderness, because like all wild areas it has its hidden treasures for those willing to discover them.

The Withington Wilderness was among several wilderness areas created by the New Mexico Wilderness Act of 1980, having been identified with wilderness characteristics by the RARE II process a few years earlier. Yet despite Withington's relatively small size—third smallest wilderness in the state—only the presence of a seldom-traveled dirt road and opposition from a politically powerful local rancher prevented it from being combined with the Apache Kid Wilderness farther south to create a much larger area (which the Forest Service had recommended). And given the low number of visitors to the San Mateo Mountains, the de facto wilderness vastly exceeds the formal boundaries to include almost the entire range.

Several factors account for the low visitation. One is distance from population centers. The nearest town, Magdalena, is 25 air miles away with a population of about 1,000. The nearest large town is Socorro, population 9,000, which is 45 air miles away. In addition to isolation, the area lacks a focus of interest. No singular geologic feature, no dramatic historical incident, no unusual natural characteristic— nothing attracts the attention of the outside world. Few New Mexicans have heard of the San Mateo Mountains, much less the Withington Wilderness.

And for those few hikers drawn here, there are few trails to take them into the wilderness, all involving long drives over rough dirt roads. Beyond the trails through narrow canyons, the rugged, dry terrain is spotted with unstable volcanic rock debris.

It's rough cross-country travel. Water is sparse, summer's heat fierce. Small wonder that the San Mateo Mountains were among the last redoubts for the Chiricahua Apaches to seek security (see Apache Kid Wilderness).

And yet . . .

Driving on dirt Highway 107 southwest from Magdalena across the expansive, rolling grasslands separating the Magdalena Mountains from the San Mateos to the west, you can easily imagine what this country looked like thousands of years ago at the end of the Pleistocene era when humans first appeared in the New World. Most of the animals that were here then have vanished forever, but pronghorn are still abundant, their white rumps conspicuous against the straw-colored canvas of grass.

At 17.3 miles, a much smaller and rougher Forest Road 52 leaves Highway 107 to head west to the San Mateo Mountains. After 3.4 miles, Forest Road 56, smaller and rougher still, branches south to lead down into Big Rosa Canyon. Here in the canyon bottom cattle graze the dry grass. From Big Rosa Canyon, trails head into the wilderness along the stream beds in Potato and Water Canyons. Dry Canyon also heads into the wilderness, but without a trail. The name explains why. (Speaking of names, the name Withington is among New Mexico's toponymic mysteries; many people have tried different approaches to learning who Withington was, but all have failed, yet his or her name appears on a major mountain in this part of New Mexico.)

Hikers can also access the Withington Wilderness from its periphery atop 10,116-foot Mount Withington and the San Mateo crest trending south. A dirt road, Forest Road 138, starts at Monica Saddle at the range's north end and leads to the Forest Service fire observation hut on the summit. From there the road runs south along the ridge before descending to the east, passing through the decaying remains of Rosedale. This long-abandoned mining camp flourished briefly in the decades following the Apache wars of the late 1800s, but in its entire history the mining district here never produced more than $300,000 worth of gold, silver, and copper.

Geology was to blame. The San Mateo Mountains are part of the Datil-Mogollon Physiographic Section that is characterized by volcanic formations. Like their sister range, the Magdalenas across the plains to the east, the San Mateos are composed of gray or pinkish volcanic rock, the product of eruptions 24–26 million years ago. Indeed, as one hikes up Potato Canyon, you'll appreciate the fantastic shapes into which this singular rock has eroded. Sometimes the rock formations have a curious laminar quality, like thin sheets, while near the canyon's head they have eroded into giant knobs reminiscent of potatoes, hence the canyon's name.

The mountains' slopes are dry and steep: game trails abound, but human trails are infrequent. In the canyon bottoms thrive ponderosa pine, Douglas fir, juniper, cottonwood, box elder, and Arizona walnut. The arid slopes have characteristic cacti, yucca, piñon pine, scrub oak, and one-seed and alligator juniper—all plants of the Upper Sonoran Desert. This diversity—canyon-bottom forest and desert slopes—fosters abundant wildlife, including whitetail and mule deer, elk, wild turkeys, mountain lions, and black bears.

Yet despite the above somewhat discouraging portrait of the Withington Wilderness, it richly fulfills the promise of wilderness everywhere. In Potato Canyon you'll find a tiny waterfall I deem among the state's most charming: I've named it Pink Glissade. Also in the canyon you'll find rock formations resembling Gothic architecture. Once, hiking over the divide separating Potato and Water Canyons, I encountered another hiker laden with photo equipment. Simply seeing another person was a surprise, but more intriguing was why he had come here: he photographed wildlife, and on a previous trip he'd seen four black bears.

DAY HIKE: WATER CANYON
One-way length: 4.4 miles
Low and high elevations: 7,200 and 9,400 feet
Difficulty: moderate to strenuous

This hike begins at the end of Forest Road 56 in Big Rosa Canyon. It ascends Water Canyon via Trail No. 37, getting steeper as it approaches its end at the mountain crest south of Mount Withington. The route is forested, and one usually finds water in the stream bed and in the springs along the route.

DESTINATION HIKE: PINK GLISSADE WATERFALL
One-way length: 2.2 miles
Low and high elevations: 6,750 and 6,800 feet
Difficulty: easy

The lower part of Potato Canyon is paved with flat, volcanic cobbles. Rely on tree blazes to follow the Potato Trail, No. 38, but the hiking isn't really that hard and the scenery is interesting. Look for the remains of an old log cabin, and not too long after that, you'll start a long, very steep climb out of the canyon. Skip the climb and scramble over some boulders in the stream bed to the little waterfall.

LOOP HIKE: POTATO CANYON – WATER CANYON –
BIG ROSA CANYON
Round-trip length: 11.0 miles
Low and high elevations: 6,800 and 8,405 feet
Difficulty: strenuous

A 2.5-mile trail marked in 1996 connects this loop between Potato Canyon and Water Canyon, if you hike along the road in Big Rosa Canyon for about three miles. For the easiest grades and a pleasant finish, park at the mouth of Potato Canyon, walk up Big Rosa, continue up Water Canyon to the connector, and then descend Potato Canyon to your vehicle.

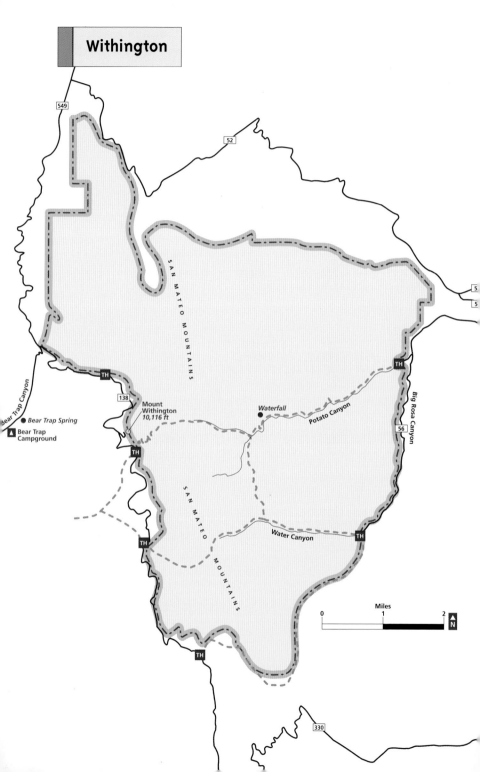

Withington

549

52

5

5

SAN MATEO MOUNTAINS

Bear Trap Canyon

TH

138

Mount
Withington
10,116 ft

● Bear Trap Spring

▲ Bear Trap
Campground

TH

Waterfall

Potato Canyon

Big Rosa Canyon

56

SAN MATEO MOUNTAINS

Water Canyon

TH

TH

TH

Miles

0   1   2

N

330

SHUTTLE HIKE: POTATO CANYON
One-way length: 6.2 miles
Low and high elevations: 6,800 and 10,116 feet
Difficulty: moderate

Begin this hike at the Forest Service fire lookout atop Mount Withington. The Potato Canyon Trail, No. 38, descends the steep slope to the east, affording views of huge potato-shaped knobs. The trail becomes more level as it descends Potato Canyon, but the tread often is obscure, so pay attention to tree blazes and your map. In South Potato Canyon, just above its junction with Potato Canyon, are some interesting rock formations. Just below this junction in a tight gorge you'll see what I call the Pink Glissade, a delightful pink-rock waterfall. The hike ends at the junction with Big Rosa Canyon.

OTHER RECREATIONAL OPPORTUNITIES

The Big Rosa Canyon Trail, No. 36, is mostly outside the wilderness as it climbs 4.9 miles to the mountain crest. It follows an old road through the canyon for most of that distance and is open for mountain biking.

FOR MORE INFORMATION

CIBOLA NATIONAL FOREST – MAGDALENA RANGER DISTRICT, P.O. Box 45, Magdalena, NM 87825; (505) 854-2281.

The East Central Region

The East Central Region is bounded on the west by the San Andres and Oscura ranges, which include some of New Mexico's largest tracts of wildland. However, these are not likely to have wilderness designation because they are within the White Sands Missile Range. On the east, the region grades onto the high plains of eastern New Mexico. To the north, plains again define the region, while to the south the region stops at the Mexican border.

Within this small, compact region the wildlands have little in common except proximity. Here is found New Mexico's greatest topographical relief: 8,000 feet from the Tularosa Basin to Sierra Blanca's 12,003-foot summit. The ecological gradient is almost as steep: the gypsum dunes of White Sands support just a few, highly adapted xerophytic plants while within the White Mountain and Capitan Mountain Wildernesses are diverse, well-watered forest ecosystems—habitat for deer, elk, mountain lions, and black bears.

The landscape within this region owes much of its character to the last Ice Age, which seems ironic given that the southern New Mexico environment here hardly fits the image of a classic cold-climate land-scape. Yet Sierra Blanca was the southernmost glaciated mountain in North America. The glaciers were small and ephemeral (erase from your mind images of the Talkeetna Glacier in Alaska), but they did shape the high mountain valleys here. Sierra Blanca, a long-extinct volcano, is the region's dominant mountain, a landmark visible throughout southeastern New Mexico. But the wilderness named for this peak doesn't include it; Sierra Blanca is within the Mescalero Apache Indian Reservation, and the Mescaleros, who venerate the peak, discourage hiking. Rather, the wilderness extends northward from the peak, through public lands administered by the Lincoln National Forest, along the mountain crest that ends just south of Highway 380. Along this crest—cool, lush, a cushy quilt of conifer forests, aspen groves, and meadows, with water and good campsites readily at hand—is some of New Mexico's finest hiking and backpacking.

That doesn't mean, however, that very many hikers take advantage of this. The mountains are not close to any large population centers, and although the nearby resort town of Ruidoso is a hive of tourists in the

Rainbow over dunes, White Sands National Monument

summer, most visitors are more interested in the wildflowers on souvenir T-shirts than those along mountain trails. Furthermore, with the Mescaleros now operating a casino as well as a resort hotel, the closest most visitors to the reservation get to Sierra Blanca is the Mescaleros' resort hotel named the Inn of the Mountain Gods.

To the northeast of the White Mountain Wilderness is the Lincoln National Forest wilderness centered on the Capitan Mountains. This wilderness is also aligned along a mountain crest, although here running east to west (the Capitans are the only New Mexico range oriented in this way). Here, as in the White Mountains, Pleistocene glaciers played a role in shaping the mountains' character, although in the Capitans the glaciers were comprised of rock flowing downhill in a matrix of ice. Huge boulder fields, the remains of these rock glaciers, still drape the mountains' steep slopes.

The Capitan Mountains are less hiker-friendly than the White Mountains: water is more problematic, trails are rougher and steeper, and access is more difficult. Geologically, the Capitan Mountains are a huge granitic intrusion, called a laccolith, which formed beneath sedimentary layers that have since eroded away. (Imagine a huge egg-shaped boulder embedded in the midst of plains; then imagine the boulder three to four miles wide, 12 miles long, and rising 3,000 feet above the surrounding plains to an elevation of 10,000 feet.) Precipitation falling on the mountains' upper slopes sometimes reappears as springs of varying reliability. On the steep slopes grow piñon pines, alligator junipers, scrub oak, and, at higher elevations, ponderosa pine, spruce, and fir. Doughty day-hikers routinely trek to Capitan Peak, but backpackers are generally deterred by daunting terrain and logistical obstacles.

At the other elevational and climatic extreme from the nearby mountains is White Sands National Monument, located in the parched, 4,000-feet elevation basin once occupied by a huge Pleistocene lake. At 147,200 acres, the monument is almost twice as large as the two mountain wildernesses combined. But large as the monument seems, its expanse of gypsum dunes is only part of the even larger whole, a white desert conspicuous even from space. Most of the whole, however, is within White Sands Missile Range and consequently off-limits to the public.

Tourists by the thousands annually visit White Sands National Monument to frolic on the dunes, and frankly, any visitor who doesn't succumb to frolicking should go back and try again. White Sands National Monument isn't really a hikers' wilderness—and backpacking is prohibited except on the short designated trail. Still, no portrait of New Mexico's wilderness landscape would be complete without this vast roadless area with its unique ecology.

At the other extreme in terms of texture and color is the unit of two contiguous BLM Wilderness Study Areas called Carrizozo Lava Flow–Little Black Peak, located northwest of Carrizozo. Instead of being soft and white, these wildlands are jagged and black. About 1,000 years ago, lava oozed from fissures associated with Little Black Peak, eventually creating a flow extending 44 miles into the Tularosa Basin. The appropriately named Valley of Fires State Park features this flow on Highway 380, which is also the main access for the two wilderness study areas. Day hikers who've not experienced lava flows would find this volcanic area interesting, and the plant and animal life is surprisingly abundant and diverse. But this is not a backpacking destination, and even day hikers will find hiking the lava is a tough test of their balance and boots.

50 Capitan Mountains Wilderness

The Capitan Mountains are characterized by steep, rocky slopes and a ridge capped by numerous summits.

Majestic Chimney Rock

LOCATION	East of Carrizozo, north of Lincoln
SIZE	35,822 acres
ELEVATION RANGE	5,500 to 10,201 feet
MILES OF TRAILS	32
ECOSYSTEMS	Semidesert; piñon-juniper, ponderosa pine, and aspen; Douglas fir, Engelmann spruce, and corkbark fir at higher elevations
ADMINISTRATION	Lincoln National Forest – Smokey Bear Ranger District
TOPOGRAPHIC MAPS	Lincoln National Forest – Capitan Mountains Wilderness
BEST SEASONS	Spring, summer, fall
GETTING THERE	The Capitan Mountains Wilderness is north of Highway 380, linking the villages of Lincoln and Capitan. Highway 246 goes around the mountains' western and northern perimeter, while Highway 368 goes past the eastern section. From these highways forest roads head toward the mountains.
HIKING	Though the mountains have an extensive system of maintained trails, logistical obstacles limit most hiking here to day trips, although a backpack trip along the range's crest is certainly possible.

GEOGRAPHERS LIKE TO POINT OUT that the Capitan Mountains are among the nation's few east-west trending ranges. Cultural historians remind us that these mountains gave us Smokey the Bear, and that this landscape was the backdrop for the infamous Lincoln County War and the many exploits of Billy the Kid. But what hikers likely will remember of the Capitans is long miles of rough trail through country as rugged as anyone could possibly desire.

Geologically, the Capitan Mountains are a laccolith, a mass of intrusive igneous rock that heaved the surrounding sedimentary layers into a dome. Over time, the sedimentary rocks eroded away, except for a few remnants capping the crest summits leaving the igneous core rising more than 3,000 feet above the surrounding countryside. Knowing this geologic history makes it easier to understand the mountains' ridgelike character, with steep slopes and dramatic rock glaciers. Occurring on both the range's north and south flanks, these "glaciers" formed during the recent Ice Ages when ice welded together the rocks of giant talus slopes; then as a unit the entire mass flowed downhill, just as a glacier would. When the ice eventually melted, the stones remained.

Because the mountains are essentially an east-west ridge, the trail system consists of feeder trails leading from the range's north and south foothills to connect with the trail along the crest. Consequently, these feeder trails are often quite steep, typically rising 3,000 feet in a few miles. Hikers begin walking among semidesert plants and piñon-juniper woodland, then through open ponderosa forest leading to Douglas fir, Engelmann spruce, and corkbark fir interspersed with meadows and aspen groves. This diversity, coupled with springs and streams fed by snow accumulations on the crest, make the mountains an outstanding habitat for animals such as black bears, mule deer, elk, mountain lions, and numerous smaller mammals. Wild turkeys are also common here.

The feeder trails rising to the crest are linked by base trails on the north and south sides of the range. The North Base Trail, No. 65, is 4.6 miles long with gentle gradients; the more heavily used South Base Trail, No. 57, is 11.8 miles long, also with gentle gradients, although portions can be rough due to erosion. Water is usually available along both base trails. Although the feeder trails receive very little use, the trails are well-marked and water is generally available along routes that parallel drainages (check with local rangers before counting on it and, of course, treat all water before drinking).

Most hikers gain access to the range's crest from its west end, leaving much of the elevation gain to their vehicle. From Capitan Pass a very rough four-wheel-drive route skirts the southern boundary of the wilderness until it nears the unnamed 10,179-foot summit (the high point of the range where the road ends at the wilderness boundary). From here the Summit Trail, No. 58, heads east along a series of summits to end near 10,083-foot Capitan Peak at the junction with the Capitan Peak Trail, No. 57. Hiking on the Summit Trail along the ridge doesn't require as much climbing as the feeder trails, but there's still plenty of up and down, and hikers often return saying the mountains are among the rockiest they've ever encountered. You won't have trouble finding a good campsite along the crest. Regrettably, however, there is little or no water along the crest.

The Capitan Mountains Wilderness is challenging—no doubt about that. Challenging, rugged, and wild, and filled with all the unexpected difficulties and joys that wilderness is all about.

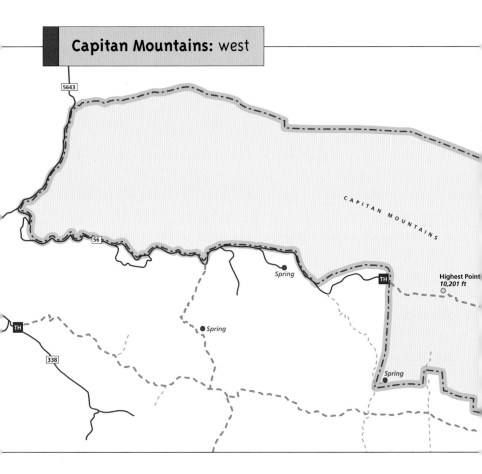

Capitan Mountains: west

5643

56

Spring

CAPITAN MOUNTAINS

TH

Highest Point
10,201 ft

TH

● *Spring*

338

Spring

DESTINATION HIKE: SUMMIT TRAIL
One-way length: 8.5 miles
Low and high elevations: 9,200 and 10,179 feet
Difficulty: strenuous

This is a trip for strong cars and strong hikers. East of Capitan on Highway 380, Forest Road 56 heads north to Capitan Pass, where it then runs east along the crest to the wilderness boundary near the 10,179-foot unnamed summit. Here you'll find a good site for car camping. This road is very rough and unsuited for passenger cars. From the wilderness boundary, Summit Trail No. 58 continues east along the crest, connecting several high points, until at 8.5 miles it reaches Capitan Peak (10,083 feet). The trail is long and often rocky, but from the summit you can see as many as 17 other mountain ranges.

Capitan Mountains: east

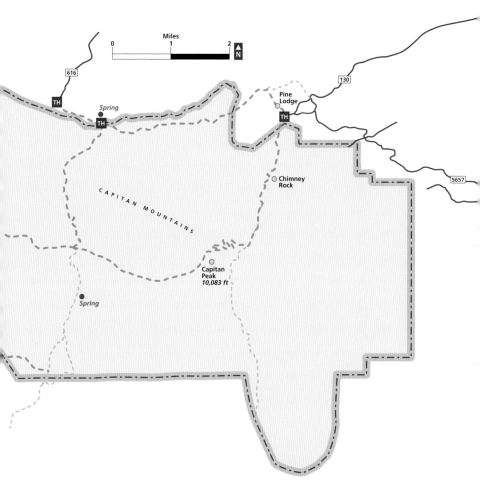

DESTINATION HIKE: CAPITAN PEAK
One-way length: 5.7 miles
Low and high elevations: 6,300 and 10,083 feet
Difficulty: strenuous

This steep but scenic trail includes spectacular vistas and interesting rock formations, including Chimney Rock, which is two miles up the trail. The trail climaxes at 10,083-foot Capitan Peak, where it connects with the Summit Trail, No. 58.

The trail continues running west along the crest of the Capitan Mountains. Most hikers on the Capitan Peak Trail, however, simply return as they came. The trailhead is on the range's north side. You can reach it by driving Highway 246 out of Capitan, heading north and then east to parallel the range's north side. When you reach Forest Road 130, turn right and drive to the Pine Lodge Cabins.

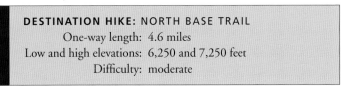

DESTINATION HIKE: SOUTH BASE TRAIL
One-way length: 11.8 miles
Low and high elevations: 6,750 and 7,000 feet
Difficulty: moderate

While this trail is among the easiest in the Capitan Mountains, most people don't hike it. But because it connects the trails heading north to the crest, it's a perfect part of different loop hikes. You can reach the head of the South Base Trail, No. 57, by taking Highway 380 east from Capitan. Then take Forest Road 56 north into the foothills to where Forest Road 338 heads east. The South Base Trail begins along this road and runs east to end at its junction with the Pierce Canyon Trail. For people exploring the south side of the Capitan Mountains, the Forest Service Baca Campground is south of the South Base Trail.

DESTINATION HIKE: NORTH BASE TRAIL
One-way length: 4.6 miles
Low and high elevations: 6,250 and 7,250 feet
Difficulty: moderate

This is the northern counterpart to the South Base Trail because it links trails running from the mountains' northern foothills up canyons and ridges to the crest. The eastern terminus of the North Base Trail, No. 65, is at Pine Lodge, which you can reach by taking Highway 246 north out of Capitan to Forest Road 130 and eventually to Pine Lodge. The North Base Trail is pleasant and generally easy hiking in its own right. It ends when it meets Forest Road 616 to the west.

FOR MORE INFORMATION

LINCOLN NATIONAL FOREST - SMOKEY BEAR RANGER DISTRICT, 901 Mechem Drive, Ruidoso, NM 88345; (505) 257-4095.

LINCOLN NATIONAL FOREST, Supervisor's Office, Federal Building, 1101 New York Avenue, Alamogordo, NM 88310; (505) 434-7200.

SMOKEY THE BEAR

What is it about New Mexico that its three most famous individuals are an outlaw, an alien, and a bear? The outlaw is Billy the Kid, the alien is the one whose craft supposedly crashed near Roswell, and the bear is Smokey.

An entire generation of Americans (including me) grew up with the image of a kindly, avuncular-looking bear in a Forest Ranger's hat, urging people to fight forest fires. Smokey was as familiar as Mickey Mouse or Superman. The big difference was that Smokey was real. Every kid in the 1950s and even later knew the story:

Remember
Only you can PREVENT FOREST FIRES!
1944–1994

The weather in New Mexico was hot and dry that May in 1950 when a careless human, driving along Capitan Gap Road, flipped a lit cigarette or match onto the tinder like forest floor. It smoldered, then ignited, and soon, fanned by strong winds, caused a forest fire that roared over the Capitan Mountains and destroyed every-thing in its path. Firefighters, rushing to the scene from wherever they could be found, risked their lives—but little could be done. When the fire was finally brought under control, 17,000 acres had been devastated. The area seemed completely bereft of life until one firefighter found a badly burned bear cub, miraculously still alive, clinging to a charred tree.

They attempted to treat the little bear, and decided to fly him to a veterinarian in Santa Fe. When the cub began to recover, people wanted to adopt him, but this was not a viable long-term solution. Then state con-servation officials, including state game department head Elliott Barker, realized the increasingly famous bear had tremendous potential as a fire-prevention symbol. Already christened with the name of Smokey, he was taken to the National Zoo in Washington, D.C., where for 25 years he was the zoo's most famous resident.

When Smokey eventually died of natural causes, his remains were returned for burial at Capitan, the village where Smokey Bear Historical State Park is located. Another New Mexican black bear went to Washington as Smokey II, thus perpetuating the tradition.

Smokey's impact upon America's conservation consciousness has been enormous. In the 1980s, a poll showed that 98 percent of Americans recognized him. In Washington, at least 3 million people a year visit him at the zoo; he has his own zip code (20252) and receives 30,000 pieces of mail a year, each answered and signed with a paw print. In the years the Smokey Bear fire prevention campaign has been in place, forest and range fires have been reduced by half. Before 1950, the fires totalled 200,000 annually and destroyed some 30 million acres, with 90 percent caused by human carelessness. This reduction has produced an estimated savings of $27 billion. Smokey's influence has even spread to other countries; Mexico adopted a counterpart to Smokey called *Simon Oso*, "Simon Bear," or *El Osito Bombero*, "little bear fireman."

An outlaw, an alien, and a bear: I don't know about the other two, but I'm proud of the bear.

Little Black Peak and Carrizozo Lava Flow Wilderness Study Areas

These two closely related, contiguous WSAs are separated only by a highway. The Carrizozo Malpais dominates both areas. Extensive and relatively recent lava flows originated from fissures near Little Black Peak. Wildlife is surprisingly varied and includes several melanistic, lava-adapted species.

New Mexico Wilderness Alliance

Carrizozo Lava Flow

LOCATION	Four miles west of Carrizozo, along Highway 380
SIZE	25,312 acres (combined)
	Size recommended by the NM Wilderness Alliance: 46,083 acres (combined)
ELEVATION RANGE	4,000 to 5,676 feet
MILES OF TRAILS	No marked or maintained trails
ECOSYSTEMS	Grasses and shrubs, occasional one-seed juniper
ADMINISTRATION	BLM
TOPOGRAPHIC MAPS	Carrizozo West
BEST SEASONS	Fall, winter, spring
GETTING THERE	The only legal year-round access is from Highway 380 west of Carrizozo. The best place to explore the lava is Valley of Fires State Park, which abuts the WSAs.
HIKING	Limited; no delineated routes, and walking over the lava can be daunting.

52 White Mountain Wilderness

This north-south mountain ridge contains southern New Mexico's highest peaks. But forests and rolling meadows also characterize this area, which makes for easy and inviting hiking.

Along the South Fork

LOCATION	In the northern Sacramento Mountains, north of Ruidoso
SIZE	48,873 acres
ELEVATION RANGE	4,700 to 11,300 feet near Lookout Mountain
MILES OF TRAILS	110
ECOSYSTEMS	Semidesert shrubs and grassland, piñon-juniper, ponderosa pine, spruce-fir, and high meadow grassland
ADMINISTRATION	Lincoln National Forest – Smokey Bear Ranger District
TOPOGRAPHIC MAPS	Lincoln National Forest – White Mountain Wilderness
BEST SEASONS	Spring, summer, fall
GETTING THERE	The White Mountain Wilderness is within a rough triangle whose points are Carrizozo, Ruidoso, and Tularosa. Access to the wilderness from the south is blocked by the Mescalero Apache Indian Reservation. Most access is from the east, with forest roads heading into the wilderness from Highway 37 and connecting Ruidoso with Highway 380. From the west, the wilderness is reached from Highway 54 by Forest Road 579 leading to the Three Rivers Campground.
HIKING	A mild climate, a welcoming environment, a good system of maintained trails, and easy access make for outstanding hiking in the White Mountain Wilderness.

THE MOUNTAINS OF THE SOUTHWEST have been described as "sky islands," and nowhere is this more true than the mountain ridge known as the White Mountains, a subrange of the larger Sacramento Mountains. From the parched Chihuahuan Desert of the Tularosa Basin just to the west, the mountains rise precipitously 8,000 feet to the alpine life zone atop the 12,003-foot summit of Sierra Blanca, the southernmost occurrence of this life zone in the U.S. No place in New Mexico has greater vertical relief. To the east stretch the arid high plains. The range and the wilderness take their name from Sierra Blanca, "white mountain," the dominant peak whose retention of snow long after other peaks are bare has made it a landmark throughout southern New Mexico.

But the White Mountains are a cultural island as well. Although you can find race tracks, tourist condos, ski resorts, a casino, Stealth bombers, and space age missiles near its borders, the White Mountain Wilderness remains an enclave of serene beauty and solitude. Hikers haven't overlooked the White Mountains, but they are surprisingly scarce relative to the area's tourist hordes. The closest most visitors get to mountain wildflowers are those on the T-shirts in souvenir shops.

The mountains have been traditionally associated with the Mescalero Apaches, who once roamed all of southeastern New Mexico and whose modern reservation encompasses the White Mountains' southern portion, including Sierra Blanca. While the tribe's territory has shrunk dramatically, the Mescaleros have used their natural resources as well as formidable entrepreneurial skills to thrive. Logging, commercial hunting, and above all tourism have made the tribe among the nation's most prosperous. They operate the sumptuous Inn of the Mountain Gods, the Ski Apache ski area, and, most recently, a casino. Their reservation forms the White Mountain Wilderness's southern boundary, and hikers planning to climb Sierra Blanca must obtain permission because the mountain is considered sacred.

In 1879, gold and later silver were discovered in the northern White Mountains. A modest mining boom ensued and small mining camps sprang up. The only surviving communities of the inevitable bust are Nogal and Bonito on the wilderness's northeast side. However, mine dumps, prospect holes, and mining claims still dot the area.

Little did the miners suspect that the area's most valuable resource was its climate. If you live in El Paso, Las Cruces, Alamogordo, or elsewhere in southern New Mexico or west Texas, the Sacramento Mountains are the nearest place to escape the summer swelter. They also provide close-by skiing. Second homes, retirement homes, ski lodges and resorts, tourist shops, arts and crafts galleries, horse racing, and so forth have continually flourished since 1900. The area's popularity shows no sign of abating.

But few visitors come here for the wilderness, and I strongly suspect that most of the hikers you'd meet on the trails would be locals.

Spring hiking begins in April (depending on how mild or severe the winter), although snow can linger on higher north-facing slopes much later. High elevation and abundant moisture foster an unusually rich array of wildflowers, especially in the numerous meadows along the crest. Summer is also delightful, although subject in late summer to afternoon thundershowers. And fall . . . magnificent! Dry weather with warm days and cool nights makes the area attractive, especially with hillsides dappled with the changing foliage of oaks, aspens, and maples.

The White Mountain Wilderness is one of the few hiking areas in southern New Mexico where water is not problematic. Even along the crest, you're never far from a spring or creek, although you should always check with local rangers for current conditions. The streams are small, however, so don't bring your fishing rod. Because cattle graze the wilderness, all water should be treated.

The wilderness is aligned along a north-south ridge, which means most trails ascend ridges or canyons to the crest to intersect the Crest Trail. Given the plethora of canyons and ridges, you can choose from numerous loop and shuttle hikes. Hiking the Crest Trail itself requires a vehicle near Monjeau Peak and another at Nogal Canyon. You'll find springs along the crest, and excellent campsites abound. It's a thrill to look down to the west and see the expanse of White Sands 7,000 feet below.

Generally, the trails on the ridge's east side are more popular than those on the west, where the terrain is somewhat steeper, more exposed, and less accessible. The main trailhead from the west is at the Three Rivers Campground, which you can reach from Highway 54 north of Tularosa. From the south, trails branch off from Highway 532 leading to Ski Apache and the electronic site atop Buck Mountain. From this road branches the dirt road leading to Monjeau Peak. From the east, the major trailheads are at South Fork Campground and Argentina Canyon Campground, both of which you can reach by driving Forest Road 107 past Bonito Lake.

I have a dedicated backpacker friend who has hiked all over New Mexico. When I asked him what place was his favorite, he didn't hesitate: the Crest Trail of the White Mountain Wilderness. He returns there every chance he gets. My wife and hiking partner, Mary, agrees. Of all the places we've hiked together in New Mexico, the White Mountain Wilderness Crest Trail is the one to which she'd most like to return.

DESTINATION HIKE: THREE RIVERS
One-way length: 5.6 miles
Low and high elevations: 6,400 and 9,780 feet
Difficulty: strenuous

This is the main route by which hikers enter the wilderness from the west. It begins at the Three Rivers Campground, which you can reach from Highway 54 between Tularosa and Carrizozo by Forest Road 579. Forest Road 579 heads east past the very interesting Three Rivers Petroglyph Site to end at the campground at the wilderness boundary. The Three Rivers Trail, No. 44, for the most part goes up Three Rivers Canyon, a rare and delightful perennial stream that offers not only water but also shade and good campsites. Near the drainage's head, the trail switchbacks steeply up the range's west face to end at the junction with the Crest Trail, No. 25, just east of 10,255-foot White Horse Hill. You could make a loop by taking Trail 31 from the Three Rivers Trail to connect with the Dry Canyon Trail, No. 46, which follows a tributary of Three Rivers Creek.

LOOP HIKE: ARGENTINA CANYON – BONITO CANYON
Round-trip length: 5.6 miles
Low and high elevations: 7,820 and 8,960 feet
Difficulty: moderate

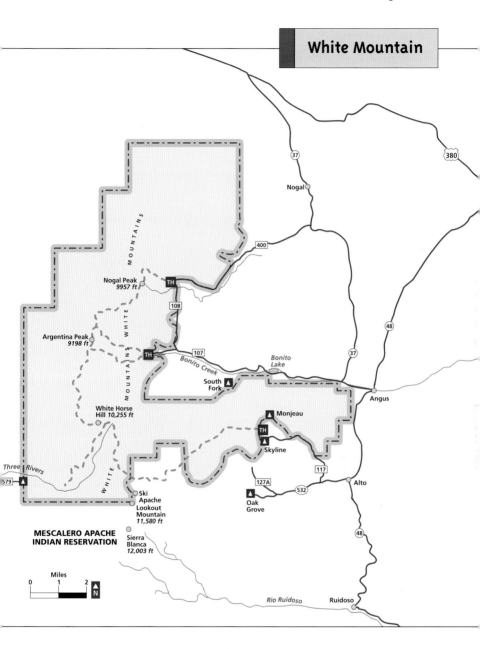

You reach this hike north of Ruidoso by driving the partly paved, partly dirt Forest Road 107 west from Highway 37 along Bonito Creek past Bonito Lake to the trailhead. This loop can be completed from either way, but the hiking is easier if you begin by hiking up Argentina Canyon, on Trail 39. After 2.5 miles the trail reaches Argentina Spring (you'll want to carry your own water) and the junction with the Crest Trail, No. 25. Hike south through high meadows on the Crest Trail about 0.5 mile past Argentina Peak to a large meadow and the junction with the Little Bonito Trail, No. 38. It's about 2.6 miles from the meadow back to the trailhead.

Before following this down to its junction with the Bonito Trail, No. 36, and on to the trailhead, hike the easy 0.25 mile west from the meadow to Spring Cabin, a locked Forest Service facility. The beautiful campsites nearby are more interesting than the cabin.

SHUTTLE HIKE: WHITE MOUNTAIN CREST TRAIL
One-way length: 22.0 miles
Low and high elevations: 8,792 and 10,400 feet
Difficulty: moderate to strenuous
(due to length of hike and pack weight)

This is the premier hike in the White Mountain Wilderness—relatively easy, ample water, beautiful campsites, and spectacular scenery. The only problem is getting back to where you started. One could argue that starting south (9,200 feet) and ending north (8,792 feet) saves 400 feet of climbing, but I doubt the difference is significant. Both routes begin with rather gentle gradients. The southern trailhead is 0.5 mile past Skyline Campground, which you can reach by taking Highway 532 west from Highway 37 north of Alto. After about a mile, Forest Road 117 goes north. Skyline Campground has no water. You can reach the northern trailhead by taking Forest Road 400 west from Highway 37 into Nogal Canyon. Near its end, Forest Road 108 heads south about 0.5 mile to the trailhead. Forest Road 108 connects Nogal Canyon with Bonito Canyon, and the intersection is not far from the Argentina Campground. Along this route several trails connect with the Crest Trail, No. 25, where you can enjoy several shorter loop or shuttle trips. Once you're on the ridge, the Crest Trail follows a rolling route through forests, aspen groves, and meadows, with several springs just down the slope from the crest. If you had to cut your trip short, you could follow one of the connecting trails downhill.

BOB JULYAN'S FAVORITE HIKE: CREST TRAIL SOUTH END
One-way length: 5.0 miles
Low and high elevations: 9,220 and 10,400 feet
Difficulty: moderate

This is a day-hike version of the multi-day Crest Trail described above. Open grassy meadows with wonderful views, aspen groves, forests, and a gentle trail make for a very pleasant experience. Take Highway 532 west from Highway 37. After about a mile, Forest Road 117 goes north. This steep and often rough road leads after 12 miles to the Lincoln National Forest fire lookout at 9,641-foot Monjeau Peak, an interesting side trip to the hike. The Forest Service Skyline Campground (no water) is about a mile before the lookout, and the trailhead for the Crest Trail is 0.5 mile before the lookout. The Crest Trail, No. 25, almost immediately enters the meadows for which it is noted. It travels through meadows, aspens, and then spruce-fir forest to emerge after 2.5 miles at another meadow, a good place to break or turn around. From here the Crest Trail continues ascending gradually another two miles to 10,400 feet as it passes along the west side of Buck Mountain, site of electronic facilities. From there it descends to junction with Trail 15, which connects with the Ski Apache facilities.

OTHER RECREATIONAL OPPORTUNITIES

You'll find excellent mountain biking near the wilderness from Forest Road 107, which runs west to the wilderness from Highway 37 north of Alto. Philadelphia Canyon, Kraut Canyon, and Littleton Canyon all run northwest along old mine roads that eventually become single-track, the latter two from Bonito Lake. Forest Road 107 itself offers easy and scenic mountain biking, part paved, part gravel. Forest Road 107 passes by Bonito Lake and ends at the Argentina Canyon Campground near the wilderness boundary. Near Ruidoso, a local favorite is the winding and climbing Perk Canyon ride. And farther south, near Cloudcroft, you'll find the Rim Trail, a 17-mile route along the crest of the Sacramento Mountains. This ride is ranked among the nation's top mountain bike rides.

Two areas near the wilderness offer downhill skiing: Ski Apache, a ski resort operated by the Mescalero Apaches, and the much more modest Ski Cloudcroft at the village's east end. No maintained cross-country ski trails exist in the wilderness, and because of the area's southern latitude, snowpack can vary widely from year to year. Still, when conditions are good, several routes lead from Bonito Canyon on Forest Road 107, which is plowed for most of its length. Backcountry skiers head to Buck Mountain, just outside the wilderness at the south. The Crest Trail can also be accessed from here, and its high, rolling character makes it eminently suited for cross-country skiing.

Horseback riding is popular in the area, often on wilderness trails. You can attribute the popularity to the famed horse race track and Museum of the Horse, both of which sit at the center of horse culture in the Ruidoso area.

FOR MORE INFORMATION

LINCOLN NATIONAL FOREST – SMOKEY BEAR RANGER DISTRICT,
901 Mechem Drive, Ruidoso, NM 88345; (505) 257-4095.

LINCOLN NATIONAL FOREST, Supervisor's Office, Federal Building,
1101 New York Avenue, Alamogordo, NM 88310-6992; (505) 434-7200.

53 White Sands National Monument

This area features a unique ecology, including a vast expanse of snow-white gypsum dunes.

Sunrise light

LOCATION	14 miles southwest of Alamogordo on Highway 70, north of the highway
SIZE	147,200 acres
ELEVATION RANGE	Approximately 4,000 feet throughout
MILES OF TRAILS	Short nature trails, no developed hiking trails
ECOSYSTEMS	Scattered alkaline-resistant and drought-resistant trees, shrubs, and grasses
ADMINISTRATION	National Park Service
TOPOGRAPHIC MAPS	Garton Lake and Heart of the Sands USGS 7.5-minute quadrangles
BEST SEASONS	Winter, spring, fall
GETTING THERE	White Sands National Monument is reached by taking Highway 70 southwest from Alamogordo to the visitor center at the monument's entrance.
HIKING	Except for walking on the dunes, hiking here is limited to officially designated nature trails and one backcountry campsite, for which a permit is required.

NO PORTRAIT OF NEW MEXICO'S WILDLANDS would be complete without White Sands, and while the national monument rarely is a hiking, much less a back-packing, destination, the unique environment here is eminently worthy of off-road exploration. Furthermore, at more than 230 square miles penetrated by only seven miles of access road, the monument is among the state's largest roadless areas.

White Sands is the result of unique geologic and meteorological circumstances. About 30,000 years ago, during the Pleistocene Epoch when the climate was cooler and wetter than today, the Tularosa Basin between the Sacramento and San Andres Mountains was filled with a vast undrained lake whose waters contained calcium sulfate—gypsum—that had washed down from the *Yeso,* "gypsum," formation in the San Andres Mountains to the west. About 20,000 years ago, as the lake began to dry up, gypsum crystals known as selenite began precipitating from the mineral-saturated water. This process of evaporation and precipitation continues today, south of the monument at Lake Lucero, whose shallow waters are all that remain of the huge Pleistocene lake.

But at the same time the basin was drying up, the prevailing winds began changing, blowing from the south and west. These winds picked up gypsum particles from the dry lake bed and deposited them into the dunes known as White Sands. Again, this process continues today.

People naturally associate dunes with sand, but these dunes are distinct from sand dunes. They're not only snow-white, but the gypsum particles are distinctly softer than the quartz grains that normally make up sand dunes.

Similarly, people assume the dunes to be devoid of plant and animal life, but in fact plant and animal communities do exist here. Plants at White Sands must be able to tolerate high alkalinity; fourwing saltbush is an example. Plants must also have roots that can cope with the deep, shifting dunes; the soaptree yucca, for example, can send its roots up to 40 feet deep and thus stay atop the dunes. Hoary rosemary mint has fast-growing vinelike roots that quickly spread over the surface. Skunkbush sumac has a tough, extensive root system that provides a firm anchor. In between the dunes are flat areas with high water tables.

Because the sand readily records animal tracks, hikers will immediately notice that the dunes are home to lizards, insects, rodents, foxes, coyotes, roadrunners, and other birds, and many more.

White Sands National Monument has no campground; the nearest public campground is at Oliver Lee Memorial State Park, south of Alamogordo, east of Highway 54 at the mouth of Dog Canyon (which is a spectacular canyon). From the monument's visitor center a paved road heads into the dunes. At three miles is the one-mile Big Dunes Nature Trail. After another four miles you'll reach the area known as Heart of the Dunes (which has picnic tables and toilets).

While a backcountry campsite is available, most people simply take day hikes. In summer, the heat can be brutal, and in all seasons the light reflected at midday from the white dunes is intense. Wear dark glasses, a hat, and sunscreen. Also, any water you encounter (not likely) will be undrinkable because of dissolved minerals. The topography is confusing—the dunes quickly all begin to look alike, so plan on retracing your footsteps or using a GPS receiver.

White Sands National Monument

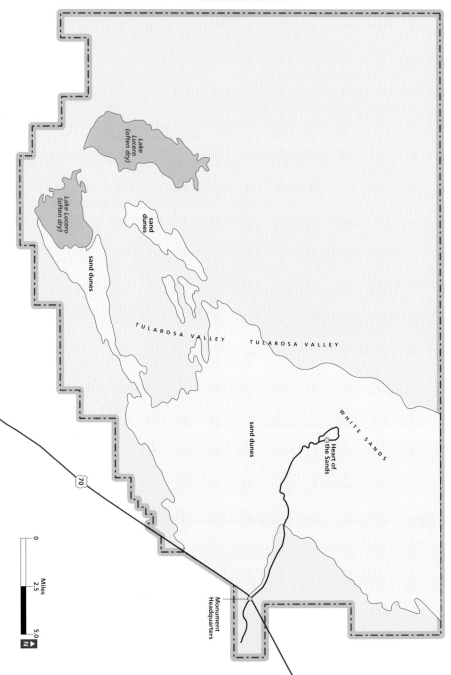

WHITE SANDS MISSiLE RANGE

Lake Lucero (often dry)

Lake Lucero (often dry)

sand dunes

sand dunes

sand dunes

sand dunes

TULAROSA VALLEY

TULAROSA VALLEY

WHITE SANDS

Heart of the Sands

Monument Headquarters

70

Miles
0
2.5
5.0
N

But let's face it: White Sands isn't really where you come for serious hiking. To me it's a place to bring the kids or come be a kid again myself. I take off my shoes, put on loose clothing I know will get filled with gypsum, and go romping and exploring. This is the playful side of wilderness!

DAY HIKE: BIG DUNES NATURE TRAIL
One-way length: 1.0 mile
Low and high elevations: approximately 4,000 feet throughout
Difficulty: easy

An interpretive trail is located about three miles from the monument's visitor center.

BACKPACK HIKE: OVERNIGHT BACKCOUNTRY CAMPSITE
One-way length: typically very short
Low and high elevations: approximately 4,000 feet throughout
Difficulty: easy

A permit is required for this site, whose location changes. Backcountry camping here is especially appealing during the summer, on nights when the moon is full and the air soft and warm.

OTHER RECREATIONAL OPPORTUNITIES

As one of the world's premier sandpiles, White Sands National Monument is perfect for, well . . . playing in the sand—sliding, tumbling and rolling, leaping and bounding, and building sand castles. The area also lends itself to dramatic outdoor photography, although photographers must take into account the sand's extreme whiteness. (Photography tip: when shooting people on the dunes, adjust the aperture according to light reflected from your hand, not the dunes.) Riding a bicycle along the paved road leading into the dunes would be an excellent way to explore the monument.

FOR MORE INFORMATION

White Sands National Monument, P.O. Box 1086, Holloman AFB, NM 88330; (505) 679-2599.

The South Central Desert Region

The Chihuahuan Desert is one of New Mexico's major ecosystems and is well-represented in the wildlands of the South Central Desert Region centered around Las Cruces—New Mexico's third largest city and among the nation's fastest growing. No wilderness has been formally designated here, but several BLM Wilderness Study Areas exist within an hour's drive of the city. In addition to these, several areas of de facto wilderness exist here, although as with the acreage held by White Sands Missile Range, public entry is often forbidden.

The most conspicuous of these WSAs is within the BLM's Organ Mountains, whose dramatic spires, reminiscent of an organ's huge pipes (hence the name), are a dramatic backdrop for the city immediately to the west. The mountains, however, are generally too small, rugged, and hot to provide the recreational escape that the Sandia Mountains do for Albuquerque. Moreover, large sections are within the missile range or otherwise off-limits. Still, easy access and high visibility mean the Organs receive intense recreational use, especially by rock climbers: the climbing here is among the state's best, and a small but well-developed hiking trail network exists here. The mountains are wonderfully scenic, and I can think of no better place to discover the varied and interesting plants of the Chihuahuan Desert—alligator juniper, sotol, mountain mahogany, prickly pear cactus, Apache plume, squawbush, mesquite, and many more. Water is scarce here, although a few springs and intermittent streams exist. The Organ Mountains' small size and brief trails argue against backpacking, unless, of course, one simply wishes to hike a short distance and spend a magnificent night beneath the stars. (Why do we always associate backpacking with long hikes?)

In contrast to the Organ Mountains, the region's other wildlands are little known and seldom visited. Southwest of Las Cruces and northwest of El Paso are several large BLM Wilderness Study Areas that, except for geologists, naturalists, and a few local outdoor recreationists, are little known to hikers. These wildlands include the West Potrillo Mountains, Mount Riley, and the Aden Lava Flow, all volcanic in origin. Access is often difficult, although not impossible; the main reason these areas receive so little attention is that they simply don't appear at first glance to be inviting. After all, who would want to hike on a lava flow in

Our Lord's Candle Yucca in Organ Mountains at dawn

Yucca and limestone ridges, Robledo Mountains Study Area

southern New Mexico when the Organ Mountains are closer at hand? Still, among the lessons wilderness has for us is that beyond surface appearances, things exist that are far more interesting and important than we'd ever imagined.

This is especially true in the Robledo Mountains and the Las Uvas Mountains BLM Wilderness Study Areas, northwest of Las Cruces. These are true desert mountains, where yucca stalks sometimes rival the height of trees (which are scarce). In the Robledos, the WSA is primarily on the mountains' western side. Seemingly featureless hills are carpeted with creosote bush and mesquite, and dotted with huge barrel cacti. Mule deer abound, and some hikers report seeing oryx, an exotic species that has colonized here from White Sands Missile Range to the east. The Robledos are a good destination for day hikers.

The Las Uvas Mountains to the northwest have more difficult access and terrain. Here high sandstone bluffs overlook much the same vegetation as in the Robledos. Engraved on canyon walls in some drainages (usually dry) are petroglyphs made by the prehistoric Jornada–Mogollon Culture.

These are do-it-yourself wildernesses. Again, there are no designated trails, but simply following an arroyo or a ridge is sure to lead to something interesting. Water is scarce. But for these reasons alone these mountains are wild. No park ranger will ask for your backcountry permit; you won't be assigned a campsite; no one will care how long you stay or where you go—and no one will intrude upon your solitude. If you're among those who seek in wilderness the excitement of discovery, you'll find much here to reward you.

Still farther north are the Caballo Mountains, east of the Rio Grande and south of Truth or Consequences. Like the Robledos, these mountains are long, sinuous, pale sedimentary layers. The Caballo Mountains are laced with numerous roads and mining claims, causing the BLM to drop the Caballos from wilderness consideration, but the New Mexico Wilderness Alliance says they deserve another look.

Caballo Mountains
54 Wilderness Inventory Unit

A steep, rugged western escarpment reveals the fault-block origin of this dramatic desert range. The gentle eastern slope overlooks the desert basin known as the Jornada del Muerto.

LOCATION	On the east side of the Rio Grande overlooking Caballo Reservoir, south of Truth or Consequences
SIZE	Recommended by the NM Wilderness Alliance: 28,800 acres
ELEVATION RANGE	4,900 to 7,300 feet
MILES OF TRAILS	No marked or maintained trails
ECOSYSTEMS	Desert scrub and grassland, piñon-juniper forest
ADMINISTRATION	BLM
TOPOGRAPHIC MAPS	Palomas Gap, Upham, Apache Gap, McLeod Tank, and Alivio USGS 7.5-minute quadrangles
BEST SEASONS	Fall, winter, spring
GETTING THERE	Improved dirt roads lead to the area from up Green Canyon just north of Derry, from Caballo Dam east to the beginning of Apache Canyon, and from the east by way of Timber Mountain.
HIKING	Old roads and tracks substitute for trails here. The area's relief and openness provide spectacular vistas, which makes this destination worth overcoming the rugged terrain and aridity.

THE BLM DROPPED this area from its wilderness inventory because of past and possibly future mining, but the New Mexico Wilderness Alliance notes that their proposal avoids conflicts with mining areas.

OrganeMountains Wilderness Study Area 55

This small but extremely rugged and scenic desert range is easy to access from population centers in south-central New Mexico and El Paso, Texas.

Indian blanket flowers

LOCATION	East of Las Cruces, west of White Sands Missile Range
SIZE	7,283 acres
	Recommended by the NM Wilderness Alliance: 64,992 acres
ELEVATION RANGE	4,600 to 9,012 feet at Organ Needle
MILES OF TRAILS	Approximately 30 miles in the Organ Mountains, including the WSA
ECOSYSTEMS	Chihuahuan Desert shrub, piñon-juniper, ponderosa pine
ADMINISTRATION	BLM
TOPOGRAPHIC MAPS	Organ Peak, Organ, Bishop Cap USGS 7.5-minute quadrangles
BEST SEASONS	Fall, winter, spring
GETTING THERE	The range's western foothills are an easy 10-mile drive east from Las Cruces. From Highway 70-82 near the village of Organ, the mountains are even closer. Yet the overwhelming percentage of visitation is concentrated on the few trails radiating from the BLM A.B. Cox Visitor Center on the west side, which you can reach from Las Cruces by taking University Boulevard east until it becomes Dripping Springs Road. You can access the BLM Aguirre Spring Campground via the paved road heading south from Highway 70-82, which is east of San Augustin Pass.
HIKING	Existing trails offer several interesting day hikes; backpack trips generally are limited by the paucity of long-distance trails, difficulty of cross-country travel, and the range's relatively small size.

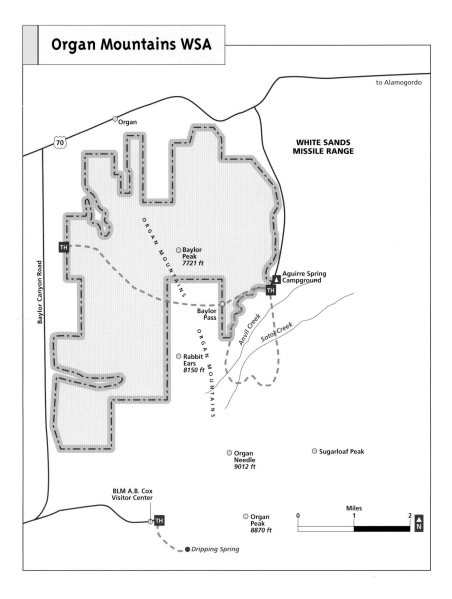

TO EARLY SPANISH SETTLERS traveling along the Rio Grande north from El Paso, the dramatic sky-reaching granite spires of the Organ Mountains resembled massive organ pipes, hence the name. Certainly the range's striking profile provides a scenic backdrop to the city of Las Cruces, and there are countless photos taken with a bayonet yucca's gracile flower stalk in the foreground and the craggy peaks in the background.

Visitors are rare in many areas in the range; the extreme ruggedness of the terrain discourages casual off-trail exploration. This, as well as off-limits military land, has prevented an extensive network of hiking trails in the Organ Mountains, and the existing trails hardly count as wilderness treks. The hikers who know the range best are rock climbers. The large and numerous high-angle faces and formations have a national reputation in the climbing community; indeed, many summits can be reached only by technical climbers, and the peaks' names reflect not only their distinctive appearance but also climbers' characteristic whimsy and irreverence in naming: Nordspitz, Rabbit Ears (this mutated rabbit has three ears), Low Horns, Spire, Razorback, Wildcat, Dingleberry, Organ Needle, Sugarloaf, and Organ Peak.

Below the rocks, the terrain is varied and interesting as well, and includes three major life zones: Lower Sonoran, Transition, and Upper Sonoran. This is desert country. Common plants include yucca, ocotillo, black grama grass, mountain mahogany, and creosote bush. You'll find the threatened southwestern barrel cactus here. Animal species include mule deer, mountain lions, golden eagles, and peregrine falcons.

Most people are introduced first to the range's western side via the trails radiating from the BLM's A.B. Cox Visitor Center at the site of an historic ranch. You can reach the center by taking University Boulevard east over I-25, then 10.5 miles on what becomes the Dripping Springs Road. The 1.75-mile Dripping Springs – Ice Canyon Trail, easy and heavily used, is very scenic and interesting. The Fillmore Canyon Trail also begins near the visitor center, five steep and strenuous miles to the summit of Organ Peak.

Farther north is the Baylor Pass National Recreation Trail, a six-mile, well-blazed route connecting Baylor Canyon Road with Aguirre Spring. Each fall mountain runners traverse this trail in a race. The main trailhead from the east is at the BLM Aguirre Springs Campground. The most popular trail is the Pine Tree Trail, a 4.5-mile loop that ascends the range's eastern flanks.

56 Robledo Mountains and Las Uvas Mountains Wilderness Study Areas

These roughly contiguous WSAs are both centered on small but scenic desert mountain ranges. They are an important habitat for desert wildlife and feature archaeological and paleontological sites of major significance.

View from the Las Uvas Mountains

LOCATION	The Robledo Mountains are 8 miles northwest of Las Cruces, immediately west of the Rio Grande. The Las Uvas Mountains are 30 miles northwest of Las Cruces.
SIZE	Robledo Mountains, 12,496 acres; Las Uvas Mountains, 11,067 acres Size recommended by the NM Wilderness Alliance: 210,000 acres (combined)
ELEVATION RANGE	4,600 to 6,198 feet
MILES OF TRAILS	No marked or maintained trails
ECOSYSTEMS	Scattered junipers, diverse cacti, mesquite, creosote bush, grassland
ADMINISTRATION	BLM
TOPOGRAPHIC MAPS	Souse Springs and Leasburg USGS 7.5-minute quadrangles
BEST SEASONS	Fall, winter, spring

GETTING THERE   **Approach the Robledo Mountains** from the northeast by taking Highway 85 north through Radium Springs, continuing 0.5 mile west of the Blue Moon Bar and Cafe then turning south onto dirt Faulkner Canyon Road (County Road D59). At 1.25 miles a rough two-track heads up an arroyo. Park about 100 yards farther up the county road and hike along the two-track until it peters out. Then go cross-country.

To approach the mountains from the southwest, take the I-10 frontage road marked "Airport" at the Highway 70 and I-10 junction west of Las Cruces, then take Corralitos Road (County Road CO9) north about 7 miles to where County Road CO7 branches northeast, leading to the mountains.

To approach the Las Uvas Mountains from the east, take Highway 85 to a point about halfway between Radium Springs and Hatch. Then take dirt County Road EOO6 west. After about 12 miles is the WSA's southern boundary, characterized by high mesas.

HIKING   While designated hiking trails are lacking here, old roads, drainages, and ridges provide walking routes, and the terrain is amenable to cross-country travel, though lack of water discourages backpack trips.

EXPLORING THE ROBLEDO MOUNTAINS AND LAS UVAS MOUNTAINS WSAS is exciting. Despite their proximity to Las Cruces, with a population of 74,000 and growing very rapidly, these two ranges are remarkable for the sense of remoteness they inspire in visitors.

Robledo Peak and nearby hills are limestone formations laid down when this area was under an inland sea. Later, when the sea had receded during the Jurassic Period, dinosaurs walked across mud flats here. Their tracks survive on the mountains' west side at a site among the best of its kind in the world. Much later—by geologic standards but still ancient on the human time scale—Paleo-Indians, the first human inhabitants of North America, camped around the mountains. The first European colonists in New Mexico moved up along the Rio Grande under the leadership of Don Juan de Oñate. On May 21, 1598, the expedition suffered its first death when a 60-year-old man named Pedro Robledo died of natural causes. He left behind his name on the mountains overlooking his unmarked grave.

Don't look for *uvas* ("grapes") in the Sierra de las Uvas. The name refers to a huge wild grape thicket at a spring in the mountains. Rather, look for barrel cacti, ocotillo, prickly pear, mesquite, creosote bush, and other plants of the Chihuahuan Desert. And as you hike cross-country (for there are no trails), you might be fortunate to find petroglyphs made centuries ago by Indians of the Jornada Mogollon Culture. Failing that, you're almost certain to see raptors, who nest in the basaltic cliffs capping the mesas.

When exploring either the Robledo or the Las Uvas Mountains, carry water, wear a hat and sunscreen, wear sturdy, thorn-resistant shoes, and, if possible, save your exploration for any season but summer.

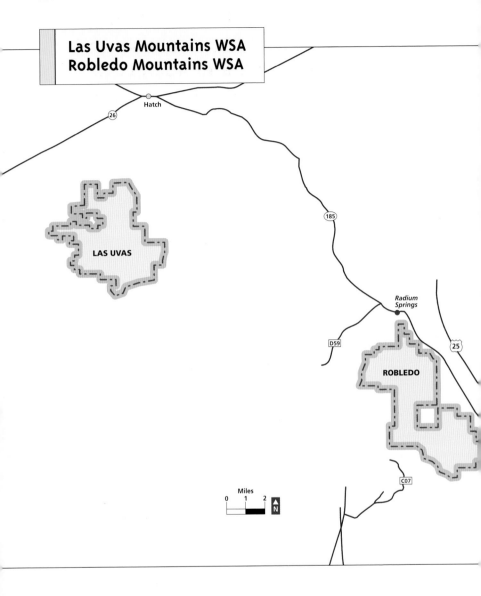

Las Uvas Mountains WSA
Robledo Mountains WSA

Hatch
(26)

(185)

LAS UVAS

Radium
Springs

D59

(25)

ROBLEDO

Miles
0   1   2
N

C07

West Potrillo Mountains, East Potrillo Mountains, Mount Riley, and Aden Lava Flow Wilderness Study Areas

These four, roughly contiguous wild areas encompass arid plains, lava flows, desert mountains, and volcanic cinder cones. Although this region is geologically and ecologically interesting, it is nonetheless largely unknown to the public.

LOCATION	Southwest of Las Cruces, just north of the Mexican border
SIZE	159,972 acres Size recommended by the NM Wilderness Alliance: 288,557 acres
ELEVATION RANGE	4,225 to 5,957 feet at Cox Peak
MILES OF TRAILS	No marked or maintained trails
ECOSYSTEMS	Chihuahuan Desert scrub, semidesert grassland
ADMINISTRATION	BLM
TOPOGRAPHIC MAPS	Mount Riley, Potrillo Peak, P O L Ranch, Guzmans Lookout Mountain, Camel Mountain, Coyote Hill, Mount Aden SW, and X 7 Ranch USGS 7.5-minute quadrangles
BEST SEASONS	Fall, winter, spring
GETTING THERE	County Road A3-B2, connecting Columbus to Santa Teresa along the Mexican border, provides general access from the south, while County Road A17 – B4 allows access from the northeast.
HIKING	The West Potrillo Mountains WSA is the largest in New Mexico, and if the entire NM Wilderness Alliance proposal were adopted, this complex would handily surpass the Pecos as the state's second largest wilderness. Despite this, the arid, exposed, unwelcoming terrain is unlikely to attract many hikers. Trails are few to none, although jeep tracks used by hunters and ranchers could be used as hiking routes. The East Potrillo Mountains are a small limestone ridge, the highest point of elevation reaching 5,185 feet. The West Potrillo Mountains, on the other hand, are more extensive and volcanic in origin (the highest elevation is 5,297 feet). In Spanish, *potrillo* means "colt," perhaps referring to wild horses once found here. Mount Riley is a volcanic cinder cone (elevation 5,905 feet). The Aden Lava Flows are associated with Aden Crater, that erupted about 10,000 years ago. Most hiking here focuses on gaining the tops of the summits, which provide spectacular desert vistas. The vegetation is mostly desert scrub. Trees are few, and water sources even fewer. Still, the area's size allows ample opportunities for solitude, which could become more valued as the population of southern New Mexico continues to increase dramatically.

The Desert Southwest

The Desert Southwest Region is one of the hottest, most remote, least accessible, and least known parts of New Mexico. If you're familiar with the state's outline, you'll understand why this region is often referred to as the state's Bootheel. But the term is descriptive of more than just the shape. Here is where the state scuffs up against Mexico. And like a bootheel, it receives scant notice, except when something goes wrong.

The Desert Southwest is the region beginning at Deming and running west to the Arizona border, south of I-10, although Cookes Peak slightly north of Deming is included. Deming is a small, pleasant town, serving interstate traffic and a large retirement population. Farther west from Deming is Lordsburg, which makes Deming seem metropolitan. And after Lordsburg…well, suffice it to say that state maps sometimes still label Cloverdale—consisting of one abandoned and decaying building, without any residents for decades. Tens of thousands of tourists annually pass through the region, on I-10, but they rarely stop. So to most humans, the region's wildlands are like mirages, distant and ambiguous in the heat-shimmer, ignored by all except for a few ranchers—and ecologists.

To ecologists, this is a very interesting region. Indeed, here is one of the nation's most significant ecological research sites—the vast natural area, including the Animas Mountains, known as the Gray Ranch, once held by the Nature Conservancy and now managed for ecological research by the Animas Foundation. South of the Bootheel are the wild Sierra Madrean ecosystems of Mexico; to the north are the wild uplands and riparian areas of the Gila Country. And in between, sharing plants and animals of both ecosystems, are the basins and ranges of the Bootheel. Here are some of the Southwest's most exotic species—coatimundi, ring-tails, javelinas, Gila monsters, and numerous bird species rarely found in the U.S. In 1997, a jaguar was sighted and photographed in the Peloncillo Mountains. The list of rare and endangered plants here is long. This is due in part to the "sky island" effect—small, geographically isolated mountains separated by vast, arid basins, blocking the intermingling of species. The Sky Island Alliance has been working to promote and pro-tect the region's biodiversity through management of habitats in New Mexico, Arizona, and even Mexico as a whole rather than as isolated, fragmented units.

No wildernesses have been designated here, although the region includes numerous BLM Wilderness Study Areas. The most conspicuous WSA is in

Jim Norton

Bighorn Sheep

the Florida Mountains, a small, sawtooth-rugged desert range immediately south of Deming. Road access to at least the range's northeastern part is easy from Deming, but only a few trails traverse the Florida Mountains' difficult terrain. The persons who most often use them are hunters and naturalists seeking glimpses of the introduced Persian ibex who live among the crags.

Also well-known but rarely visited is the Cookes Range, a small mountain group north of Deming whose fang-like apex, Cookes Peak, has for centuries been a major landmark in southwestern New Mexico. Surrounding the peak are numerous significant historical and archaeological sites—the ruins of Fort Cummings, Cookes Canyon, the ghost town of Cookes, prehistoric petroglyphs, and more. But while the wildland here is scenic and interesting, it attracts few hikers, most content just to bag Cookes Peak.

The region's largest proposed wilderness is the Peloncillo Complex put forward by the New Mexico Wilderness Alliance in cooperation with the Sky Islands project. This complex would link several existing and proposed public wildlands in New Mexico and Arizona, including the BLM Bunk Robinson and Whitmire Canyon WSAs in the southern Peloncillos, into a 194,513-acre megawilderness that could support endangered wildlife in ways that fragmented wildlands cannot.

The Peloncillo Mountains straddle the New Mexico–Arizona border. Very rugged, they see few hikers. Of these, many are trekking to the historical sites here: where Geronimo surrendered in 1886, and where the Clanton Gang of Tombstone infamy ambushed and massacred Mexican smugglers. Public lands in the Peloncillos are administered by the Coronado National Forest, with district offices in Douglas, Arizona. Public access is generally much better in Arizona than in New Mexico.

The New Mexico Wilderness Alliance has also proposed wilderness status for an area north of I-10 near the Arizona border known as the Lordsburg Playas. These are extensive flats that become shallow lakes in wet seasons, attracting migratory birds and creating a distinctive ecology.

Immediately east of and paralleling the Peloncillo Mountains is the Animas Range. Along its crest runs the Continental Divide—but not the Continental Divide Trail. The Animas Foundation, which manages the former Gray Ranch for ecological research, resolutely forbids public access. So the CDT must begin still farther east in the Alamo Hueco and Big Hatchet Mountains (depending upon the route hikers choose).

On the Animas Range's eastern slopes, however, is the BLM Cowboy Spring WSA. Here is a highly scenic and interesting area of peaks, ridges, valleys, and alluvial fans—but as is typical with this region's wildlands, it is virtually unknown to the public and has no legal access except to hunters during hunting season.

Farther east still, across the vast Playas Valley, are two desert ranges, the Alamo Hueco Mountains and, just to the north, the Big Hatchet Mountains that also include BLM WSAs. The Alamo Hueco Mountains rise dramatically above the plains like a herd of giant prehistoric animals. They also contain numerous endangered plant and animal species as well as nationally significant archaeological sites. Yet no trails exist in the Alamo Huecos, and until recently no legal access existed. Even now, access is only via a long, rough dirt road that passes between the Alamo Huecos and the Big Hatchets. Mention to anyone that you've gone hiking in the Alamo Huecos, and they'll assume you've gone to the famous rock-climbing area northeast of El Paso in Texas. The Big Hatchets are slightly better known and slightly more accessible. In both ranges, cross-country hiking is difficult not only because of steep, complex, trackless terrain but also because the desert flora—ocotillo, prickly pear cactus, cholla, yucca, agave—is very well-armed with spines, thorns, and other protective gear. Furthermore, surface water is rare to nonexistent; without windmill-fed stock tanks, extended travel here would be all but impossible. Despite this, two of at least three alternative routes for the Continental Divide Trail go through the Big Hatchets.

The hiking situation gets somewhat better with the BLM Cedar Mountains WSA to the north between Hachita and I-10. The Cedars, a low range of gently rolling hills, lack the dramatic appeal of the Big Hatchets and the Alamo Huecos. Access is somewhat better, although entry to the WSA is blocked by private land (except for a dirt county road). The Continental Divide Trail goes through the Cedars, but the persons who most often visit these mountains are deer and quail hunters.

The recurring access problems in this region result from complex land ownership: BLM lands, state lands, railroad leases, ecological research areas, and private ranches. Relations between these groups have often been thorny, and accommodating recreational users has been a low priority. Furthermore, border tensions sometimes exacerbate local suspicion of outsiders.

But having said all that, I must say that for many hikers the region gains appeal from being remote, poorly accessible, challenging, and seldom-visited. For such hikers, these are true mountains of mystery, the "blank spots on the map" that have always attracted adventurers. And while not completely "blank," the wildlands here certainly have not yet yielded all their secrets. In the deepening light of evening, these distant desert ranges shine with an almost mystical glow whose allure has always been irresistible.

58 Alamo Hueco Mountains Wilderness Study Area

This small but scenic desert range features highly eroded mesas, cliffs, and long, sinuous canyons. An ecological transition zone between the northern and southern Chihuahuan Desert ecosystems, this WSA is nearly contiguous with the Big Hatchet Mountains WSA just to the north.

New Mexico Wilderness Alliance

Looking south into Alamo Hueco

LOCATION	In the southeast corner of the Bootheel, just northwest of the Mexican border
SIZE	16,264 acres Size recommended by the NM Wilderness Alliance: 31,984 acres
ELEVATION RANGE	4,800 to 6,838 feet
MILES OF TRAILS	No marked or maintained trails
ECOSYSTEMS	Evergreen oak, piñon and Chihuahuan pines, Chihuahuan Desert scrub and semidesert grassland
ADMINISTRATION	BLM
TOPOGRAPHIC MAPS	Pierce Peak and Sentinel Butte USGS 7.5-minute quadrangles
BEST SEASONS	Fall, winter, spring

GETTING THERE   Until very recently no vehicular access existed for the Alamo Hueco Mountains WSA, but the BLM has put in a new gravel road running between the Big Hatchets and the Alamo Huecos, providing access to both ranges.

HIKING   Lack of access has kept recreational use of these mountains very low. Now that access has improved, hiking might increase somewhat, with most hikers attracted by desert scenery, archaeological sites, and diverse wildlife. Still, remoteness, lack of trails, and rugged, arid terrain are likely to keep hiking infrequent at best, at least for now.

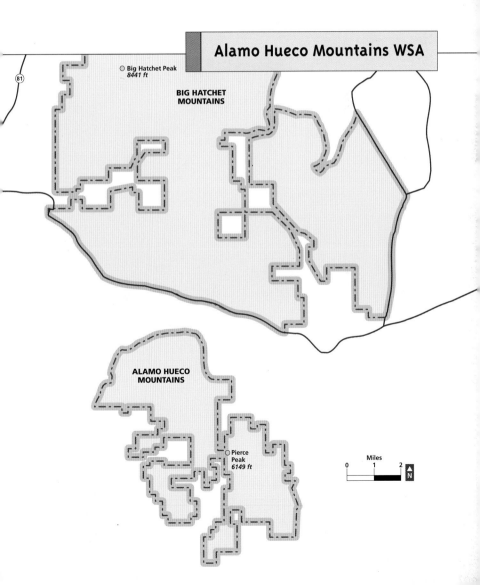

Alamo Hueco Mountains WSA

Big Hatchet Peak
8441 ft

BIG HATCHET
MOUNTAINS

81

ALAMO HUECO
MOUNTAINS

Pierce
Peak
6149 ft

Miles
0   1   2
N

59 Big Hatchet Mountains Wilderness Study Area

This rugged and scenic desert range is nearly contiguous with the Alamo Hueco Mountains WSA just to the south. Its diverse wildlife includes several endangered species.

Jim Norton

Big Hatchets from the west

LOCATION	In the east section of the Bootheel, just west of the Mexican border, 70 miles south-southeast of Lordsburg
SIZE	48,720 acres Size recommended by the NM Wilderness Alliance: 91,219 acres
ELEVATION RANGE	4,400 to 8,366 feet at Big Hatchet Peak
MILES OF TRAILS	No marked or maintained trails
ECOSYSTEMS	Evergreen oak, piñon and Chihuahuan pines, chaparral, semidesert grassland, Chihuahuan desert scrub
ADMINISTRATION	BLM
TOPOGRAPHIC MAPS	Hatchet Ranch, Big Hatchet Peak, Sheridan Canyon, and U Bar Ridge USGS 7.5-minute quadrangles
BEST SEASONS	Fall, winter, spring
GETTING THERE	Until very recently, no vehicular access existed for the Big Hatchet Mountains WSA, but the BLM has put in a new gravel road that runs along the mountains' southeast side between the Big Hatchets and the Alamo Huecos and then along the Big Hatchets' east side.
HIKING	Hiking here is limited by lack of trails, difficult terrain, torrid warm-weather temperatures, lack of water, and poor access.

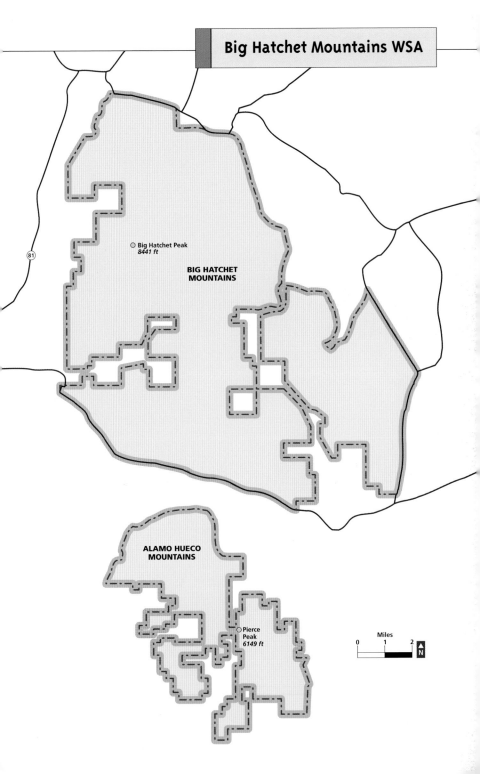

Big Hatchet Mountains WSA

○ Big Hatchet Peak
8441 ft

BIG HATCHET MOUNTAINS

ALAMO HUECO MOUNTAINS

○ Pierce Peak
6149 ft

Miles
0   1   2

N

ECOLOGISTS RECOGNIZE THIS PART OF NEW MEXICO as a transition area, and thus exceptionally rich in plants and animals. The list of rare and endangered species found in the Big Hatchet Mountains WSA is long. Plants include night-blooming cereus and at least two species of pincushion cacti. One of the last indigenous populations of desert bighorn sheep is here. Other mammals include javelina, coatimundi, pygmy mouse, thick-billed kingbird, golden eagles, giant spotted whiptail lizard, and Sonora mountain king snake.

Much of this diversity results from the mountains' rugged, diverse topography, which also makes it an appealing area for hikers.

Until recently, access difficulties have discouraged hiking here, although hikers who are familiar with the Big Hatchets are very fond of them. Only a single hiking trail exists in the mountains; it starts near the mouth of Big Thompson Canyon and leads to the top of Big Hatchet Peak. A possible route of the Continental Divide National Scenic Trail passes through the Big Hatchets, even though the Continental Divide itself runs across the Animas Mountains to the west (with even worse access problems). Still, distance from population centers likely will continue to mean that hikers in the Big Hatchet Mountains don't have to worry about crowds.

Bunk Robinson Wilderness Study Area

60

This WSA includes a number of ridges and canyons along the eastern slopes of the very rugged Peloncillo Mountains.

Cliffs at Bunk Robinson

LOCATION	Extreme southwestern New Mexico, northeast of Douglas, Arizona
SIZE	7,000 acres
ELEVATION RANGE	5,400 to 6,444 feet at Guadalupe Mountain
MILES OF TRAILS	Undetermined
ECOSYSTEMS	Chihuahuan pine, piñon-juniper, Chihuahuan Desert scrub, Arizona sycamore and Fremont cottonwood along drainages
ADMINISTRATION	Coronado National Forest
TOPOGRAPHIC MAPS	Clanton Draw, Black Point, Skeleton Canyon, and Guadalupe Spring USGS 7.5-minute quadrangles
BEST SEASONS	Fall, winter, spring
GETTING THERE	From Highway 338 south of Animas, County Road 2 heads west and crosses the Peloncillo Mountains toward Douglas. This road is also called the Geronimo Trail. The Bunk Robinson WSA is south of this, abutting the Arizona border. The Whitmire Canyon WSA is to the north.
HIKING	From County Road 2, at the saddle separating Clanton Draw draining to the east and Cottonwood Draw draining west, a trail runs north and south along the crest of the Peloncillos. Other trails may enter the WSA from the west. The area is extremely rugged, and water is scarce.

61 Cedar Mountains Wilderness Study Area

This segment of the Cedar Mountains features a low range of rolling, grass-covered hills and valleys, as well as occasional summits with spectacular views of southwestern New Mexico's mountains. This WSA is also known for its significant archaeological sites.

New Mexico Wilderness Alliance

Broad vista of the Cedar Mountains

LOCATION	Northeast of Hachita, southwest of Deming, north of Highway 9
SIZE	14,911 acres
	Size recommended by the NM Wilderness Alliance: 172,921 acres
ELEVATION RANGE	4,700 to 6,215 feet at Flying W Mountain
MILES OF TRAILS	No marked or maintained trails
ECOSYSTEMS	Semidesert grassland, chaparral, Chihuahuan Desert scrub, occasional Madrean evergreens
ADMINISTRATION	BLM
TOPOGRAPHIC MAPS	Flying W Mountain and Hat Top Mountain USGS 7.5-minute quadrangles
BEST SEASONS	Fall, winter, spring
GETTING THERE	About 7 miles southeast of Hachita, a county road heads northeast into the WSA; other approaches require crossing private land.
HIKING	At present far fewer hikers visit the Cedar Mountains than do hunters of mule deer and quail, which abound here. Nonetheless, a portion of the Continental Divide Trail passes through the Cedar Mountains, and those willing to hike cross-country to explore this region will be well rewarded.

Cookes Range Wilderness Study Area

This small range centers on 8,404-foot Cookes Peak, a conspicuous landmark visible throughout southwestern New Mexico. Cookes Range is rich in ecological, archaeological, and historical resources.

New Mexico Wilderness Alliance

Cookes Peak

LOCATION	North of Deming, south of the Sierra-Luna County line
SIZE	19,608 acres Size recommended by the NM Wilderness Alliance: 23,848 acres
ELEVATION RANGE	4,750 to 8,404 feet at Cookes Peak
MILES OF TRAILS	No marked or maintained trails
ECOSYSTEMS	Conifer woodland, chaparral, semidesert grassland, and Chihuahuan Desert scrub
ADMINISTRATION	BLM
TOPOGRAPHIC MAPS	Massacre Peak and OK Canyon USGS 7.5-minute quadrangles
BEST SEASONS	Fall, winter, spring
GETTING THERE	You can access the Cookes Range WSA via County Roads A019 from the east, A008 from the west, and A016 from the southwest.
HIKING	Except for the route to Cookes Peak described below, little hiking occurs here except for foot travel on old roads.

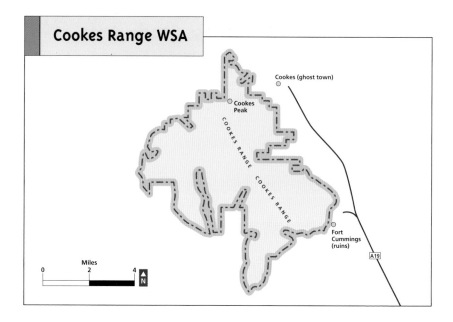

PROBABLY NO WILDERNESS STUDY AREA in New Mexico has greater historical significance than the Cookes Range WSA, a fact illustrated by important historic sites located just outside the WSA boundary. Petroglyphs left by the long-vanished Mogollon Culture are here, as well as Mimbres Culture lithic and dwelling sites. Fort Cummings, whose ruins are in Cookes Canyon just 0.5 mile east of the WSA, played an important role in the Apache wars of the latter 1800s. In 1882, the mining boomtown of Cookes sprang up on the side of Cookes Peak, along the WSA's northeast boundary. The WSA's southeast boundary coincides with the Butterfield Overland Mail route.

In addition, the Cookes Range WSA, with its rugged and varied topography, supports a rich diversity of plants and animals including rare and endangered species. Rockhounds collect gem-quality carnelian agate in an area extending along County Road A016 to the base of Cookes Peak. The area offers rock climbing and outstanding opportunities for photography. And it's large enough for multi-day backpack trips.

Most hikers will want to climb Cookes Peak. A good route goes up County Road A016 from Highway 26 through Cookes Canyon, passing en route the turnoff to the ruins of Fort Cummings. Near a corral you'll see a locked gate. Park here, then follow a fence line to a wash, which you'll follow upstream to rejoin the road, once again on public land. This old road takes you by the weathered crosses of the Cookes Cemetery, about two miles from the locked gate. Two miles farther is what little remains of this abandoned mining town. Another mile northwest along the road brings you to a saddle leading south to the summit's base, which you reach after about 4.5 miles. The summit is surrounded by cliffs and talus slopes. To minimize scrambling, approach from the south. Eliminate some of the distance on the return trip by following the ridge back down to the mining camp.

Cowboy Spring Wilderness Study Area

63

Cowboy Spring is characterized by peaks, ridges,
valleys, and alluvial fans, all dominated by 6,300-foot
Cowboy Rim.

LOCATION	On the eastern slopes of the Animas Mountains, 50 miles south of Lordsburg
SIZE	6,999 acres Size recommended by the NM Wilderness Alliance: 40,989 acres
ELEVATION RANGE	4,900 to 5,445 feet
MILES OF TRAILS	No marked or maintained trails
ECOSYSTEMS	Evergreen oak, semidesert grassland, riparian deciduous forest
ADMINISTRATION	BLM
TOPOGRAPHIC MAPS	Center Peak USGS 7.5-minute quadrangle
BEST SEASONS	Fall, winter, spring
GETTING THERE	There is no legal access, although people with New Mexico hunting licenses may cross state land to the south and east during hunting season.
HIKING	Very limited, primarily because of remoteness and limited access.

Lordsburg Playas (Proposed Wilderness)

64

For the most part, this area features large, flat, and usually
dry lake beds, as well as occasional low peaks and stabilized
sand dunes in a basin surrounded by mountains.

LOCATION	Northwest of Lordsburg, north of I-10
SIZE	Size recommended by the NM Wilderness Alliance: 35,680 acres
ELEVATION RANGE	4,140 to 5,050 feet
MILES OF TRAILS	No marked or maintained trails
ECOSYSTEMS	Flat, bare lakebed surrounded by alkali-adapted grasses
ADMINISTRATION	BLM
TOPOGRAPHIC MAPS	Summit and Mondel USGS 7.5-minute quadrangles
BEST SEASONS	Fall, winter, spring
GETTING THERE	Dirt roads running northeast of Steins and southwest from Highway 70 northwest of Lordsburg, provide access to the area.
HIKING	This area, representative of the distinctive basin-and-range ecology, is of more interest to naturalists than to hikers; ecological value is the primary reason that the NM Wilderness Alliance is recommending this area be considered for wilderness designation. People go wind-sailing just north of the proposed wilderness.

Peloncillo Mountains Wilderness Complex

65

This "super-wilderness" features many ecological and administrative units linked along the rugged Peloncillo Mountains.

LOCATION	Along both sides of the Peloncillo Mountains in New Mexico and Arizona
SIZE	Size recommended by the NM Wilderness Alliance: 194,513 acres
ELEVATION RANGE	5,400 to 6,928 feet at Gray Mountain
MILES OF TRAILS	Undetermined
ECOSYSTEMS	Chihuahuan and Sonoran Desert plants, as well as mountain conifer and riparian ecosystems
ADMINISTRATION	BLM, Forest Service
TOPOGRAPHIC MAPS	Numerous maps cover this large area
BEST SEASONS	Fall, winter, spring
GETTING THERE	In New Mexico take Highway 338, south of I-10, by County Road A12, north of I-10. You can also get here via Highway 80 in New Mexico and Arizona.
HIKING	The enormous size and diversity of this proposed wilderness translates into outstanding hiking, despite terrain that often is difficult and lacking water. A few trails exist in the region now; more will likely be created.

As proposed by the New Mexico Wilderness Alliance, this area would unite several Wilderness Study Areas, Areas of Critical Environmental Concern, and Research Natural Areas into a large ecotone straddling the Sonoran and Chihuahuan Deserts. The Alliance has proposed three units to this. The North Unit would consist of the Peloncillo WSA, which is adjacent to the already designated Peloncillo Mountains Wilderness in Arizona. Eight miles south, the Middle Unit would consist of the roadless Preacher Mountain area in the north and the Granite Gap Inventory Unit in the south. Four miles south, the South Unit would consist of the Whitmire Canyon WSA, the Bunk Robinson WSA, the Guadalupe Canyon Instant Study Area, and Arizona's Baker Canyon.

Because the area does merge two desert ecosystems, the diversity of plants and animals is extraordinary, as evidenced by the many endangered species living here ranging from Gila monsters to several species of pincushion cacti. The only confirmed sighting of a jaguar recently in New Mexico occurred in this area in 1997.

The area also has exceptional historical interest and significance. The mountains were a stronghold of the Chiricahua Apaches; Geronimo surrendered in these mountains. The mountains were along a major route to southeastern mining camps such as Tombstone, and names like Clanton Draw (the Clantons were involved in the shootout at the OK Corral) and Skeleton Canyon reflect incidents that occurred during this turbulent period of the nation's history.

Few hikers have discovered the remote and rugged Peloncillo Mountains, but people who have explored them say they epitomize the qualities inherent in wilderness.

Whitmire Canyon Wilderness Study Area

Steep, rugged canyons and ridges flank a canyon in the eastern Peloncillo Mountains.

LOCATION	Extreme southwestern part of New Mexico, northeast of Douglas, Arizona
SIZE	18,000 acres
ELEVATION RANGE	5,450 to 6,358 feet
MILES OF TRAILS	Undetermined
ECOSYSTEMS	Chihuahuan pine, piñon-juniper, oak, Chihuahuan Desert scrub, Arizona sycamore and Fremont cottonwood along drainages
ADMINISTRATION	Coronado National Forest
TOPOGRAPHIC MAPS	Clanton Draw and Skeleton Canyon USGS 7.5-minute quadrangles
BEST SEASONS	Fall, winter, spring
GETTING THERE	From Highway 338 south of Animas, County Road 2 heads west and crosses the Peloncillo Mountains toward Douglas. This road also is called the Geronimo Trail. The Whitmire Canyon WSA is north of this, abutting the Arizona border; the Bunk Robinson WSA is to the south.
HIKING	From County Road 2, at the saddle separating Clanton Draw draining to the east and Cottonwood Draw draining west, a trail runs north and south along the crest of the Peloncillos. Other trails may enter the WSA from the west. The area is extremely rugged, and water is scarce, yet its remoteness appeals to wilderness enthusiasts. And the rich array of wildlife includes peregrine falcons, Gould's wild turkey, white-tailed deer, coatimundi, javelina, mountain lions, and bobcats. New Mexico's only confirmed sighting of a jaguar in recent times occurred in the Peloncillo Mountains.

The Desert Southeast

The wildlands of the Desert Southeast owe their existence, as well as their character, to water. During the Permian Period—about 250 million years ago—this area lay beneath the shallow coastal waters of an ancient sea. Great reefs formed in these waters and, as time passed, were buried and compressed into limestone. Later, due to movements in the earth's crust, these compressed reefs were uplifted to form the mountains that exist in southeastern New Mexico today.

It is easy to imagine the ancient reefs as you gaze at the mountains' pale horizontal layers—stacked hundreds of feet high to form precipitous walls. Rainwater readily percolates through the porous rock, leaving the surface conspicuously bereft of water. As the slightly acidic water passes through the rock layers, it slowly dissolves the subsurface limestone to produce the vast and intricate subterranean chambers that have made Carlsbad Caverns and Lechuguilla Cave so famous. Other caves are found throughout the backcountry, and although not as famous as Carlsbad or Lechuguilla, are equally complex and beautiful. These "wild caves," as they are called, can be hard to find, as spelunkers jealously guard their locations. In any case, hikers without training or proper equipment should avoid these caves, as they can be extremely dangerous.

The most impressive of the reef mountains are the Guadalupes. They reach their greatest height just south of New Mexico in Guadalupe Mountains National Park. Here Guadalupe Peak rises 8,749 feet, making it the highest point in Texas. The park, however, is only part of the Guadalupes' southern tip; most of the range is in New Mexico.

No one would dispute that the Guadalupes are indeed mountains, but they usually aren't defined by peaks and summits. Rather, the mountains are characterized by long, high ridges flanked by deep, steep-sided canyons. Elevations along the ridges are approximately 6,000 to 6,500 feet, and they have a vertical rise of 2,000 to 2,500 feet from the adjacent plains and valleys.

Although these are extremely dry mountains, water—like the miracle it is—sometimes finds its way into the Guadalupes. Indeed, one of New Mexico's most spectacular waterfalls, Sitting Bull Falls, is located in an otherwise parched canyon in the mountains' northeastern foothills. Elsewhere, tiny streams flow in deep and remote canyons, slipping over rocks and forming clear, cool pools. These delicate threads of water

Photo courtesy of Carlsbad Caverns National Park

Yucca Canyon, Carlsbad Caverns National Park

vanish beneath the desert at canyon mouths, if they make it even that far, but have a sinewy toughness evidenced by the riparian vegetation they have sustained for centuries. In the fall, when much of the land is drab and brown, these deciduous plants turn color with an almost defiant brilliance.

Elsewhere in these mountains, vegetation must cope with heat and dryness. On the plains and extending into the foothills are widely spaced Chihuahuan Desert shrubs, including creosote bush, snakeweed, and four-wing saltbush. On rocky outcrops among the foothills are desert succulents—cacti such as prickly pear, cholla, and several species of agave. The latter was an important food source for the Apaches, and the pits where they roasted mescal roots are still found today in the backcountry. The Spaniards called these Apaches Mescaleros, a name by which they are still known. At higher elevations, dominant plants include piñon pine, alligator juniper, gray oak, Texas madrone, and skunkbush. Occasionally in the mountains, at the highest elevations in sheltered locations, are remnants of the coniferous forest that existed here in cooler, moister times—limber pine, ponderosa pine, and Douglas fir.

Wildlife is diverse and surprisingly abundant within this region; we aren't aware of these animals because most are nocturnal—a common desert adaptation. Mammals include mule deer, elk, rabbits, porcupines, skunks, ringtails, bobcats, foxes, black bears, mountain lions, and, due to the many caves, bats. Snakes and lizards flourish here, and birdlife likewise is varied and abundant. For naturalists, the Guadalupe Mountains are a place of endless fascination and discovery.

The only designated wilderness in New Mexico's Guadalupe Mountains is the 33,125-acre Carlsbad Caverns National Park Wilderness, but the actual extent of the wildlands is almost as great as the mountains them-selves. The Guadalupe Mountains Unit of the Lincoln National Forest links the Carlsbad Caverns and Guadalupe Mountains national park wildernesses. Furthermore, Forest Service lands join BLM lands and all together include several Wilderness Study Areas, including one in the Brokeoff Mountains—a western subrange of the Guadalupes. Other WSAs include Guadalupe Escarpment, Devils Den Canyon, McKittrick Canyon, Last Chance Canyon, Lonesome Ridge, Pup Canyon, and Rawhide Canyon. The New Mexico Wilderness Alliance has proposed linking several of these areas along Guadalupe Ridge into a more com-prehensive 98,171-acre wilderness.

Many areas outside the designated wilderness areas are far more wild than the two national park wildernesses. Terrain and land ownership have much to do with this. The steepness and ruggedness of the canyon walls —really steep and very rugged—mean that cross-country travel between canyons is usually extremely difficult. To get a real sense of this country, you need to look at a topographic map; rarely are contour lines as tortuous or as close together as they are here. And because access to many canyon mouths is blocked by private land, some canyons are rarely visited.

In fact, the entire area is seldom visited. Carlsbad, with 25,000 residents, is the region's largest population center, and except for Roswell, 76 miles to the north, no other city is within one hundred miles. To be sure, Carlsbad Caverns, among the world's most scenic wonders, attracts thousands of visitors annually. But they come for the caverns, not the backcountry, and besides, the temperature underground is constant and pleasant— unlike the surface temperatures. Indeed, torrid summer temperatures and surprisingly severe winter weather mean rather narrow spring-fall hiking windows in the Guadalupe Mountains. So, despite the wilderness's vastness and spectacular scenery, the Guadalupe Mountains have yet to be truly explored by most hikers.

The other mountain range in the Desert Southeast Region is the Sacramento Mountains, east of the Tularosa Basin. Like the Guadalupe Mountains immediately to the southeast, the Sacramentos consist of uplifted sedimentary deposits, usually limestone, although the Sacramentos were formed by the uplifting of fault blocks. This has resulted in the Sacramentos' eastern slopes being gradual and forested, rising to a crest that drops off precipitously to the west. This escarpment of pale strata, incised by deep, steep-walled canyons, is reminiscent of the Guadalupe Mountains. One of the most interesting and dramatic hikes in all New Mexico is into Dog Canyon along the escarpment about 10 miles south of Alamogordo in Oliver M. Lee Memorial State Park.

Being more accessible and more hospitable than the Guadalupes, the Sacramentos are more traveled and settled by humans. Extensive logging occurred here around 1900, and the mountain's high elevation and cool summer temperatures have attracted residential developments. Toward the range's northern end is the White Mountain Wilderness, but in the southern end no wilderness has been designated.

This is not to say that the Sacramento Mountains are devoid of wilderness. Along the southwest escarpment is the Culp Canyon Wilderness Study Area, and contiguous with this is the proposed Sacramento Escarpment Wilderness. If created, this wilderness would include 65,000 acres of Forest Service, BLM, and state lands. Furthermore, at the range's southern end are extensive lands now controlled by the military; if released to the public as expected, these lands, too, could have wilderness potential.

Brokeoff Mountains Wilderness Study Area

67

Several endangered plant and animal species thrive in this remote Chihuahuan Desert range. The Brokeoff Mountains WSA consists of a dominant north-south ridge and two canyons more than 500 feet deep.

Eroded limestone plateaus

LOCATION	80 miles east of El Paso, contiguous on the south with Guadalupe Mountains National Park
SIZE	31,606 acres Size recommended by the NM Wilderness Alliance: 66,350 acres
ELEVATION RANGE	4,600 to 6,500 feet on Cutoff Ridge
MILES OF TRAILS	No marked or maintained trails
ECOSYSTEMS	Chihuahuan Desert scrub, cacti, agaves, soaptree yuccas, creosote bush, mesquite, semidesert grassland, pines at higher elevations
ADMINISTRATION	BLM
TOPOGRAPHIC MAPS	La Paloma Canyon and Panther Canyon USGS 7.5-minute quadrangles
BEST SEASONS	Fall, spring
GETTING THERE	You can access this WSA via Highway 506, which begins in Texas and heads north into New Mexico. Privately maintained ranch roads lead into the WSA.
HIKING	While designated hiking trails are lacking here, old roads, drainages, and ridges provide walking routes, and the terrain is amenable to cross-country travel, though remoteness, poor access, and lack of water discourage most hikers.

THE BROKEOFF MOUNTAINS get their name by being isolated—or broken off—from the main body of the Guadalupe Mountains. The ranges, which are separated by Big Dog Canyon in New Mexico, connect again in Texas at Guadalupe Mountains National Park. You can tell the two ranges are related because they both have deep canyons cutting through their thick limestone layers. These layers are remnants of the Capitan Reef, which formed—like Australia's Great Barrier Reef—near land in an ancient sea. Reef limestone is very porous and water readily percolates through it. This porosity also means surface water is scarce—something hikers here must consider.

The best vehicular access is from the north, via private ranch roads; permission should be obtained to use them. If you wish to enter the WSA from the south, you'll likely have to walk in. Start at the Dog Canyon Campground and Trailhead at the north end of Guadalupe Mountains National Park, then take the Bush Mountain Trail 3.5 miles to its junction with the Marcus Trail, which heads 1.2 miles past the Marcus camping area and ends at the park border (also the Texas–New Mexico border.) Access from the south to Cutoff Ridge, which dominates the WSA, involves cross-country travel over very difficult terrain.

Whichever route you take, be aware that this is a harsh, challenging environment. Hiking the trails of Guadalupe Mountains National Park would be good preparation for the Brokeoff Mountains WSA.

68 Carlsbad Caverns National Park Wilderness

With its deep, steep canyons and limestone hills, this area in the Guadalupe Mountains is both challenging and interesting.

Courtesy of Carlsbad Caverns National Park

Slaughter Canyon

LOCATION	Runs southwest from Carlsbad Caverns National Park, south of Guadalupe Ridge
SIZE	33,125 acres
ELEVATION RANGE	3,800 to 6,432 feet at Wild Cow Mesa
MILES OF TRAILS	50 plus
ECOSYSTEMS	Chihuahuan Desert grassland and scrub, including creosote bush and mesquite; piñon and ponderosa pines
ADMINISTRATION	National Park Service
TOPOGRAPHIC MAPS	Trails Illustrated map for Carlsbad Caverns National Park
BEST SEASONS	Spring, fall
GETTING THERE	Carlsbad Caverns National Park is reached by taking Highway 62-180 southwest from Carlsbad to Whites City and the park's official entrance leading to the visitor center.
HIKING	Though several maintained and interesting backcountry trails exist here, torrid warm-season temperatures, lack of water, and difficult terrain discourage many hikers.

OF THE THOUSANDS OF VISITORS to Carlsbad Caverns National Park each year, only a handful come for what is above ground rather than beneath it. And admittedly, the underground wonders of the great cave, with constant and pleasant temperatures, an elevator, snack bar and water fountains, paved trail, and friendly rangers, are tough competition for the Chihuahuan Desert backcountry, where widely fluctuating temperatures, steep and rugged terrain, little or no water, and often-rocky trails may not be so attractive. But if the Guadalupe Mountains just to the south warrant a national park, then the mountains here warrant a second look, for both share the same mountain range and the same geologic origin.

The Guadalupe Mountains are the expression of the Capitan Reef (named for the prominent peak at the range's south end). It is the world's largest exposed reef. To imagine how it appeared during its formation during the Permian Period, 250 million years ago, think of Australia's Great Barrier Reef. Over the vastness of geologic time, the remains of lime-secreting organisms accumulated, then the reef subsided, to be buried by other sediments. During later mountain-building, the area was uplifted, the overlying sediments eroded away, and the ancient reef exposed to form today's Guadalupe Mountains.

From this geologic history, the Guadalupe Mountains derive their distinctive topography. Precipitous slopes flank deep canyons. Mountaintops are capped by a long, relatively level, plateau-like ridge. The limestone is porous and precipitation readily percolates through it, meaning surface water is rare. If you're lucky to find water, it will be in canyon bottoms, not above.

As water seeps downward, minute amounts of acid dissolve the limestone, over time resulting in the caves for which the area is famous. In addition to the famous cavern, Carlsbad Caverns National Park (including the wilderness) has more than 80 other caves, and within those, cavers are always discovering new chambers and passages. But unless you're an experienced caver with appropriate equipment, stay out of any caves you discover in the backcountry. They're simply too dangerous. Besides, the Park Service requires written permission to enter "wild caves" in the park.

The Carlsbad Caverns National Park Wilderness is part of the Chihuahuan Desert, the largest yet arguably the least known of America's deserts. As a desert, it demands of hikers special knowledge and skills. Foremost among these is knowing when to hike here. No one hikes here in the summer. The highest temperature ever recorded in New Mexico, 122 degrees Fahrenheit, occurred at a site not far from Carlsbad on June 27, 1994. 'Nuff said. But don't assume that winters are mild and balmy. Severe storms often scour the area, cloaking desert plants in seemingly incongruous snow. Winter hiking can be delightful here, but there are no guarantees! The best seasons are early spring and late fall, typically dry seasons in New Mexico. In nearby Carlsbad, the average high temperature in April is 80 degrees, which is pretty hot; in October it's 79 degrees (compared to 96 degrees in July). The average high in January is 57 degrees. Plan to carry water; the rule of thumb among backpackers here is a gallon per person per day. That means a heavy pack.

You also should have good route-finding skills, or at least the good sense to stay on the trails. The topography here is extremely complex, and the Capitan Reef is dissected by a maze of canyons. Furthermore, cliffs often obscure the ridges and highlands;

you easily could find yourself high on a ridge without any obvious way to get down to where you need to be. It's an unsettling experience to scramble down a slope only to find yourself facing hundreds of feet of thin air, then to look along the ridge and realize the cliff extends as far as you can see.

Carlsbad Caverns began attracting national attention not long after cowboy Jim White first explored them in 1901. By 1923 President Coolidge, responding to public sentiment, proclaimed the area Carlsbad Caverns National Monument. In 1930, Congress made the area a national park, the only one in New Mexico. The wilderness was formally designated in 1978. Since then, advocates have proposed a wilderness of at least 44,000 acres on Lincoln National Forest and BLM land to link the wilderness here with that of Guadalupe Mountains National Park just to the south. In 1995 the park became a World Heritage Site.

Because this is a national park, it has a goodly number of regulations. Permits (free) are required for backcountry camping, which is limited to designated wilderness areas. No campfires are allowed. The Apaches once built huge fires here to roast the mescal plant for food; the fact that you can still see these Apache fire pits speaks volumes about why modern fires aren't allowed. Pets are not allowed in the backcountry. Limited kennel facilities are available at the visitor center for day hikers, while Carlsbad has overnight kennels. Firearms are not allowed in the backcountry.

But despite all the rigors of this environment, and beyond all the regulations, the wild Guadalupe Mountains backcountry has a welcoming, almost flirtatious side to its nature.

The intensely red blossoms of claret-cup cacti, the whirr of opalescent hummingbirds, unexpected pools of water, and animals—such as javelinas, Mexican spotted owls, mule deer and elk, coyotes and foxes, mountain lions and bobcats, rabbits and squirrels—remind us that for all the environment's harshness, life is also here, varied and abundant. And perhaps most beguiling of all—the desert night when the air is warm and rabbit-fur soft, and the sky is filled with more stars than you've ever seen before. You don't get that in a cave.

DAY HIKE: JUNIPER RIDGE
One-way length: 3.5 miles
Low and high elevations: 4,110 and 4,790 feet
Difficulty: easy to moderate

This day hike begins 0.9 mile past Mile Marker 15 on the Desert Loop Drive. The easy-to-follow trail heads north to the park boundary (the round-trip is two miles if you turn around here), then follows the fence line west to overlook Crooked Canyon. The hike is exposed, so plan it for cooler times of day.

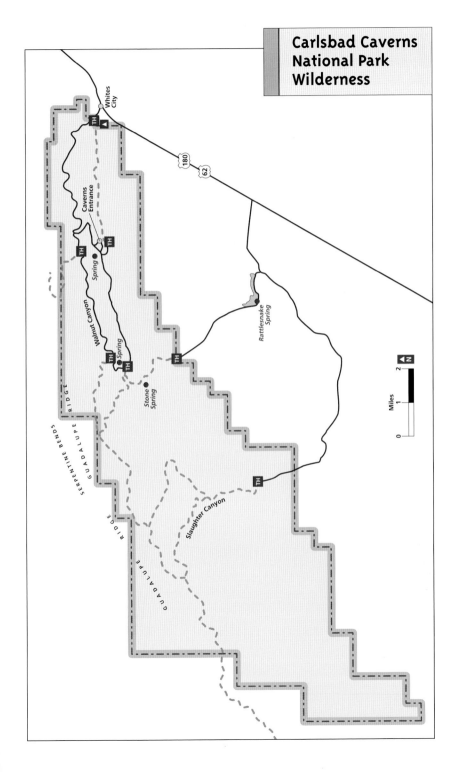

**Carlsbad Caverns
National Park
Wilderness**

Whites
City

TH

180

62

Caverns
Entrance

TH

Spring

TH

Walnut Canyon

Spring

TH

Rattlesnake
Spring

TH

Stone
Spring

SERPENTINE BENDS

GUADALUPE RIDGE

GUADALUPE RIDGE

Slaughter Canyon

TH

Miles

0   1   2

N

BACKPACK HIKE: GUADALUPE RIDGE
One-way length: 13.5 miles
Low and high elevations: 4,077 and 6,240 feet
Difficulty: strenuous

The Guadalupe Ridge Trail is marked by a sign on Desert Loop Drive. You begin by following a rough road up Walnut Canyon (a high-clearance vehicle can go about 2.5 miles up this). From the end of this you have a pleasant, level walk in Walnut Canyon for three miles before climbing steeply onto Guadalupe Ridge, where you follow an unmaintained jeep road to the park's western boundary. En route you'll pass two intersections with different prongs of the Slaughter Canyon Trail, so if you had a vehicle spotted at the Slaughter Canyon trailhead, you could make this a shuttle hike. (You definitely want to hike down Slaughter Canyon rather than up!) Because of its length, the Guadalupe Ridge Trail is best done as an overnighter, which means carrying extra water. Still, this trail has the reputation of showcasing the park's best backcountry. From the ridge, the entire area is spread out before you.

LOOP HIKE: RATTLESNAKE CANYON TRAIL
Round-trip length: 5.0 miles
Low and high elevations: 4,120 and 4,600 feet
Difficulty: moderate

Scenic and readily accessible, this hike begins at Mile Marker 9 of Desert Loop Drive. The trail drops into Rattlesnake Canyon to meet the Rattlesnake Canyon Trail. Follow this south (downstream) to eventually end at the park boundary, at which point you'll retrace your steps, a total distance of six miles. To make the loop, marked Guadalupe Ridge, turn right when you reach the canyon and go north. The trail follows the canyon until it climbs out to cross a divide and drops into Walnut Canyon, joining the Guadalupe Ridge Trail. Follow this downstream east back to Desert Loop Drive. A mile walk brings you back to Mile Marker 9 and your vehicle.

LOOP HIKE: SLAUGHTER CANYON – GUADALUPE RIDGE
Round-trip length: 14.0 miles
Low and high elevations: 4,207 and 6,240 feet
Difficulty: strenuous

From Highway 62-180, six miles south of Whites City, paved County Road 410 goes 10 miles to the start of this, perhaps the park's most challenging backcountry trail. The first challenge is to start on the right trail. The Slaughter Canyon Trail and the Slaughter Canyon Cave Trail both start at the same trailhead, but the cave trail is better defined. So take the lesser-used trail just to the right of the cave trail. If you go up the wash, you're headed in the right direction. Stay in the wash, ignoring several cairn-marked side trails, for about three miles. At this point the trail splits, the left fork going up the ridge between North Slaughter Canyon and Middle Slaughter

Canyon, while the right fork goes up Slaughter Ridge, the steeper of the two. By taking the left fork, you still have a steep climb up onto Guadalupe Ridge. Here is where you likely would camp. To make the loop, hike east on the Guadalupe Ridge Trail 2.5 miles to where the other prong of the Slaughter Canyon Trail comes in. Follow this downhill back to the wash and eventually your vehicle. If you had a vehicle at the Guadalupe Ridge Trailhead on Desert Loop Drive, you could do this as a very scenic shuttle hike.

SHUTTLE HIKE: GUANO ROAD TRAIL
One-way length: 3.5 miles
Low and high elevations: 3,610 and 4,320 feet
Difficulty: easy

This pleasant hike follows the route that guano (bat dung) miners used to haul this prized fertilizer from Carlsbad Cavern to Whites City. The easiest way to do this hike is to spot a car at Whites City, then get to the park headquarters at the cavern and hike back. This strategy means the hike is gently downhill. The trail begins at the Bat Flight Amphitheater and for the first 0.25 mile coincides with the Chihuahuan Desert Nature Trail. The Guano Road Trail is well-marked, with cairns and brown trail markers. Refreshments and a very interesting museum await you in Whites City.

OTHER RECREATIONAL OPPORTUNITIES

Caving is deservedly very popular not only in the national park but throughout the Guadalupe Mountains. However, training, experience, and special skills and equipment are mandatory. The national park visitor center can answer questions about which caves are open to the public and how one can learn more about caving. If you already are a caver, then the local grotto of cavers would be a good information source.

Horseback riding is popular in the area, with approximately 60 percent of the trails in Carlsbad Caverns and Guadalupe Mountains National Parks open to horses, although only day use is allowed. Both parks have stock corrals. As with hikers, free permits are required. Check at the visitor center to see what other regulations might be in effect. And remember: the backcountry has neither feed nor water, and some trails are so steep and rocky that taking a horse on them would constitute cruelty toward animals.

Because some backcountry trails follow old roads, such as the Guadalupe Ridge Trail, the park allows mountain biking, although bikers must stay on the trail. Check with the visitor center for which trails are open for mountain biking.

FOR MORE INFORMATION

CARLSBAD CAVERNS NATIONAL PARK, 3225 National Parks Highway, Carlsbad, NM 88220; (505) 785-2232.

GUADALUPE MOUNTAINS NATIONAL PARK, HC 60, Box 400, Salt Flat, TX 79847; (915) 828-3251.

Culp Canyon
Wilderness Study Area

Alluvial fans, hills, and canyons cut into the steep western escarpment of the Sacramento Mountains.

LOCATION 22 miles south by southeast of Alamogordo, between Lincoln National Forest and the McGregor Range missile testing area

SIZE 10,937 acres
Size recommended by the NM Wilderness Alliance: 14,462 acres

ELEVATION RANGE 4,500 to 6,500-plus feet

MILES OF TRAILS No marked or maintained trails

ECOSYSTEMS Chihuahuan Desert shrubs, including mesquite and creosote bush; semidesert grassland

ADMINISTRATION BLM

TOPOGRAPHIC MAPS Culp Canyon USGS 7.5-minute quadrangle

BEST SEASONS Fall, winter, spring

GETTING THERE From Highway 54, take all-weather dirt Highway 506 east 6 miles to another, smaller dirt road that runs north to Culp Canyon.

HIKING Outstanding vistas abound and wildlife is plentiful, which explains why this WSA's main use at present is deer hunting.

Devils Den Canyon, McKittrick Canyon and Lonesome Ridge Wilderness Study Areas

70

These three small, nearly contiguous areas showcase the steep eastern and western slopes of the Guadalupe Mountains.

LOCATION
On the eastern and western sides of the Guadalupe Mountains, adjacent to the Forest Service's Guadalupe Escarpment WSA

SIZE
Devils Den Canyon, 320 acres; McKittrick Canyon, 200 acres; Lonesome Ridge, 3,505 acres

ELEVATION RANGE
4,800 to 6,825 feet

MILES OF TRAILS
Undetermined

ECOSYSTEMS
Chihuahuan Desert grassland and scrub, including creosote bush and mesquite, piñon-juniper woodlands, riparian deciduous

ADMINISTRATION
BLM

TOPOGRAPHIC MAPS
El Paso Gap and Gunsight Canyon USGS 7.5-minute quadrangles

BEST SEASONS
Fall, winter, spring

GETTING THERE
From Highway 285, northwest of Carlsbad, take Highway 137 to the Dog Canyon Campground in Guadalupe Mountains National Park. Before you reach the campground, a road branches east to approach the mouth of Devils Den Canyon. Continuing south on Highway 137 you can see the steep slopes of the McKittrick Canyon WSA to the east. To get to Lonesome Ridge from Highway 62-180 in Texas, a network of ranch roads leads to the fork at the two upper prongs of Big Canyon.

HIKING
The small size of the Devils Den Canyon and McKittrick Canyon WSAs makes hiking limited. Devils Den Canyon is the northwest terminus of a long route that begins at the McKittrick Canyon Visitor Center in Guadalupe Mountains National Park, follows the Permian Reef Trail to the park boundary, and then follows trails and old roads along Camp Wilderness Ridge to end near Devils Den Spring and the canyon.

From Big Canyon, the Lonesome Ridge Trail, Trail No. 56, climbs steeply up to Lonesome Ridge, connecting eventually with the Forest Service trails along Guadalupe Ridge. The round-trip length is 14.2 miles, with spectacular views along the way. This is very rugged, very isolated country, with little if any water in the backcountry; hikers should plan accordingly.

Guadalupe Escarpment Wilderness Study Area

71

New Mexico's extension of the Capitan Reef and the Guadalupe Mountains, this area features deep canyons plunging off Guadalupe Ridge.

Cliffs of the Guadalupe Mountains

LOCATION	Southwest of Carlsbad, adjacent to Carlsbad Caverns National Park Wilderness on the east and Guadalupe Mountains National Park Wilderness on the south
SIZE	20,936 acres
ELEVATION RANGE	3,500 to 7,400 feet
MILES OF TRAILS	Undetermined
ECOSYSTEMS	Ponderosa pine and Douglas fir, piñon-juniper, Chihuahuan Desert scrub, small stands of Texas madrone and Rocky Mountain maples
ADMINISTRATION	Lincoln National Forest
TOPOGRAPHIC MAPS	El Paso Gap, Gunsight Canyon, and Queen USGS 7.5-minute quadrangles

BEST SEASONS   Fall, spring

GETTING THERE   Access this area from the north via Highway 137. Then take Forest Road 540, which runs south along the WSA's western border. People with high-clearance four-wheel-drive vehicles can drive along Guadalupe Ridge via Forest Road 201. Access from the south is possible via the Guadalupe National Park backcountry. Access this area from the east by taking BLM and private roads from Highway 180, southwest of Carlsbad.

HIKING   The Guadalupe Escarpment WSA offers spectacular backcountry hiking for people willing to meet its challenges. Such people are few; most hikers enter the area from the south, through the Guadalupe Mountains National Park backcountry. Forest Road 201, along Guadalupe Ridge, is rough enough to convince many people to hike it instead of driving. (It is also suitable for mountain biking.) Connecting with this ridge are trails along Camp Wilderness Ridge, Lonesome Ridge, and the Ussery Trail. On the east, Guadalupe Ridge is flanked by several dramatic canyons, including 1,500-foot Deep Canyon, North McKittrick Canyon, and Big Canyon. These canyons have perennial water; you'll find little, if any, water along the ridge.

72 Last Chance Canyon (Proposed Wilderness)

This area of steep-sided canyons and limestone hills in the Guadalupe Mountains is both challenging and interesting.

LOCATION	In the eastern foothills of the Guadalupe Mountains, southwest of Carlsbad
SIZE	Size recommended by the NM Wilderness Alliance: 27,380 acres
ELEVATION RANGE	4,600 to 5,775 feet
MILES OF TRAILS	Undetermined
ECOSYSTEMS	Chihuahuan Desert scrub, plus a rare Chihuahuan Desert riparian area with cottonwoods, walnuts, and willows
ADMINISTRATION	BLM, Lincoln National Forest
TOPOGRAPHIC MAPS	Red Bluff Draw, Ares Peak, and Queen USGS 7.5-minute quadrangles
BEST SEASONS	Fall, winter, spring
GETTING THERE	This area can be accessed from Sitting Bull Falls Recreation Area, which is an interesting and scenic area complete with restrooms, parking, and picnic tables. A trail leads up Sitting Bull Canyon to the plateau above, from which several other canyons may be reached. The falls are reached from Carlsbad by driving approximately 9 miles northwest on Highway 285 to Highway 137, then driving southwest 24 miles to Forest Road 276; the falls are 7.6 miles away, in a narrow, scenic limestone canyon. On the way to the falls is the trailhead for Last Chance Canyon, a main hiking access point.
	You can also reach the area by driving farther southwest on Highway 137.
HIKING	Perhaps the best hike here is up Last Chance Canyon (named around 1881 because it was some cowboys' "last chance" to find water, and they did!). After turning off Highway 137, drive 6.5 miles on Forest Road 276 to where Forest Road 276B branches right. A quarter mile up this route you'll find the trailhead. After about a mile the trail drops down into the canyon, where you soon encounter spring-fed water pools from White Oak Spring. Farther into the canyon you'll encounter other springs and pools. The availability of water and campsites makes Last Chance Canyon a perfect base for exploring other canyons in this proposed wilderness.
	The Sitting Bull Falls Trail, Number 68, begins at Sitting Bull Falls and leads up Sitting Bull Falls Canyon. The trail winds past emerald pools to Sitting Bull Spring, where it ascends a side canyon to the plateau. The trail joins Highway 137 approximately 3.6 miles from the falls.

Mudgetts Wilderness Study Area

73

Like the adjacent Carlsbad Caverns Wilderness, this is an area of steeply rolling limestone hills along Guadalupe Ridge. Cut by deep and sinuous canyons, such as the Serpentine Bends of Dark Canyon, this area features several significant caves including Big Man Hole Cave.

LOCATION	Southwest of Carlsbad, contiguous on the south with the Carlsbad Caverns Wilderness
SIZE	2,941 acres Size recommended by the NM Wilderness Alliance: 3,490 acres
ELEVATION RANGE	4,000 to 4,900 feet
MILES OF TRAILS	No marked or maintained trails
ECOSYSTEMS	Chihuahuan Desert scrub, including sotol, agave, and juniper
ADMINISTRATION	BLM
TOPOGRAPHIC MAPS	Carlsbad Caverns USGS 7.5-minute quadrangle
BEST SEASONS	Fall, winter, spring
GETTING THERE	All vehicular access means crossing private land; short hikes over BLM land allow foot access.
HIKING	Lack of access, difficult terrain, and better-known hiking alternatives nearby have kept visitation here very low.

Pup Canyon (Proposed Wilderness)

74

Two extremely rugged canyons—Little Dog and Pup—lead onto the Guadalupe Rim where wildlife flourishes.

LOCATION	On the west side of the Guadalupe Mountains' rim
SIZE	Size recommended by the NM Wilderness Alliance: 43,900 acres
ELEVATION RANGE	4,000 to 6,400 feet
MILES OF TRAILS	No marked or maintained trails
ECOSYSTEMS	Chihuahuan Desert scrub and grassland
ADMINISTRATION	BLM, Lincoln National Forest
TOPOGRAPHIC MAPS	Sixteen-mile Draw West USGS 7.5-minute quadrangle
BEST SEASONS	Fall, winter, spring
GETTING THERE	From County Road G14, dirt roads lead across BLM land to the mouth of Little Dog Canyon. All roads leading to Pup Canyon cross private land.
HIKING	Very steep, rugged terrain, characterized by remoteness, lack of water, and poor access. These factors have limited the use of this area by hikers.

75 Rawhide Canyon (Proposed Wilderness)

Sheer limestone cliffs flank canyon bottoms here in the Guadalupe Mountains.

LOCATION	In the eastern foothills of the Guadalupe Mountains
SIZE	Size recommended by the NM Wilderness Alliance: 26,400 acres
ELEVATION RANGE	4,725 to 5,450 feet
MILES OF TRAILS	No marked or maintained trails
ECOSYSTEMS	Chihuahuan Desert scrub; piñon-juniper; riparian willows, hackberry, and walnut
ADMINISTRATION	BLM, Lincoln National Forest
TOPOGRAPHIC MAPS	Sixteen-mile Draw East USGS 7.5-minute quadrangle
BEST SEASONS	Spring, fall
GETTING THERE	From Highway 137, west of Carlsbad, Forest Road 67 heads north along the Guadalupe Mountains' rim. From here, Forest Road 277 heads northeast; rougher Forest Road 277A continues heading northeast towards the Rawhide Canyon area.
HIKING	Hiking here has been very limited, primarily because of poor access and limited public awareness of the area. The Rawhide Canyon area is immediately south of the BLM-designated South Texas Hill Canyon Research Natural Area, and is similarly an excellent example of Chihuahuan Desert deciduous woodland and grassland.

76 Sacramento Escarpment (Proposed Wilderness)

A dramatic limestone face rises nearly a mile here, cut by deep, rugged canyons and topped with a high, forested ridge.

LOCATION	On the east side of the Tularosa Basin, south of Alamogordo
SIZE	Size recommended by the NM Wilderness Alliance: 50,840 acres
ELEVATION RANGE	4,250 to 8,100 feet
MILES OF TRAILS	Undetermined
ECOSYSTEMS	Chihuahuan Desert scrub, piñon-juniper, canyon riparian
ADMINISTRATION	BLM, Lincoln National Forest
TOPOGRAPHIC MAPS	Lincoln National Forest–Smokey Bear, Cloudcroft, and Mayhill Ranger Districts
BEST SEASONS	Fall, winter, spring
GETTING THERE	Numerous routes lead east from Highway 54 toward the escarpment. The most convenient access is via Oliver M. Lee Memorial State Park, at the mouth of Dog Canyon.
HIKING	Anyone who's hiked in Dog Canyon knows the Sacramento Escarpment is one of the most spectacular, interesting, and rugged areas in southern New Mexico. The BLM WSA consisted of 3,510 acres and abutted the much larger Forest Service WSA. But when the Forest Service dropped its WSA, the BLM did likewise. The Wilderness Alliance, however, believes that significant wilderness potential exists among the complex of land-management units here.

Salt Creek Wilderness 77

*Affiliated with the U.S. Fish and Wildlife Service's
Bitter Lake Wildlife Refuge, this area features creek-
bottom wetlands, grasslands, and sand dune habitats.*

LOCATION	Northwest of Roswell, north of Highway 70
SIZE	9,621 acres
ELEVATION RANGE	3,520 to 3,670 feet
MILES OF TRAILS	No designated trails
ECOSYSTEMS	Creek bottom riparian, tamarisk, grasses
ADMINISTRATION	U.S. Fish and Wildlife Service
TOPOGRAPHIC MAPS	Coyote Draw USGS 7.5-minute quadrangle
BEST SEASONS	Spring, fall
GETTING THERE	Highway 70 northeast of Roswell abuts the wilderness's southeastern border, while Old Horse Road and Cottonwood Road heading east from Highway 285 go along its northwest border.
HIKING	Hiking here is severely limited by lack of trails and because it is primarily a wildlife refuge rather than a recreation area.

ALTHOUGH THE SALT CREEK WILDERNESS is near Roswell and a major highway, hikers can experience a high degree of solitude in this seldom visited area. Salt Creek Wilderness is maintained to complement the nearby Bitter Lake Wildlife Refuge and thus exists more for plants and animals than for humans. Salt Creek runs through the wilderness, giving it its name, but the creek is usually dry or intermittent, partly because some of its moisture is absorbed by dense stands of tamarisk. This plant, introduced as an exotic species in 1916, first appeared along the Pecos River immediately east of the wilderness. Since then it has become a serious pest. Thousands of dollars have been spent to eradicate it, with little success.

A red bluff overlooks the lowlands from the north. A major feature here is a 40-foot-deep gypsum sinkhole that inspired the name "the Ink Pot."

FOR MORE INFORMATION

BITTER LAKE NATIONAL WILDLIFE REFUGE, P.O. Box 7, Roswell, NM 88202; (505) 622-6755.

Appendix 1: Wilderness Areas

NAME	ACRES	AGENCY	YEAR DESIGNATED
Gila	558,065	Gila National Forest	1924
Pecos	222,673	Santa Fe and Carson National Forests	1955
Aldo Leopold	202,016	Gila National Forest	1970
Cebolla	62,800	BLM	1987
Chama River Canyon	50,300	Santa Fe and Carson National Forests, BLM	1988
White Mountain	48,873	Lincoln National Forest	1964
Apache Kid	44,650	Cibola National Forest	1980
Bisti—De-na-zin	37,100	BLM	1984
San Pedro Parks	41,132	Santa Fe and Carson National Forests	1964
West Malpais	39,700	BLM	1987
Sandia Mountain	37,232	Cibola National Forest	1978
Manzano Mountain	36,970	Cibola National Forest	1978
Capitan	35,822	Lincoln National Forest	1980
Carlsbad Caverns	33,125	National Park Service	1978
Bandelier National Monument	32,727	National Park Service	1976
San Pascual/ Chupadera/Indian Wells	30,287	U.S. Fish and Wildlife Service	
Blue Range	29,304	Apache National Forest	1980
Latir Peak	20,506	Carson National Forest	1980
Wheeler Peak	19,150	Carson National Forest	1960
Cruces Basin	18,902	Carson National Forest	1980
Withington	18,869	Cibola National Forest	1980
Salt Creek	9,621	U.S. Fish and Wildlife Service	
Dome	5,200	Santa Fe National Forest	1980

TOTAL: Approximately 1.6 million acres, or 2 percent of the state's total land area.

Appendix 2: Useful Addresses

BUREAU OF LAND MANAGEMENT
Albuquerque Field Office
435 Montano Road NE, Albuquerque,
NM 87107; (505) 761-8700

BUREAU OF LAND MANAGEMENT
Farmington Field Office
1235 La Plata Highway, Farmington,
NM 87401; (505) 599-8900

BUREAU OF LAND MANAGEMENT
Las Cruces Field Office
1800 Marquess Street, Las Cruces,
NM 88005; (505) 525-4300

BUREAU OF LAND MANAGEMENT
Socorro Field Office
198 Neel Avenue NW, Socorro,
NM 87801; (505) 835-0412

BUREAU OF LAND MANAGEMENT
Taos Field Office
226 Cruz Alta Road, Taos, NM 87571
(505) 758-8851

FOREST GUARDIANS
1413 Second Street SW, Suite 1
Santa Fe, NM 87505
e-mail: swwild@fguardians.org

NEW MEXICO WILDERNESS ALLIANCE
P.O. Box 13116
Albuquerque, NM 87192
Web site: http://www.sdc.org/nmwa

NEW MEXICO MOUNTAIN CLUB
P.O. Box 4151, University Station
Albuquerque, NM 87196

SIERRA CLUB, RIO GRANDE CHAPTER
c/o John Buscher
606 Alto, Santa Fe, NM 87501

SKY ISLAND ALLIANCE
Web site: http://www.lobo.net/~skisland

WILDERNESS SOCIETY
P.O. Box 29241, San Francisco, CA 94129
(415) 561-6641
Web site: http://www.wilderness.org

WILDLANDS PROJECT
1955 West Grant Road, Suite 148
Tucson, AZ 85745; (520) 884-0875
Web site: http://www.wild-lands.org

Appendix 3: Selected References

NEW MEXICO HIKING GUIDES

Evans, Harry. *50 Hikes in New Mexico.* Gem Guides Book Co: Baldwin Park, CA 1995.

Hill, Mike. *Guide to the Hiking Areas of New Mexico.* University of New Mexico Press: Albuquerque. 1995.

Julyan, Bob. *Best Hikes with Children in New Mexico.* The Mountaineers Books: Seattle, WA. 1994.

Martin, Craig. *75 Hikes in New Mexico.* The Mountaineers Books: Seattle. 1995.

Parent, Laurence. *The Hiker's Guide to New Mexico.* Falcon Press Publishing Company: Helena, MT 1991.

Ungnade, Herbert. *Guide to the New Mexico Mountains.* University of New Mexico Press: Albuquerque. 1965.

LOCAL AND REGIONAL HIKING GUIDES
THE SANTA FE–LOS ALAMOS–TAOS AREA:

Hoard, Dorothy. *A Guide to Bandelier National Monument.* Los Alamos Historical Society: Los Alamos. 1983.

Hoard, Dorothy. *Los Alamos Outdoors.* 2nd ed. Los Alamos Historical Society: Los Alamos, NM. 1995.

Matthews, Kay. *Hiking the Mountain Trails of Santa Fe.* Acequia Madre Press: Chamisal, NM 1995.

Matthews, Kay. *Hiking the Wilderness: A Backpacking Guide to the Wheeler Peak, Pecos, and San Pedro Parks Wilderness Areas.* Acequia Madre Press: Chamisal. 1992.

Overhage, Carl. *One-day Walks in the Pecos Wilderness.* Sunstone Press: Santa Fe. 1980.

Day Hikes in the Santa Fe Area. 4th ed. The Santa Fe Group of the Sierra Club.

Appendix 3: continued

Pecos Wilderness Trail Guide, Santa Fe National Forest. Public Lands Interpretive Association: Albuquerque. 1991.

THE ALBUQUERQUE AREA:

Hill, Mike. *Hikers and Climbers Guide to the Sandia Mountains.* 2nd ed. University of New Mexico Press: Albuquerque. 1993.

Matthews, Kay. *Hiking Trails of the Sandia and Manzano Mountains.* 3rd ed., revised. Acequia Madre Press: Chamisal. 1995.

The Visitor's Guide to the Sandia Mountains. Public Lands Interpretive Association: Albuquerque. 1994.

SOUTHERN NEW MEXICO:

Kurtz, Don, and Goran, William D. *Trails of the Guadalupes: A Hiker's Guide to the Trails of Guadalupe Mountains National Park.* Environmental Associates: Champaign, IL. 1982.

Magee, Greg S. *A Hiking Guide to Doña Ana County.* Naturescapes: Las Cruces, NM. 1989.

Murray, John. *The Gila Wilderness: A Hiking Guide.* University of New Mexico Press: Albuquerque. 1988.

Schneider, Bill. *Hiking Carlsbad Caverns and Guadalupe Mountains National Parks.* Falcon Press Publishing Co.: Helena, MT. 1996.

WESTERN NEW MEXICO:

Robinson, Sherry. *El Malpais, Mount Taylor, and the Zuni Mountains: A Hiking Guide and History.* University of New Mexico Press: Albuquerque. 1994.

NORTHWESTERN NEW MEXICO:

Chaco Back Country Trails. Chaco Culture National Historical Park: Southwest Parks and Monuments Association.

Hinchman, Sandra. *Hiking the Southwest's Canyon Country.* The Mountaineers Books: Seattle. 1990.

NATURAL HISTORY GUIDES

Chronic, Halka. *The Roadside Geology of New Mexico.* Mountain Press Publishing Co.: Missoula, MT. 1987.

Fish, Jim, ed. *Wildlands: New Mexico BLM Wilderness Coalition Statewide Proposal.* 1987. A revised and current edition of this was in preparation early in 1998.

Foreman, Dave, and Wolke Howie. *The Big Outside.* Ned. Ludd Books: Tucson. 1989.

Ivey, Robert DeWitt. *Flowering Plants of New Mexico.* Robert DeWitt: Albuquerque. 1995.

MacCarter, Jane S. *New Mexico Wildlife Viewing Guide.* Falcon Books: Helena. 1994.

Mitchell, James R. *Gem Trails of New Mexico.* Gem Guides Book Co.

Northrup, Stuart A. *Minerals of New Mexico.* University of New Mexico Press: Albuquerque. 1996.

CULTURAL HISTORY GUIDES

Chilton, Lance, et al. *New Mexico: A New Guide to the Colorful State.* University of New Mexico Press: Albuquerque. 1984.

Christiansen, Paige, and Kottlowski, Frank. *Mosaic of New Mexico's Scenery, Rocks, and History.* N.M. Bureau of Mines and Mineral Resources: Socorro, NM. 1972.

Fugate, Francis L. and Roberta B. *Roadside History of New Mexico.* Mountain Press Publishing Co.: Missoula. 1989.

Horgan, Paul. *Great River.* Texas Monthly Press: Austin, TX. 1984.

Julyan, Robert. *The Place Names of New Mexico.* University of New Mexico Press: Albuquerque. 1996.

Sherman, James E. and Barbara H. *Ghost Towns and Mining Camps of New Mexico.* University of Oklahoma Press: Norman. 1975.

Simmons, Marc. *New Mexico: An Interpretive History.* University of New Mexico Press: Albuquerque. 1988.

Williams, Jerry L., ed. *New Mexico in Maps.* 2nd ed. University of New Mexico Press: Albuquerque. 1986.

Young, John V. *The State Parks of New Mexico.* University of New Mexico Press: Albuquerque. 1984.

Appendix 4: Glossary of Spanish Words

Agua   water
Alamo   cottonwood tree
Alto, alta   high
Amarillo   yellow
Ancho, ancha   wide
Angostura   narrow
Arroyo   eroded, intermittent drainage
Azul   blue
Bajada   gradual descent, slope
Barranca   gorge, ravine, gully, but also hillside
Blanco, blanca   white
Boca   mouth
Bonita, bonito   pretty, attractive
Borrego   sheep
Bosque   forest, often referring to the thicket of trees bordering a stream or river
Brazo   arm, usually referring to branches of a stream or canyon; dim. *brazito*
Caballo   horse
Cabra   goat
Caja   box, often referring to a box or narrow, constricted canyon
Caliente   hot, as in a hot spring
Camino   road
Campana   bell
Canjilon   deer antler
Cañada   ravine, gulch, canyon
Cañon   canyon, gulch; dim. *cañoncito*
Capilla   hood, cowl, sometimes a descriptive metaphor for peaks
Capulin   chokecherry
Carrizo   reed grass
Casa   house; dim. *casita*
Cebolla   wild onion; dim. *cebolleta*
Cedro   juniper
Ceja   eyebrow, but usually referring to a fringe, border, or the edge of a cliff or mesa
Cerro   hill, but often applied to mountains; dim. *cerrito*
Chamisa   a shrub whose English name is rabbitbrush
Chiquito, chiquita   small, little
Chivato   kid, young goat
Cholla   a shrubby, many-branched cactus
Chupadero   sinkhole, occasionally a tick
Cobre   copper
Colorado, colorada   reddish in color
Concha   shell, as in snail or clam

Conejo   rabbit
Corona   crown, but also high point or top
Costilla   rib, sometimes a metaphor for a ridge or drainage
Crestón   hogback
Cuate   twin
Cuchillo   knife, a descriptive metaphor for a ridge
Cuesta   slope, hill, grade
Cueva   cave
Cumbre   summit
Diablo   devil
Diente   tooth, spire
Dulce   sweet, as in spring water
Embudo   funnel, often describing broad canyons with narrow mouths; dim. *embudito*
Encino   evergreen oak
Escondido, escondida   hidden, as in a spring
Florido, florida   flowery
Frijoles   beans
Frío, fría   cold
Gallina   chicken, but often referring to *gallina de la tierra,* or wild turkey
Gigante   giant, huge
Gordo, gorda   stout, fat
Grande   big
Hermano, hermana   brother, sister, often referring to closely related landforms
Hermoso, hermosa   handsome, beautiful
Hondo, honda   deep, as in a canyon or arroyo
Huerfano   orphan, often describing isolated landforms
Indio   Indian
Jara   scrub willow
Joya   basin, valley, hole
Junta   junction, confluence
Ladera   hillside, slope
Lago   lake
Laguna   lake; dim. *lagunita*
Largo, larga   long
Lindo, linda   pretty
Liso, lisa   smooth, as of a rock
Llano   plain (the noun)
Lobo   wolf
Loma   hill, typically small; dim. *lomita*
Madera   wood
Madre   mother
Malpais   badland, in New Mexico usually referring to lava flows
Manga   sleeve, fringe
Medio, media   middle

Appendix 4: continued

Mesa   table but also flat-topped landforms; dim. *mesita*
Mina   mine
Mogote   isolated grove or clump of trees or shrub
Monte   mountain
Montosa   well-wooded, mountainous
Morro   butte, headland
Nacimiento   birth, origin
Negro, negra   black
Nogal   walnut tree
Norte   north
Nuevo, nueva   new
Nutria   beaver
Ojo   spring; dim. *ojito*
Olla   earthen water jar, a descriptive metaphor for some landforms
Orilla   border, edge, margin
Oro   gold
Oscuro, oscura   dark, somber
Osha   medicinal herb, English name lovage
Oso   bear
Padre   father, priest
Pajarito   little bird
Palo   stick
Paloma   dove
Pardo, parda   gray
Paso   pass
Pavo   turkey
Pedernal   flint
Pedregoso, pedregosa   rocky, stony
Pelado   bare, bald
Pelon, pelona   bald
Peñasco   rocky bluff or spire
Petaca   box, metaphor for landforms
Picacho   peak
Piedra   rock
Pilar   pillar
Pinabete   spruce
Pino   pine
Pintado, pintada   painted
Plata   silver
Playa   beach, dry lake bed
Plaza   settlement, village; dim. *placita*
Polvadera   dust
Potrero   long finger mesa
Potrillo   colt
Prieto, prieta   dark, black
Pueblo   town, in New Mexico used typically for Indian settlements

Puente   bridge
Puerco   dirty, muddy
Puerta   gate, gap
Puerto   pass; dim. *puertecito*
Punta   point, tip
Quemado, quemada   burned
Ratón   rodent
Redondo, redonda   round
Rincon   box canyon, crossroads, corner; adj. *rinconada*
Rio   river
Rito   stream
Rojo   red
Salado   salty
Sangre   blood
Sarco   clear blue
Seco, seca   dry
Sierra   mountain range, mountain
Sur   south
Tecolote   owl
Tejón   badger
Tetilla   small breast, metaphor for landforms
Tierra   earth
Truchas   trout
Tularosa   characterized by reeds
Tusa   prairie dog
Uva   grape
Vaca   cow
Vado   ford
Valle   valley; dim. *vallecito*
Vega   meadow
Venado   deer
Verde   green
Vermejo   brown, auburn
Viejo, vieja   old; old man, old woman
Volcán   volcano
Yerba   herb
Yeso   gypsum
Zorro   fox

Index

NOTE: Entries in boldface denote major areas; citations followed by the letter "p" denote photos; citations followed by the letter "m" denote maps.

Bob Julyan
author

BORN AND RAISED in Colorado, author and lecturer Bob Julyan has lived in New Mexico for 20 years and hiked every corner of the state. He holds a master's degree in Natural Resources Conservation from Cornell University, and is well-known as a writer and conservationist. In addition to writing about hiking and the outdoors for the *Albuquerque Journal*, his books include *Best Hikes with Children in New Mexico* and *The Place Names of New Mexico.* Active in conservation issues, Julyan has been a member of the New Mexico Wilderness Alliance, the New Mexico Mountain Club, and the New Mexico Historical Society. Julyan lives with his family in Albuquerque.

Tom Till
photographer

TOM TILL, a resident of Moab, Utah, has traveled to the four corners of the globe photographing landscape, nature, and history subjects. His images have appeared in countless publications worldwide, including Sierra Club, Audubon, and National Geographic Calendars. Till has been sole photographer for twenty books including *Utah: A Celebration of the Landscape,* and *Utah: Magnificent Wilderness,* both published by Westcliffe Publishers. Fine art prints and books by Till can be purchased at the Till Gallery at 61 North Main in Moab, or at www.tomtill.com. Till lives near Behind-the-Rocks with wife Marcy, and children Mikenna and Bryce.